BLUE OCEAN
SHIFT

BLUE OCEAN
SHIFT

BEYOND COMPETING

PROVEN STEPS TO INSPIRE CONFIDENCE
AND SEIZE NEW GROWTH

W. CHAN KIM | RENÉE MAUBORGNE

MACMILLAN

First published 2017 by Hachette Books,
a division of Hachette Book Group, Inc., New York

First published in the UK 2017 by Macmillan
an imprint of Pan Macmillan
20 New Wharf Road, London N1 9RR
Associated companies throughout the world
www.panmacmillan.com

ISBN 978-1-5098-3216-3

Pan Macmillan does not have any control over, or any responsibility for,
any author or third-party websites referred to in or on this book.

3 5 7 9 8 6 4

A CIP catalogue record for this book is available from the British Library.

Printed and bound by CPI Group (UK) Ltd, Croydon, CR0 4YY

Visit **www.panmacmillan.com** to read more about all our books
and to buy them. You will also find features, author interviews and
news of any author events, and you can sign up for e-newsletters
so that you're always first to hear about our new releases.

To strive, to seek, to find, and not to yield.

–Alfred Lord Tennyson

Contents

Preface

In the poem "O Me! O Life!" Walt Whitman, the American poet and essayist, reflects on the trials and tribulations that define the human experience. "What good amid these, O me! O life?" he asks. His answer—that all of us, individually and collectively, may contribute a verse to the powerful play that is life—has never left us.

Life has its challenges and tribulations, no doubt. But it is not beyond our ability to shape. By our very existence, we all are able to contribute a verse and, in doing so, influence life's course, and maybe even its beauty, if only by an inch.

What will your verse be? What will ours? We have never stopped asking ourselves this question. What do we want to stand for? What narrative arc do we want to focus our efforts on in the hopes of adding a small verse to the powerful play that is life that can help our world to advance?

For us, as business scholars, the world we aspired to help advance wasn't one defined by competing and dividing up markets or the globe, where one's gain comes at the expense of others. Competition exists, and win-lose scenarios abound, but they weren't what captured our imaginations, nor what we believed our world needed more of. What we admired, what inspired us, were the organizations and individuals that went beyond competing to create new frontiers of opportunity, growth, and jobs, where success was not about dividing up an existing, often shrinking pie, but about creating a larger economic pie for all—what we refer to as *blue oceans*. Blue oceans are less about disruption and more about *non*disruptive creation, where one's gain doesn't have to come at the expense of others.

But how do you translate aspiration into action, intention into reality?

We need a road map that can shift our perspective and free our imaginations, allowing us to suspend belief in the limits of today so we can see and create the possibilities of tomorrow. And for that we need to inspire confidence in ourselves and in our people because, although we all are replete with creative energy and resilience, at our core, most of us are also incredibly tender and vulnerable. Without the confidence to act, few will venture down a new path, no matter how clear the road map. We aspire to make a difference, yet at the same time fear we cannot. Confidence is that magical quality that allows us to transcend the quiet self-doubts that tug at us. It shows us the emotional way forward by allowing us to believe in ourselves and trust the process.

The book you are holding in your hands is our answer to this challenge. It is based on our nearly 30-year research journey to the blue ocean in which we studied organizations large and small, for-profit, nonprofit, and governments that moved beyond competing in existing crowded markets—what we think of as red oceans—to new heights of confidence, market creation, and growth. What we learned in studying those who succeeded in making this shift as well as those who failed is that for any process to work, it must acknowledge our doubts and build our confidence as much as unlock people's requisite creativity with proven steps.

In *Blue Ocean Shift,* people and our human spirit are put on an equal plane with a tested process and market-creating tools to move you, your team, and your organization from red to blue oceans in a way that people own and drive the process to succeed. It provides a step-by-step guide anyone can follow with battle-tested lessons learned from the field on what works, what doesn't, and how to avoid potential pitfalls along the way.

We made our choice of what verse we want to bring to the world. We firmly believe that we all are capable of creating new frontiers and verses of our own. As Nelson Mandela once noted, "It always seems impossible until it's done." We hope that this book can help you make yours.

PART ONE

Blue Ocean Shift

CHAPTER 1

Reach Beyond the Best

"WHEN I PLAY MUSIC, I feel like I'm in a beautiful world that is endless."

In 2008, amid the devastation that is Iraq—a country of religious and ethnic divisions, hardship, and war—Zuhal Sultan had a dream. The 17-year-old Iraqi pianist wanted to create her country's first national youth orchestra and travel with it abroad. Iraq, however, had few formally trained musicians or music teachers, and few quality instruments to speak of, not to mention cultural chasms dating back centuries that divided Iraqi youth.

Where to begin? Using the Internet, Zuhal reached out to find a conductor. Paul MacAlindin, a Scottish conductor and classically trained musician, responded and signed on to lead the National Youth Orchestra of Iraq (NYOI).

It didn't take Paul long to see that he would need to be a strategist as well as a musician, since the orchestra would have no chance if it competed on the same terms as other national youth orchestras. The industry was intensely competitive, dominated by venerable European youth orchestras from countries such as France, Italy, Spain, and the UK. Comprised of highly trained young musicians with great technical skills, these orchestras engaged world-class guest soloists and conductors, and featured polished performances of classical masterpieces by composers such as Brahms, Beethoven, and Chopin. To stand apart, while keeping costs low, Paul realized that NYOI would have to break with industry tradition and redefine what it meant to be a national youth orchestra.

Rather than focus on technical excellence and musical sophistication, NYOI would focus on the power of music to heal, bridge the deepest divides, and showcase the hidden glory of Iraq's rich heritage. To this end, Paul reduced the orchestra's reliance on musical excellence and a sophisticated European repertoire, and eliminated renowned guest soloists and guest conductors, which dramatically dropped its cost structure.

In its place, Paul and Zuhal assembled a group of youthful musicians who would play original Iraqi music of both Kurdish and Arab origin and put it on an equal footing with the likes of Hayden, Beethoven, and Schubert, which they also played. Much to the disbelief of many, NYOI brought together young men and women musicians who were Sunni and Shia, Arab and Kurdish. In this way, Paul and Zuhal built an orchestra that demonstrated the young Iraqis' hope and commitment to building a brighter future together out of the destruction of war. As NYOI member Mohammed Adnan Abdallah put it, "Music is the language of peace, and it makes people love each other. When musicians sit and play together, they communicate that."[1]

The result: NYOI became known as the "Bravest Orchestra in the World," a title first bestowed on it by the British broadcaster Sky News. It might not be the most technically accomplished group of young musicians. But it was, perhaps, the most inspired. It broke away from other national youth orchestras, winning accolades, standing ovations, and attention across the globe. It attracted new audiences who had never gone to classical music concerts before and enjoyed one of the largest social media followings of any youth orchestra. More than that, it showed young Iraqi people they could create a different narrative for their country other than one of destruction, hate, and war—one of peace, hope, and solidarity.[2]

Paul MacAlindin is smart and a fine conductor. He is hardworking, strives to do his best, and has a passion for making a difference. He will be the first to admit, though, that he is not a genius or your typical entrepreneur. In many ways, Paul is just like most of us. Yet, despite organizational constraints, ranging from scant resources to limited top talent, Paul and his young orchestra members developed a strategy that was both creative and low cost, allowing the orchestra to stand apart from fierce, entrenched competition.

Paul and NYOI's youthful musicians are not alone.

From Orchestras to French Fry Makers

Take Groupe SEB, the French multinational founded in 1857. Like most large, well-established multinationals, Groupe SEB is run by professional managers, many of whom have been with the company for years, with an established culture and its share of bureaucracy and internal politics. Like most small appliance makers at the time, its businesses were facing increasingly intense competition and margin pressure. In particular, its electric French fry makers, struggling to stand apart in a market that was shrinking 10 percent a year in value, were a case in point.

Recognizing the need to break out of this intense competition, Christian Grob, the head of electric cooking at the time, and his team set out to turn the situation around. The professional managers of Groupe SEB were somewhat skeptical. After all, what could you do with a French fry maker when price was the only thing that seemed to drive sales?

Christian and his team reasoned differently. What if all the players in the industry were operating under the same set of assumptions, but those assumptions limited the attractiveness of and the demand for their products? What would happen if those assumptions were rethought? Christian and his team set about to do just that—to identify and challenge the industry's most basic assumptions. When they did, they had a revelation.

Christian's team discovered that there were two facts that everyone accepted without question—two facts that in essence defined the industry. The first was that making fresh French fries required frying. The second was that frying required a lot of oil.

Obvious? Yes. However, these unexamined assumptions drove the industry to overlook a host of problems. The 2.5 liters of cooking oil that were required were expensive. Once hot, the oil makes fryers dangerous. When the fries are done, it's hard to dispose of the cooking oil, making cleanup difficult. To top it off, all that oil makes fries both unhealthy and incredibly fattening.

Challenging this accepted wisdom led the team to redefine the problem from the one the industry focused on—how to make a best-in-class fryer—to how to make mouthwatering, healthy, fresh fries without frying. The result was ActiFry—a whole new type of French fry maker, first launched in France in 2006 and since rolled out globally. ActiFry requires no frying, and uses only one tablespoon of oil to make two pounds of fries, with roughly 40 percent fewer calories and 80 percent less fat than the same size serving of traditional fries. What's more, the appliance is easy to clean and has no safety or oil disposal issues. The fries are great, too—crunchy on the outside and soft on the inside. The winning combination of healthy, lower-calorie, yet yummy fries inspired Oprah Winfrey to tweet about how much she loves her ActiFry. "This machine...actifry has changed my life," she tweeted, "And they're not paying me to say it."[3] Not only did demand outstrip supply across Europe, but after Oprah's comments, Groupe SEB's stock price jumped 5 percent based on this one product. It took competitors five years to dive into the market, and even so they didn't succeed in capturing a significant share, since they couldn't match what ActiFry offered, thanks to the patents Groupe SEB secured. To this day, more than ten years out, ActiFry remains the global market leader. With the launch of ActiFry, the industry also grew by nearly 40 percent in value, pulling into the market brand-new customers who had never bought an electric fry maker before.

The industries of national youth orchestras and French fry makers are clearly worlds apart. They deliver different offerings, compete in different ways, and have completely different sets of players. The two organizations are also different. The National Youth Orchestra of Iraq is a new nonprofit, essentially a start-up. Groupe SEB is a for-profit multinational with over 150 years of history behind it.

As different as these two organizations and their industry settings are, however, they succeeded in the same way. Both shifted from competing in crowded existing markets to creating new market space. And while both faced organizational hurdles—as all organizations do—they overcame them by winning people's confidence and cooperation. This is what we call *blue ocean shift*. Blue ocean shift is a systematic process to move your organization from cutthroat markets with bloody competition—what we think of as red oceans full of sharks—to wide-open blue oceans, or new markets devoid of competition, in a way that brings your people along.

To deepen our understanding of blue ocean shift, let's look at another example, this one launched by government, arguably one of the most bureaucratic, resistant-to-change entities, and one that few would describe as creative or innovative.

The Gift of a Second Chance

Many countries today face rising crime, overcrowded prisons, and high recidivism rates. The implications of this situation are huge. It is costly to taxpayers. It threatens the security of citizens. It is debilitating to people who have turned to crime and can't break out of its vicious cycle. It is also heartbreaking for their families.

Most governments deal with overcrowded prisons in conventional ways: by building more of them, or maximizing utilization by mixing petty criminals in with harder-core inmates. Neither option works very well. Building more prisons is expensive and time-consuming, and mixing petty and harder-core criminals turns prisons into crime schools.

Either way, the focus is mainly on incarceration and providing a strict security environment, not on rehabilitation. California, for instance, has built 22 prisons since 1980. Its annual prison budget is now some US$9 billion. Yet its prisons remain massively overcrowded, and its recidivism rate hovers at a whopping 65 percent. In short, the existing strategies for managing prisons may succeed at punishment, but they fail at what society needs most—rehabilitating inmates to become productive members of the community.

When the government of Malaysia faced this precise challenge in 2010, it recognized that only a shift in strategy and organizational focus could break the vicious cycle of incarceration and reduce crime. To that end, the government turned to the National Blue Ocean Strategy (NBOS) Summit. The government had created the NBOS Summit in 2009 to pioneer innovative strategies and new practices that could achieve high social impact at low cost. Each month the NBOS Summit brings together national leaders like the prime minister, the deputy prime minister, and other top ministers, as well as the highest-level civil servants, including those from the nation's security forces. Depending on the issue, Summit participants vary and relevant private sector leaders are also involved.

In seeking a creative solution to the prison problem, the Summit stopped using global best practices as the benchmark. Instead, as Paul MacAlindin did at NYOI and Christian Grob did at Groupe SEB, it sought to identify and challenge the industry's fundamental assumptions. Chief among these was the long-held assumption that all criminals need to be put in prisons. Was there an alternative to very costly, high-security prisons, which could have high impact at far lower cost?

As the Summit explored these questions, it saw an opportunity that the ministers and security professionals had never previously recognized. Many military bases around the country had idle land. These bases had a robust security infrastructure, meant to keep trespassers out. But it was equally well suited to keeping prisoners in. For petty criminals, who were the largest inmate population, this idle land could be converted into an effective, low-cost security environment.

Summit participants also surfaced a second long-held practice that was keeping the government from recognizing rehabilitation opportunities; that is, the key expertise to rehabilitate prisoners lay outside the domain of the ministry in charge of prisons. Traditionally, prison officials were put in charge of rehabilitation, but their expertise was in confinement and high security—not in education, training, employment, and family needs. These were the keys to rehabilitation, and they could be much better provided by other ministries.

As the Summit challenged and overturned these long-held assumptions, it made a blue ocean shift, and the Community Rehabilitation Program (CRP) was born. Instead of building more expensive prisons, the Summit created CRP centers for petty criminals on the military bases' idle land, a first in the world. CRP offered a solution to overcrowding that could be delivered quickly and cheaply, and it ensured that petty criminals would be separated from, and not influenced by, hardened criminals. That was just the start.

At the CRP centers, the Ministries of Agriculture and Higher Education were brought in to provide high-value vocational training in cultivating fish and growing high-yield crops, which are then sold in open markets. The inmates earn

and save money through the sale of the products they produce. Such training not only teaches valuable skills, but also
shows these minor offenders a financial alternative to crime.
CRP also reaches out, via the human rights commissioner, to
inmates' family members, encouraging more regular contact
and even providing housing facilities nearby to allow visiting
families to stay longer.

Visitation at conventional prisons normally occurs behind
a glass window for 30 minutes. By contrast, at the CRP centers, inmates and their spouses and children are allowed to
not only hug and hold each other but also play together. This
heals wounds and reminds inmates how much they are loved
and how important their rehabilitation is. Upon release, the
Ministry of Human Resources provides departing prisoners
with job-matching services, and loans are available from the
Ministry of Women, Family and Community Development,
should they wish to start their own business.

The result: CRP delivered a leap in value to prisoners,
their families, and society while keeping costs to the government low. Here are the facts: Since the CRP centers started
in 2011, the recidivism rate for petty criminals has dropped
around 90 percent and stands at some 0.6 percent of California prisons. Their families are thrilled. Society is safer. As for
cost, compared with a conventional prison, a CRP center is 85
percent cheaper to build and 58 percent cheaper to run. Based
on the current rehabilitation level, CRP is expected to deliver
over US$1 billion in reduced costs and benefits to society in
its first decade.

Perhaps the greatest gift, however, is how CRP transforms
the lives of former inmates, giving them hope, dignity, and the
tools to restart their lives and become productive members of
society. As one former CRP inmate put it, "I really feel like I've
been given a second chance. I've learned new skills and have
been able to set up my own motorcycle repair business with
the funds I made at CRP. I now see a new future for myself."

From Market Competing to Market Creating

Organizational leaders often accept and act on two fundamental assumptions. One is that market boundaries and industry conditions are given. You cannot change them. You have to build your strategy based on them.[4] The other is that, to succeed within these environmental constraints, an organization must make a strategic choice between differentiation and low cost. Either it can deliver greater value to customers at a greater cost and hence a higher price, or it can deliver reasonable value at a lower cost. But it can't do both. Hence, the essence of strategy is seen as making a value-cost trade-off.[5]

Is it, though? Can't organizations shape the market boundaries and industry conditions they face? Can't organizations create strategies that break the value-cost trade-off in pursuit of differentiation and low cost?[6]

Think about CRP. Did the NBOS Summit accept the industry or environmental conditions of escalating prison costs, high recidivism rates, and rising crime as givens? No. It redefined the boundaries of what it means to incarcerate and rehabilitate criminals. It looked across prisons, police, military, and other ministries, and made a strategic and organizational shift that changed and reshaped these environmental conditions.

As for differentiation and low cost, CRP didn't make the value-cost trade-off. It broke it. It created a leap in value for petty criminals, families, and society at low cost to the government. By not benchmarking and following the existing global best practices, CRP made a blue ocean shift beyond what the prison industry had ever known while winning the confidence and support of all members of the relevant ministries.

Figure 1-1 captures this dynamic visually. The solid curve shows the productivity frontier depicted by Michael Porter, which defines the existing boundary of an industry, the sum total of all its best practices.[7] The curve represents

Figure 1-1

From Market Competing to Market Creating

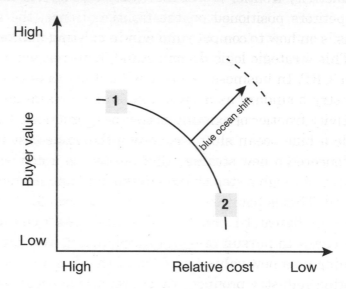

In pursuit of differentiation *or* low cost to compete on the existing productivity frontier of an industry as depicted by Michael Porter

In pursuit of differentiation *and* low cost to open up a new value-cost frontier

the highest levels of value and the corresponding costs an organization can achieve, given currently available technology and business best practices. As such, the frontier is the edge at which strategy in an existing market space, or red ocean, takes place. On this edge, all industry players have equal productivity—the ratio of value to cost. Hence changes in buyer value and cost are positively related: More of one necessarily means more of the other. What this means is that for a market-competing or red ocean strategy to succeed, an organization has to make a value-cost trade-off: It can stand out either in value, which is called differentiation (position 1), or in low cost (position 2). But it cannot stand out in both.[8] If an organization's offering is positioned behind its industry's productivity frontier it will inevitably be outperformed by its competitors positioned on the frontier. Hence, the strategic focus is on how to compete and win in existing market space.

This strategic logic doesn't stand, however, when we consider CRP. In business terms, CRP did not take the existing industry boundary as a given and stake a claim on the productivity frontier of existing prison best practices. Instead, it made a blue ocean shift that broke the value-cost trade-off. It pioneered a new strategy that opened up a new value-cost frontier through a step change in the *kind* and *degree* of value offered. This is how new market space is created. The dashed curve in figure 1-1 captures this alternate dynamic. Here strategy is in pursuit of both differentiation and low cost. By opening up a new value-cost frontier that is a leap beyond the existing industry productivity curve, a blue ocean is created and competition on the existing frontier is made irrelevant.[9]

While achieving a blue ocean shift may seem like magic, it is not. There is actually a systematic process that is accessible to everyone, whether you see yourself as particularly creative or not. The process not only maps out the path from red to blue oceans, but does so in a way that inspires people's confidence and brings them along from the beginning, so that they understand it and feel invested in the shift. Groupe SEB's ActiFry, the National Youth Orchestra of Iraq, and the Malaysian government's Community Rehabilitation Program are just a few of the blue ocean shifts made by organizations across the globe that have been applying this process, either in whole or in part.

Our Journey to the Blue Ocean

Our understanding of blue ocean shift and the process to achieve it did not come overnight. It is the result of a nearly

30-year research journey that we ventured together, often against all odds. Three decades ago we witnessed a disconcerting phenomenon that captured our minds and hearts and set us on this path. Back in the mid-1980s, global competition was heating up as never before, and, for the first time in history, American companies were fast losing ground in industry after industry. From motorcycles to cars, from earthmoving equipment to consumer electronics, they were being overtaken by a new set of competitors—Japanese corporations.

As researchers based in Ann Arbor, Michigan, at the time, we not only read about this, we witnessed it firsthand. The auto capital of America, just next door in Detroit, was devastated. The Big Three—General Motors, Ford, and Chrysler— were hemorrhaging jobs. Businesses were shutting down. People were scared. In Michigan, some had even taken to vandalizing Japanese cars on the street out of fear and anxiety over the onslaught of the new, strong competitors. Never was this more apparent to us than when we drove into Detroit. Street after street felt like a ghost town, slowly falling to ruin. We were both broke at the time, driving beat-up old cars. The city felt beat up, too—both its spirit and its economy.

Essentially, the economy of the developed world was easing into a new phase that posed a new challenge. It was shifting from a situation of demand outstripping supply following World War II to a tougher game of supply outstripping demand, which meant ever-greater competition. American companies may have been the first to feel the brunt of this emerging challenge, but we were convinced it was only a matter of time before companies throughout the developed world would face it too—including the Japanese. Unless prepared, they would fall like once-powerful Detroit.

With this perspective, and disheartened by what we saw, we set out to understand not how to cope with or slow this emerging reality, but what it would take to thrive, not merely survive, as competition heated up across the globe. With growing clarity and focus, our research questions emerged. Specifically, how can a company break out of this red ocean of bloody competition and generate strong, profitable growth? What does it take to reach beyond the best, to create new market space and make the competition irrelevant?

The initial results of our research were a series of articles on strategy and management published in *Harvard Business Review* as well as academic journals.[10] They culminated in our first book, *Blue Ocean Strategy*. Originally published in 2005, and updated and expanded in 2015, *Blue Ocean Strategy* was translated into 44 languages and became a bestseller across five continents. Long years of dogged focus, struggle, and persistence are the true story behind this "overnight" global bestseller.

In a nutshell, *Blue Ocean Strategy* articulated a view of the market universe as composed of two types of oceans—red oceans and blue oceans. Red oceans are all the industries in existence today that most organizations fight over. Blue oceans are all the industries yet to be created, where profit and growth increasingly come from. Based on our study of 150 strategic moves, spanning more than 100 years and 30 industries, the book laid out the conceptual differences and underlying patterns that separate ***market-competing moves***—what we call ***red ocean strategy***—from ***market-creating moves***—what we call ***blue ocean strategy***. It provided analytic tools to create blue oceans and highlighted why red ocean strategy is a theory of market competition and blue ocean strategy is a theory of market creation that makes competition irrelevant. The terms *red oceans*, *blue oceans*, and *blue ocean strategy* soon entered the business vernacular.

With a speed we hadn't expected, a tidal wave of interest grew as individuals, governments, companies, and nonprofits around the globe started to look at their world through the lens of red and blue oceans. Established organizations saw themselves as in a red ocean, with a call to action to get out and create blue oceans. Entrepreneurs argued for the need to seek blue ocean opportunities and avoid red oceans altogether. The focus of interest and discussion moved to a whole new level: from "What is blue ocean strategy?" to "How do we actually apply its theory and tools to shift from red to blue oceans?"

Entrepreneurs and start-ups were looking for concrete steps and a systematic process they could follow to create and capture blue oceans at minimal risk. Established companies stuck in the red ocean sought to understand how to move to open water. Their reasoning went like this: Our culture is bureaucratic and resistant to change. Where do we start this process? And how do we get people to buy into the idea and bring them along, when all they know and are comfortable with is how to compete within established industry rules? Past experience had taught them that however creative their ideas and change efforts, no shift would happen unless the human element was addressed. To ensure a successful shift, they wanted to know how to win their people's confidence and cooperation, despite facing organizational hurdles.

To meet this new research challenge, we set out to study those who had applied our theory and methodology to their organizations to create and capture blue oceans. They included individuals and organizations like Paul MacAlindin and the National Youth Orchestra of Iraq, Christian Grob and his team at Groupe SEB, and the Malaysian government's NBOS Summit, which has created and implemented more than 100 blue ocean national projects since its commencement in 2009.[11] We analyzed the patterns of their successes and failures and drew lessons from their experiences to understand what worked, what didn't work, and how to avoid potential pitfalls.

Many of these individuals and organizations came to us or to members of our blue ocean global network for guidance. They wanted to know how and where to start the journey, how to apply the tools to new opportunities, how to scope a meaningful blue ocean initiative, and how to put the right team together to make it happen. They also wanted to know how to build people's trust and confidence in the process, because only with these could they create the will and commitment to make the needed shift. As you will see later, one of them is Kimberly-Clark Brazil, a consumer-goods company that swam out of the bloody red ocean of the hypercompetitive US$1.5 billion–plus Brazilian toilet tissue industry and set the new industry standard with its blue ocean "Compacto" format.

Others applied our blue ocean theory and methodology on their own. We came to know them through word of mouth, correspondence, or reading about their experiences in the press, and reached out to them. citizenM Hotels, the affordable luxury chain, is one of these. It is currently expanding globally from its home base in Amsterdam and enjoys among the highest guest satisfaction ratings in the field of hospitality while having the lowest costs. HealthMedia, is another— a struggling company in 2006, with a mere US$6 million in sales—which, under Ted Dacko's leadership, created the new market space of digital health coaching and in two short years was sold to Johnson & Johnson for US$185 million. And then there's Wawa, the American convenience/food/gas chain, the 36th largest private company in America, which achieved explosive growth under its former CEO and current vice chairman Howard Stoeckel using the tools and ideas of a blue ocean approach. With its blue ocean offering, Wawa continues to grow under the leadership of its current CEO Chris Gheysens.

Overall, our analysis encompassed cases from Business to Customer (B2C) and Business to Business (B2B) as well as the public and nonprofit sectors. Through these field applications and our follow-up studies, we learned not only the common factors leading to a successful blue ocean shift but also the pitfalls and hurdles that got in the way.

To assess the validity and general applicability of our findings on a larger scale, we also analyzed and compared the patterns behind the strategic moves of other organizations that made the shift from red to blue oceans, based on their own processes. The aim here was to continue to broaden and deepen our understanding of how to escape cutthroat competition and create new markets. Studying both organizations that made the shift explicitly using our tools and ideas and those that did not is key to grasping a more complete picture of the pattern and dynamic process of market creation.

So, after over a decade of new study and analysis, we have arrived at a deeper understanding of what it takes to succeed in the blue ocean shift process. It comes down to three key components.

The Three Key Components of a Successful Blue Ocean Shift

The first component is adopting a blue ocean perspective, so that you expand your horizons and shift your understanding of where opportunity resides.

Organizations that open up new value-cost frontiers think differently. That is, they think about different things than those that are focused only on competing in their current markets. They raise fundamentally different sets of questions that enable them to see and understand opportunities and risk in fresh and innovative ways. This allows them to conceive of different *kinds* and *degrees* of value to offer customers that others either can't see at all or dismiss as impossible or irrelevant. With an expanded field of vision, they can, for instance, imagine creating a national youth orchestra worthy of global praise, even though it lacks highly trained musicians or quality instruments, by reconceiving it as a showcase for bridging cultural divides and promoting peace. They can imagine building rehabilitation centers on military bases for petty criminals, even though that defies the historical separation of the military, police, and prison administrations. They can imagine creating a new kind of home French fry maker that produces fresh, tasty, and healthier fries without frying.

Too many organizations are wedded to industry best practices even as they strive to break away from them. Adopting the perspective of a blue ocean strategist opens your mind to what could be, instead of limiting it to what is. It expands your horizons and ensures that you are looking in the right direction. Without expanding and reorienting your perspective, striving to open up a new value-cost frontier is like running west looking for the sunrise. No matter how fast you run, you're not going to find it.

While the right perspective is critical, for most of us it is not sufficient to actually conceive of and open up a new value-cost frontier. This is one of the greatest challenges organizations face. They want to get out of the red ocean. They want to make a blue ocean shift. They may even have a blue ocean perspective. However, they lack market-creating tools and guidance to turn their blue ocean perspective into reality.

The second component, therefore, is having practical tools for market creation with proper guidance on how to apply them to translate a blue ocean perspective into a commercially compelling new offering that creates new market space.

If the right perspective is a matter of shifting one's strategic thinking by asking different questions, market-creating tools and guidance enable you to ask the right questions at the right point in the process and to see the significance of the answers. Taken together, they build people's creative competence and provide the structure and parameters within which to organize your thinking so you can conceive and discover what others don't see, and avoid the potential pitfalls that trip up most organizations. Step-by-step, they guide you through the central questions for opening up a breakthrough value-cost frontier: How do you challenge the explicit and implicit assumptions you hold regarding your business and your marketplace? How do you go about identifying the ocean of noncustomers to create new demand? How can you systematically redefine market boundaries to open up a new value-cost frontier that makes the competition irrelevant? How can you create offerings that stand apart while simultaneously achieving lower costs? And how do you go about building a supporting business model that your organization will follow to profitably bring your strategic vision to market?

What makes these tools and frameworks so powerful is that they are visual, which renders them easy to understand and apply, no matter what an individual's level of education or creativity. By showing in a single-page graphic or diagram how the critical factors relate to one another, each tool enables everyone to see the answer to each question emerge, thus keeping everyone, well, on the same page.

Our book *Blue Ocean Strategy* introduced these tools, but the devil, as they say, is in the operational details. Here we delve deeply into those details: We show you how to put the right team together, set up the process, and systematically apply each tool, in what sequence, to produce results and avoid and overcome potential stumbling blocks along the way. We are not talking about offering lessons from a 30,000-foot perch. Instead, what we do here is empower managers with practical, hands-on guidance at every step of the journey from the red ocean to the blue.

Making a blue ocean shift is a transformational journey. It requires more than a clear idea and strategy to open up a new value-cost frontier. To move toward the new frontier, you have to bring people along. Without people's voluntary cooperation, you will be stopped dead in your tracks, as every professional of a certain age knows. While most strategy work does not delve into the human side of organizations, yours should.

Accordingly, the third component is having a humanistic process, something we have come to call "humanness" in the process, which inspires and builds people's confidence to own and drive the process for effective execution.

Most organizations face internal hurdles to change. This might be a cognitive hurdle, because people are wedded to the status quo. Or a political hurdle created by deep divisions or structural silos that breed internal tensions and infighting. Or a motivational hurdle, because people focus on doing what it takes to get by, but lack the energy, passion, and drive to make a real difference. Paul MacAlindin and the National Youth Orchestra of Iraq, for example, faced the daunting hurdle of bringing people who had been divided by years of fratricidal war together as a team. In Groupe SEB, ingrained ways of doing things and skepticism presented tough organizational hurdles to get over. The Malaysian government faced the classic hurdles stifling most governments today— ministerial silos and cross-ministerial tensions, not to mention the motivational hurdle of a bureaucratic, civil servant mentality.

Ironically, our research shows that the two most common practices organizations rely on for execution are also the reason most transformative efforts fail. First, most organizations treat strategy creation and execution as separate and sequential activities. One group of people devises a strategy and then hands it off to another to execute. For the most part, academic research on strategy and innovation reinforces this bifurcation and sequence. Second, when it comes to execution, most of the time and attention get focused on making structural changes and using carrot and stick approaches, such as changing spans of control, aligning incentives, setting up key performance indicators, and the like.

While carrots, sticks, and structural shifts have their roles to play, they do little to inspire and build people's confidence, which is critical to creating transformative change.

To do that, organizations should essentially do the opposite of what they commonly do.

Instead of treating execution as something that happens after the strategy has been set, it needs to be built into the strategy from the start or people won't own it. Also, you need to focus on the emotions and psychology of your people, instead of putting most of your energy into manipulating the mechanistic levers of structure, punishments, and rewards. If you can move people by inspiring and building their confidence to own and drive your new strategy, they will be committed to seeing change through and overcoming the organizational constraints you confront.

How can you capture people's hearts and minds and align them with your new strategy? Change, after all, is threatening, and asking people to make a blue ocean shift does just that by asking them to move away from what they know to a new frontier. Yet surprisingly, as we studied organizations that had made successful blue ocean shifts, we saw that people became more creative and more energized, and that execution wasn't questioned—precisely what you want to achieve, but what's typically so elusive. Why would that be? The longer we thought, the more clearly we could see that there was something about the process that recognized people, acknowledging their fears, their insecurities, their need to be treated with dignity, their desire to matter. We struggled to figure out what word could capture this something and best describe it. The closest we could get was what we came to term *humanness*.

What we came to understand is this: At its core, a successful blue ocean shift is fundamentally a humanistic process. It does not deny but instead embraces our humanness in such a way that it makes us more competent and confident than we ever imagined. Humanness inspires us to inch along. It recognizes our skepticism and vulnerabilities, our fear that we can't do it, our doubts over whether there even are blue oceans, our need for intellectual and emotional recognition to make us feel valued. By building humanness into the process, an organization can shift its team's psychology and create an emotional land-scape for change, whether you have 5 people or 10,000.

The blue ocean shift process accomplishes this not by demanding that anyone change but by easing people's fears and building their confidence at every step of the way. It does this by weaving atomization, firsthand discovery, and fair process into the entire journey. These elements are key to humanness, our research found, because they touch people at a fundamental level. The good news, as you will learn later, is that they are reproducible in any organization.

Figure 1-2 captures the essence of making a successful blue ocean shift in one picture. The three components shown in the figure are complementary and work together to produce a shift. Make no mistake, however. We were able to identify the three key components of a successful blue ocean shift—a blue ocean perspective, practical tools for market creation with proper guidance on how to apply them, and humanness in the process—not because we got the components right every time. In fact, organizations often faced frustrations and troubles as

Figure 1-2

The Three Key Components of a Successful Blue Ocean Shift

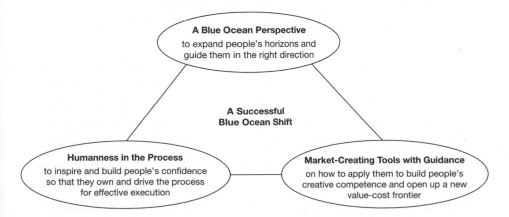

we got them wrong. We learned from lots of mistakes, most of which caused us to place even greater emphasis on the need to reinforce all three key components throughout the process.

Shifting an organization from a red to a blue ocean does not happen in one day or after one off-site. But it also doesn't take years. While the final market launch of Groupe SEB's ActiFry took over two years, because of the time required to secure complex patents, the blue ocean shifts of the National Youth Orchestra of Iraq and even the Malaysian government's large-scale Community Rehabilitation Program were made in a year or so. As organizations start to see tangible evidence of opportunities to open up breakthrough value-cost frontiers, energy climbs and momentum to move from the red to the blue ocean is unlocked in a powerful way.

Why Blue Ocean Shift Should Matter to You

There is no doubt that many, many industries are in need of new value-cost frontiers. The health-care industry, for one. Energy, for another. Public education in the United States, although not traditionally viewed as an industry per se, needs to be rethought. Its performance is unacceptably low, while costs have risen steeply. The auto industry, while currently not in free fall, clearly needs new ways to tackle environmental concerns that are not cost-prohibitive. Banking and other financial institutions beg for new strategies to achieve sustainable high performance.

UN scenarios suggest that, if current population and consumption trends continue, we will need the equivalent of two earths by the 2030s to generate sufficient resources and fresh air for all of us.[12] We need to open up new value-cost frontiers in areas as basic and diverse as the production and supply of municipal water, electricity access and use, and the way our cities are designed and run to avert what many see as otherwise unavoidable crises.

Pick any existing industry you can think of and ask if it isn't in need of a blue ocean shift. How does its demand pair against its supply? Today tighter profit margins, rising costs, stagnant or declining sales, and market share battles are hitting industries across the board, from construction to hair salons, advertising to law firms, paper mills to publishing. Even in public and nonprofit sector industries, like post offices, museums, libraries, charities, and classical orchestras, demand is down, costs and competition are up, and organizations are struggling financially.

In short, we are all paying for the red oceans around us. To turn things around, we need to produce more creative strategies that can unlock new value-cost frontiers and with them profitable new growth horizons. We need blue ocean shifts.

How about you?

Perhaps you are like Paul MacAlindin and the National Youth Orchestra of Iraq. You run or are part of a young organization, essentially a start-up, or a small Main Street business. You know you need to break out of the red ocean of head-to-head competition to grow profitably, but you don't know how. Or maybe you are part of a large, established organization with ingrained routines, culture, and its share of typical bureaucracy, as Christian Grob and his team had faced at Groupe SEB. Your organization is stuck in a red ocean of bloody competition but you doubt how, or if, it can shift away from the commoditization and price competition that is haunting it. People's mindsets seem locked in old ways of thinking, yet you know that to seize the future a strategic shift is necessary. Or you may be part of a government department, or ministry, or other public sector organization whose policies and practices are no longer cutting it. You know fundamental shifts are needed to deliver a leap in value at lower costs, but you can't even begin to imagine pulling that off.

If you can relate to any one of these situations, blue ocean shift is right for you.

What to Expect

Before diving into how to make a blue ocean shift happen, chapter 2 spells out the core concepts and mechanisms you need to know about market creation. It clarifies the existing confusion over what market-creating strategy *really* is and how it works. Here we address key issues, such as why focusing on creative destruction and disruptive innovation is limiting and captures only a partial picture of how new markets are created. How there's a whole other universe of market-creating opportunities that are often overlooked, but shouldn't be, based on *non*disruptive creation. And why the innovations that economists applaud and promote are not always synonymous with what it takes to create commercially compelling new markets that open up new value-cost frontiers, and why you need to understand what differentiates the two.

Chapters 3 and 4 then lay the foundations of blue ocean shift. Chapter 3 delineates the mindset of blue ocean strategists and their distinctive ways of thinking, so you can embrace the mental framing required to make a blue ocean shift. Chapter 4 outlines how the blue ocean shift process works. It expounds on the important concept of humanness and how it inspires and builds people's confidence in the process so that they own and drive the process and results. It also shows how the process builds people's creative competence along the journey.

Subsequent chapters then discuss the five steps involved in making a blue ocean shift. In each step, we introduce a new tool or tools that will provide structure and analytic guidance as your organization moves step-by-step to the blue ocean. We walk you through how to apply the tool to your situation, explain how to interpret the results, highlight the potential pitfalls in working with it, and discuss how to overcome those pitfalls to ensure your success. At the same time, you will learn how to build humanness naturally into each step, so your team will have the confidence to explore new possibilities and own the process and its results as it unfolds. In this way, execution is built into the process, so people are willing to drive the blue ocean shift as it is set in motion.

Specifically, the first step shows you how to get started by setting the right scope for your blue ocean initiative and constructing the right team. The second step addresses how to get a clear picture of the current state of play in your industry and align everyone around the need to make the shift. Here people learn how to get out of their functional and hierarchical silos and see the big picture. In the third step, the process pivots from what is to what could be, so a compelling future can be built. Here you learn how to uncover the hidden pain points buyers suffer and the points of intimidation limiting the size of your industry—both of which you can overturn. You also learn how to identify the landscape of noncustomers waiting to be unlocked. At this step, a blue ocean becomes more than a metaphor or an abstract concept. It becomes something you can see and feel—something whose potential you can define.

This brings us to the fourth step, where you learn how to go into the field and apply six systematic paths to create new market space. This step shows you how to reconstruct market boundaries and create new demand. In this step the process also drills down into how to convert the field insights you've gained into concrete blue ocean opportunities that both stand apart and deliver low cost. This brings us to the fifth and final step of the process. Here, we show you how to select your blue ocean move, conduct rapid market tests, and finalize, launch, and roll out your move to ensure that your value proposition and business model are delivering both differentiation and low cost. Here you learn how to choose and make your move in a way that creates a win for buyers and for yourself.

In the epilogue we pull everything together. We take you on a deep dive into a bureaucratic, conventional, and change-resistant organization—a national government—on its blue ocean shift journey. We show you how even in such an organization, characterized by formidable silos, a blue ocean shift is possible, transforming the way work is done and resulting in billions saved. In fact, today a common verb applied to emerging challenges is to *blue-ocean* it. Through the shift process, the government has augmented its ability not only to achieve high impact at low cost, but also to bring out the creativity and energy of the people who execute it. Through it, they are discovering the thrill of creating and capturing blue oceans of economic and social opportunity as they open up new value-cost frontiers. And if they can do it, we assure you, so can you.

Now, join us to learn step-by-step how to break away from the tired red ocean and seize your own blue ocean of new growth opportunities.

CHAPTER 2

The Fundamentals of Market-Creating Strategy

Before showing you how to make a blue ocean shift—how to move your organization from market competing to market creating—we first need to clarify what market-creating strategy really is and how it works.

We've seen a lot of confusion on this through the years, as some people have difficulty understanding how various perspectives on market creation fit together. Some equate market creation with creative destruction or disruption. They think you need to destroy or disrupt an existing market in order to create a new one. Others regard market creation as a matter of innovation, and often see technology as the key to unlocking new markets. Still others view market creation as synonymous with entrepreneurship and believe it to be the domain of entrepreneurs.

All these views are partly right. But they are also partly wrong, because each offers an incomplete picture of how markets are created. Without having a complete picture, efforts to make a blue ocean shift will miss many opportunities and may even be misdirected. So here we build a holistic model of market-creating strategy that shows not only the available strategic options and how they produce blue ocean shifts, but also their corresponding growth consequences. Using this model, we can understand how these existing partial views fit together in the big picture.

Creative Destruction and Disruptive Innovation Are Only Part of the Picture

In speaking with executives, entrepreneurs, and government leaders, one consistent pattern we've observed is how often they associate market creation with the concepts of creative destruction or disruption. *Creative destruction* is the iconic term coined by the Austrian economist Joseph Schumpeter, who observed that although competition in existing markets is good, diminishing returns eventually set in as buyers' needs are satisfied and profits are competed away.[1] The real engine of economic growth, he argued, is therefore the creation of new markets. But, in his view, this creation is dependent on destruction.[2]

Destruction occurs when an innovation displaces an earlier technology or an existing product or service. The word *displacement* is important here because without displacement, creative destruction does not occur. For example, the innovation of digital photography creatively destroyed the photographic film industry by effectively displacing it. So today digital photography is the norm, and photographic film is seldom used.

The concept of disruption echoes Schumpeter's insight.[3] The most well-known study on disruption directly relevant to market creation is the influential idea of disruptive innovation.[4] Whereas creative destruction occurs when a superior technology, product, or service comes along and destroys the old with the new, disruptive innovation begins with the arrival of an *inferior* technology, which then crosses the line from inferior to superior and, in doing so, displaces market leaders.

The classic example here is the disruption and eventual displacement of leading disk drive players, which were caught off guard by bottom-up disruptors that initially entered the scene with simpler technology and inferior performance.[5]

The distinguishing insight here is that the technology waltzing into an industry need not be superior, as Schumpeter suggests, but instead can come in as a Trojan horse whose initial inferiority does not appear to threaten the mainstream market. As a result, established players ignore the newcomer until it's too late. What these ideas have in common, however, is their shared focus on the displacement of existing players and markets.

As business history shows that there are ample cases of both forms of displacement, focusing singly on either creative destruction or disruptive innovation in discussions of market creation would be partial and misleading. Hence, to describe the act of market creation that embraces both forms of displacement, we coined the term *disruptive creation*.[6] This broader term captures the full, not partial, opportunity space of market creation driven by displacement.

Important as disruptive creation driven by either creative destruction or disruptive innovation is, however, it still misses another universe of market-creating opportunities. As our research shows, many new markets have also been created without disrupting existing ones.[7]

Nondisruptive Creation Also Generates New Markets and Growth

If you have children and live in any one of 147 countries around the world, from the United States, to Afghanistan, to Germany, Japan, or Yemen, you have heard of *Sesame Street*. Big Bird, Elmo, Ernie, and Bert are just a few of the lovable Muppets that teach preschool children how to count, name their colors and shapes, and recognize the letters of the

alphabet. And the best part is that children have so much
fun watching the program they don't even realize how much
they're learning. But parents do, which is why they love it too.
It's the antithesis of what many people associate with education. It seduces and amuses as it educates the very young.

Sesame Street didn't disrupt any prior market for early
childhood education. It didn't destroy and replace preschools,
or libraries, or parents reading bedtime stories to their children. Rather, *Sesame Street* opened up a new value-cost frontier that unlocked the new market of preschool edutainment
that, for the most part, had never existed before. In contrast
to "disruptive creation," *Sesame Street* is the result of what we
call "*non*disruptive creation," as it created new market space
without disrupting an existing market.

Now put children aside and turn to men. Many men's lives
were revolutionized through Pfizer's market-creating move of
Viagra. But did Viagra disrupt another market? Again, the
answer is no. It was nondisruptive creation. By alleviating
erectile dysfunction, Viagra solved a prevalent and previously
unaddressed problem and took the world by storm. Demand
for it rapidly grew into a multibillion-dollar business, creating
a new market space of lifestyle drugs.

Now think of the more than 3 billion people who live on
only a few dollars a day. Here, too, nondisruptive creation
stepped in to solve an unaddressed problem: the lack of access
to capital that was driving the poverty cycle. In 1983, Grameen Bank began offering microloans without requiring
collateral, enabling people to start businesses or engage in
agriculture and climb up the income ladder while paying off
a small debt. This strategic move created the new market of
microfinance without replacing any other market. Until then,
conventional banks had simply ignored the poor, whom they
deemed unsuitable as borrowers. Microfinance has since bal-
looned into a multibillion-dollar industry with plenty of room
for future growth. While climbing, it still reaches less than 20

percent of the potential new market, which today is served by both nonprofit and for-profit organizations around the world.

Online dating, health clubs, crowdfunding, ringtones, and routers, switches, and network devices are just some of the myriad multibillion-dollar industries that have been created in the last few decades through nondisruptive creation. Today, in fact, the fastest-growing profession in the United States, second only to information technology, is based on nondisruptive creation. It's life coaching. Just 25 years ago, the industry did not exist. Now it boasts annual revenues north of US$2 billion. The advent and growth of the life-coaching industry have not come at the expense of any existing industry. Tens of thousands of new coaching jobs have been created without destroying any other jobs. Rather, the industry has created new demand, as people flock to life coaches to become more effective in both their personal and professional lives.

As these examples illustrate, our research indeed demonstrates that growth has always been generated by market-creating moves based on both disruptive and nondisruptive creations.[8] To illustrate, consider the evolution of industrial classification standards in the United States. In 1997, the North American Industry Classification Standard (NAICS) replaced the more than half-century-old Standard Industrial Classification (SIC) system published by the US Census. In the new system, industries were not only merged or replaced but also created, with the number of sectors doubling from 10 to 20. The services sector under the old system, for example, was expanded into 7 industry sectors, ranging from information to health care and social assistance.

Since 1997, the NAICS system has been revised several times to keep up with the pace of industry creation, re-creation, and growth. For example, while the information sector was expanded significantly in the 2002 version, the 2017 version included changes to 6 out of the 20 NAICS sectors to reflect new market creation. In both these new versions, some existing industry classifications were replaced, while entirely new categories were also created to recognize the emergence of brand-new industries. Given that these systems are designed for standardization and continuity, such changes underscore the impact that both disruptive and nondisruptive creations have in shaping existing industry boundaries and creating new ones.

Getting the Full Picture

Try this short exercise. Ask a group of people to look around a room for 30 seconds and make a mental note of every red item they see. As soon as the time is up, ask them to close their eyes and recall every blue item they saw. That's right *blue*. People will have trouble recalling many items at all. What we look for determines what we see. When we assume that the only way we can create a new market is by disrupting an old one, opportunities for nondisruptive creation can be easily missed. People tend to focus their attention on the core of existing markets and what it would take to disrupt the existing order. This narrows their vision and blinds them to the wealth of nondisruptive market-creating moves they could make.

Consider the potential advantages of expressly including nondisruptive creation in your strategic thinking. First, take start-ups. When entrepreneurs set out to disrupt an existing market, they often face established players with many, many times the financial and marketing resources the start-ups have. While it's true that David sometimes beats Goliath, and the emotional pull of the story looms large, more often than not it's the other way around. As a new start-up, do you really want to be up against well-entrenched leaders? Maybe. And that's certainly one way to go. But you don't have to—that's the important point. The opportunities for nondisruptive creation loom just as large, and entrepreneurs would be unwise not to take them into account as well.

Second, consider established players. In established organizations, fear of losing one's job or current status through creative destruction or disruptive innovation can prompt managers to undermine their organization's market-creating efforts. They may starve such projects of resources. Or allocate undue overhead costs to them. Or relegate the employees working on them to corporate Siberia, which inevitably makes them want out. Microsoft and many other established organizations struggle with issues like these. Growth through nondisruptive creation is less threatening, because it doesn't directly challenge the existing order and the people who make their livelihoods through it. So, by framing their market-creating strategy in a broader context that embraces both disruptive and nondisruptive creations—as blue ocean shift does—established organizations can better manage their organizational politics and the anxieties of their key people.

Finally, consider new jobs. When disruptive creation occurs, new jobs are created. Often, a lot of jobs. But old jobs are lost. So, when the cassette tape replaced the 8-track, which was replaced by the CD, which was later challenged by the MP3 player, each successive new market created new growth and employment. But they came, in part, at the expense of jobs from, and sometimes the very existence of, the preceding businesses. By contrast, nondisruptive creation produces both growth and employment without necessarily displacing existing businesses or industries.

We do not raise these points to stress the advantages of nondisruptive over disruptive creation. Rather, we wish to show you why nondisruptive creation should also be incorporated into your strategic thinking. We need a holistic model of market-creating strategy that embraces both disruptive and nondisruptive creations, since they are complementary.[9] They separately and together open up new value-cost frontiers that are key to growth. Focusing on only one will lead to an incomplete and biased assessment of potential market-creating opportunities and limit your efforts to make a blue ocean shift.

A Holistic Model of Market-Creating Strategy

By now you may be asking yourself, "Which market-creating strategies result in disruptive creation and which result in nondisruptive creation?" In our research over the last 10 years, we found that the answer to this question comes down to the type of issue an organization sets out to address in making a market-creating strategic move.

Our research revealed three basic ways in which market-creating strategies—and hence blue ocean shifts—are made. You can:

- Offer a breakthrough solution for an industry's existing problem.
- Redefine an industry's existing problem and solve it.
- Identify and solve a brand-new problem or seize a brand-new opportunity.

Each of these approaches involves a different balance between disruptive and nondisruptive creation. The most effective way to show these relationships is through a graphic. Accordingly, figure 2-1 presents a holistic model of market-creating strategy. We call this graphic a "growth model of market-creating strategy" because it shows which strategic approach produces which kind of growth.

Let's run through each of these in turn.

Figure 2-1

A Growth Model of Market-Creating Strategy

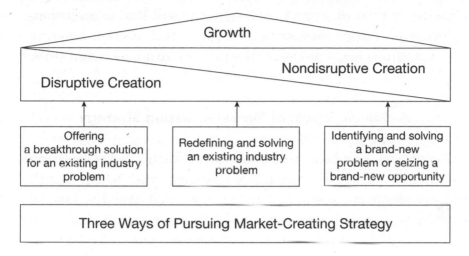

| Offering a breakthrough solution for an existing industry problem | Redefining and solving an existing industry problem | Identifying and solving a brand-new problem or seizing a brand-new opportunity |

Three Ways of Pursuing Market-Creating Strategy

Offer a Breakthrough Solution for an Existing Industry Problem

When an organization creates a breakthrough solution for an existing industry problem, it strikes at the core of existing firms and markets, whether at the outset or over time. Let's go back to our music example. CDs were a breakthrough solution to the problem of how best to store and replay sound recordings, which is a central challenge for people trying to enjoy music. In contrast to its predecessor, the CD offered "perfect sound forever," skipping effortlessly from one song to another with none of the crackling and gumming up of twisted cassette tapes. Not surprisingly, in a short time, the CD replaced the cassette as the standard music medium. For years, people were thrilled with CDs—until, that is, Apple's MP3 player, the iPod, came around and offered yet another breakthrough solution to the problem of storing and playing music. Again, people rushed in droves to replace their old, now passé and unwanted, CDs with Apple's iPod and other MP3 players, which gave them easy access to their entire music library. In each case, the existing product was essentially replaced through disruptive creation.

In the same way, the internal combustion engine replaced the steam-powered engine by offering a breakthrough solution to power generation for motorized transport. Ditto for digital photography, which effectively replaced film photography with a far better way to take, develop, share, and store photos.

The main effect, therefore of developing a breakthrough solution to an existing industry problem is the displacement of existing offerings and jobs, as the old is disrupted by the new. Existing markets are re-created from their core and expanded beyond their previous boundaries, turning red oceans into blue. Growth occurs with this market re-creation and boundary expansion as the breakthrough solution pulls in new demand, converting once noncustomers into customers. Just think, for example, of how many more people today take photos with digital photography than took pictures with film in the past.

Identify and Solve a Brand-New Problem or Seize a Brand-New Opportunity

On the other end of the spectrum, organizations that identify and solve brand-new problems or create and seize brand-new opportunities unlock new markets *beyond* existing industry boundaries. Here disruptive creation is hardly at play. Think back to Viagra and Grameen Bank, which identified and solved problems that had not previously been addressed. Or think of *Sesame Street* and life coaching, which identified and created brand-new opportunities. All these moves established new markets beyond the bounds of any existing industry.

Similarly, the multibillion-dollar industry of ringtones has delivered a brand-new opportunity for people to express their individuality and get a small boost of pleasure throughout their day, whenever their phone rings and their favorite song or sound plays. If there's been any disruption here, it's only been in eliminating monotony and boredom. This market space was created beyond the existing industry boundaries.

As our growth model indicates, solving a brand-new problem or capturing a brand-new opportunity results in nondisruptive creation because the new market hardly eats at the core, or even the margins, of existing industries. This type of growth is nondisruptive to society as well, because it grows profits, revenues, and jobs—not to mention society's imagination—without destroying any others. Areas like cybersecurity, obesity, lifelong learning, virtual reality, the environment, and health services provide ample new opportunities for nondisruptive creation. So does the bottom of the pyramid—that is, opportunities to be found and new problems to be solved among the billions of poor people at the base of the financial pyramid.[10]

Redefine and Solve an Existing Industry Problem

In between solving an existing problem and identifying and solving a brand-new problem or creating a brand-new opportunity are market-creating strategies that redefine and solve the problem an industry focuses on. Problem redefinition allows an organization to replace assumptions and reconstruct industry boundaries in new and creative ways. Here both disruptive and nondisruptive creations are in full play. Take the well-known example of Cirque du Soleil. It made a leap in the kind and degree of value the industry offered by redefining the problem it focused on, from how to maximize the fun and thrill of the circus, to how to combine the best of it—clowns, tents, and amazing acrobats—with the best of theater and ballet—their artistry, music, dance, and story lines. It created a new market space between these industries, drawing a slice of demand from each. At the same time, it enlarged the overall pie by pulling new people into this blue ocean of newly created market space. Adults without children and corporate clients, who never dreamed of going to a circus before, became customers of Cirque du Soleil.

André Rieu and the Johann Strauss Orchestra also created a new market by redefining the problem the classical music industry focused on, unlocking both disruptive and nondisruptive creation. Dubbed the "maestro for the masses," Rieu has consistently appeared on the top-ranking lists of touring concerts worldwide for the past 20 years, along with Coldplay, Beyoncé, and the Rolling Stones. Unlike traditional classical music orchestras, Rieu's orchestra combines easy listening classical and waltz music—think the "Blue Danube," "Barcarolle," and "O Mio Babbino Caro"—with contemporary music like Michael Jackson's "Ben" or Celine Dion's hit, "My Heart Will Go On" that many people find more accessible. Rieu also moved away from pretentious theaters, choosing instead to hold his concerts in large stadiums with spectacular light and sound effects and a fun, interactive atmosphere. While major concert halls can seat, on average, a maximum of 2,000 people, Rieu's stadiums can easily sell out at 10,000-plus people. While Rieu wins a slice of customers from classical music concerts, he also creates huge new demand by drawing a mass of new customers, including people who were previously put off by the formality and pretension of classical music. That's because André Rieu's orchestra, like Cirque du Soleil, strikes at the margins of these other industries, not at their core, by solving a redefined problem that doesn't go head-to-head with the problem anyone else is solving.

Groupe SEB's blue ocean shift, which we talked about in chapter 1, also belongs here. Groupe SEB redefined the problem its industry focused on from how to make the best electric French fry maker to how to make mouthwatering fresh, healthy fries with no frying. While ActiFry has won a slice of demand from the traditional electrical fryer market, the leap in the kind and degree of value the ActiFry delivers inspired people who had never bought a fryer to become customers, growing overall industry demand by nearly 40 percent in value. Likewise, by redefining conventional boundaries, the National Youth Orchestra of Iraq opened up a new value-cost frontier and brought in new customers. But, it did not replace other kinds of youth orchestras, although it drew some of the same audience.

Simply put, offering a breakthrough solution for an existing industry problem generally results in disruptive creation. Identifying and solving a brand-new problem or seizing a brand-new opportunity most often gives rise to nondisruptive creation. And redefining and solving an existing problem draws on elements of both disruptive and nondisruptive creations.

Focus on Value Innovation, Not Technology Innovation

When we speak to audiences around the world about market-creating strategy, we often begin by asking them to consider Google Glass, Motorola's Iridium satellite phone, and Apple's Newton personal digital assistant. "Were these market-creating moves innovation?" And "Were they commercial successes or failures?" Audiences usually answer "yes" to the first question and "failures" to the second.

Then we ask another set of questions: "Who invented the personal computer?" And "Who invented the home VCR?" When it comes to PCs, people most often reply Apple or IBM. As for VCRs, people come up with all sorts of consumer electronics companies, the most common being Sony or JVC. The right answers, we then tell them, are actually MITS and Ampex, respectively. Most people are not only surprised when they find that out, but also appear to be unfamiliar with either company.

Putting these conversations together reveals an important point about market creation. While technology innovators may lay extraordinary eggs, they are seldom the ones who ultimately hatch them. The focus of a successful market-creating strategy should be not on how to lay a technology egg per se, but rather on how to hatch the egg for its commercial success. Thus although MITS invented the first personal computer, it was Apple and IBM, among others, that dominated the new mass market for PCs by adapting the technology to produce a leap in buyer value. Likewise, although Ampex invented video recording technology in the 1950s, companies like Sony and JVC dominated the long-profitable home VCR industry by adopting the technology and making video recorders easy enough to use and affordable for the mass of buyers; in essence, converting a technology innovation into what we called *value innovation*.[11]

There's no inherent reason that an organization can't capitalize on its own inventions, and certainly some companies have succeeded in doing both. But history shows that egg laying and egg hatching are often performed by different players.[12] This, we suggest, may be one reason so many people don't even recognize the names of technology innovators now gone from their markets and instead mistakenly believe the value innovators—the ones that hatch new markets—are the technology pioneers as well.

It's a win for everyone if a market player lays the technology egg, hatches it, and opens up a profitable and growing new market space that others may eventually enter. But the key lesson to remember here is that to succeed in creating a new market, your focus must be on offering a quantum leap in value for buyers, not on technology innovation per se.[13] Google Glass, Motorola's Iridium, and Apple's Newton all suffered by getting this wrong. Google Glass was considered unattractive, nerdish, expensive, and raised hugely uncomfortable privacy issues. The Iridium satellite phone was a technological feat that worked in the Gobi desert but not in buildings or cars, where people needed it most.

As for Apple's Newton PDA, well, it just didn't do what it said it would, so it's not surprising that buyers didn't see value in it.

The fact is, successful market-creating strategies often don't rely on technology innovation at all. Think of Grameen Bank's microfinancing, Starbucks, or the National Youth Orchestra of Iraq—all created new markets with little or no bleeding-edge technologies. Even where technology is heavily involved, as with Salesforce.com or Groupe SEB's ActiFry, the reason buyers love these offerings isn't because of the technology. Buyers adore them because they are so simple, easy to use, fun, and effective. That is, they love them because the technology is fundamentally linked to a leap in buyer value.

Economics has long taught us that R&D and technology innovation, as measured by R&D spending and numbers of patents, are the central drivers of innovation and growth. This may be true at the macro level of the economy, which could be one reason people tend to think of technology innovation first when they think about creating new markets. But such reasoning does not necessarily hold true when we apply it to the micro level of the individual organization. To take one example, Apple's R&D spending-to-sales ratio has been among the lowest of its IT peers over the last decade. Microsoft, on the other hand, has one of the highest rates of R&D expenditures and impressive research centers the world over. But while Apple has been one of the most—if not *the* most— innovative companies in the commercial world, it's hard to think of a single market Microsoft created in the last 10 years.

As a prescient article in *Time* magazine on Dean Kamen, the inventor of the Segway Personal Transporter, noted at the time of the Segway's launch: "One of the hardest truths for any technologist to hear is that success or failure in business is rarely determined by the quality of the technology."[14] The Segway was an engineering marvel, one of the most talked-about technology innovations of its day when it was launched in 2001. But that did not convince enough people to pay

US$4,000–$5,000 for a product that left them in a quandary over where to park it, how to take it in a car, whether it could be brought on a bus or a train, and where it could be used—on sidewalks or roads? While the Segway was expected to reach breakeven six months after its launch, the company continued to lose money until it was sold in 2009.

When companies mistakenly assume new market creation hinges on breakthrough technologies, their organizations tend to push for products or services that are either too "out there"— ahead of their time, too esoteric, too complicated—or, like the Segway, lack the complementary ecosystem needed to open up a new market. In fact, many technology innovations fail to create and capture new markets even as they win accolades for their organizations. Think of TiVo, whose original DVR garnered a lot of fanfare and is in the US Patent and Trademark Office National Inventors Hall of Fame, but which left most people wondering what it did and why they would want it.

Blue ocean shift is built on this insight. Just as value innovation is a cornerstone of market-creating strategy, a successful blue ocean shift occurs only when unprecedented buyer value is created by opening up a value-cost frontier that didn't exist before. Value innovation anchors innovation to the value it gives buyers, not to the cleverness of the technology. It can be achieved with or without new technology. This holds true whether your blue ocean market-creating efforts set out to provide a breakthrough solution to an existing industry problem, to redefine the problem your industry focuses on, or to identify and solve a brand-new problem or create a brand-new opportunity.

You Don't Need to Be an Entrepreneur to Create a New Market

Are you true blue or bloody red? That's the name of a simple but telling quiz we put together a decade ago. We give it to executives when we meet to get a sense of the situation they're up against. It asks questions about, among other things, the ferocity of their competition, the pressure on their margins, and the intensity of the commoditization they face. People's overriding response: They're operating in red oceans and need to get out.[15]

Yet when we dig deep, we find that even when companies deliberately set out to create new markets, those efforts are usually geared less toward getting out of red oceans and more toward making further investments in existing, overcrowded markets. There is a mismatch between what organizations aspire and need to do and what they're actually doing. Why? Apart from the familiarity of current markets and the everyday pressure competition poses, the answer, we believe, comes down to the way people think about and manage market creation.

Ever since Schumpeter, entrepreneurs have been seen as the chief drivers of innovation and therefore of market creation. Entrepreneurs take risks and learn through trial and error as they attempt to seize opportunities by applying their intuition and ingenuity. But for market creation to be an integral part of an ongoing organization's strategy, it cannot be a random, high-risk endeavor, conducted through trial and error. It needs to be a reliable process that can be reproduced. Without that, as much as organizations may need to make market-creating moves, they will continue to shy away from investing accordingly.

Some progress has been made in this regard over the years.[16] But we still need a market-creation process built on concrete market-creating tools that systematically link innovation to buyer value and provide guidance on how to apply them. More than that, the process must recognize and address people's fear of trying new ideas and encourage them to push boundaries and overcome the forces and habits that keep them where they are. In short, it must be grounded in humanness to inspire people's confidence.

As you will see, a humanistic, teachable, and systematic process makes market creation accessible to everyone, not just highly creative people or natural-born entrepreneurs. It allows ordinary people like us to create markets and do extraordinary things. With it, Paul MacAlindin, a classically trained conductor, was able to create a new type of orchestra that could inspire peace and hold up to the world a vision of the beauty of a united Iraq. With it, government leaders and ordinary civil servants in Malaysia collectively conceived a new way to deal with petty criminals, which dramatically cuts recidivism and gives these inmates the gift of a second chance while lowering the government's costs.

It doesn't matter what industry you're in, or whether you consider yourself to be an entrepreneur. The process we will describe unlocks the potential all of us possess to see beyond what is to what could be. The success of such efforts is ultimately a probability game, of course, as all strategic initiatives are, be they red or blue ocean ones. Still, the whole point of strategy is to raise the probabilities of success, and that's precisely what the blue ocean shift process does.

With that understanding, we are now ready to dive into the mindset of a blue ocean strategist. Adopting this mindset is essential to setting the right direction for your blue ocean shift. In the next chapter, we outline its defining features and explain why those features matter, so you can grasp the mental framing you will need as you embark on your own blue ocean shift journey.

CHAPTER 3

The Mind of a Blue Ocean Strategist

How do blue ocean strategists see new opportunities where others see only red oceans of declining profits and growth? They don't get taken in by what everyone else takes for granted. They embrace a perspective that allows them to ask fundamentally different sets of questions, which, in turn, enable them to perceive and appreciate the fallacies behind long-held assumptions and the artificial boundaries we unknowingly impose upon ourselves. Their perspective is very different from the market-competing logic that dominates most executives' mental models.

To fully delineate how blue ocean strategists think, let's explore two strategic moves—one by a nonprofit B2C, and the other by a classic for-profit B2B—so you can see how this mindset applies across industries and sectors.

From Pity Pleas to Doing Something Funny for Money

Can you imagine someone hitching around town carrying a refrigerator? Or a town where highwaymen and -women dressed only in underpants accost motorists and passers-by to solicit small donations? Or your CEO coming into work, holding meetings with a soft squishy red ball the size of a golf ball affixed to her nose all day? Welcome to Comic Relief, a UK charity formed in 1985, and Red Nose Day, an event it holds once every two years. In the 16 Red Nose Days since its founding, the UK charity has raised more than £1 billion in the UK alone, with its 2017 Red Nose Day raising over £73 million.

Now imagine the UK charity fund-raising industry at the time Comic Relief was born. It was redder than red. Not only were there thousands of charities, but for most causes there was huge overlap, including more than 600 cancer charities and 200 charities for the homeless just in London. What's more, in little over a decade, the number of charities had jumped by over 60 percent. So competition was way up.

At the same time, donor fatigue was setting in, and the number of British people donating to charities had dropped by more than 25 percent. People were tired of being made to feel guilty, of the continuous solicitations, of the difficulty in choosing the right charity to support among the plethora of options. And they were suspicious of how the funds were actually being used—to cover overhead or to go to the cause?

At the time, fund-raising charities followed a fairly predictable strategy, a pattern we see played out in industry after industry. Almost in lockstep, they concentrated on competing more effectively within the boundaries of their existing industry space. They focused on their biggest customers, in this case wealthy, educated, mostly older (55–64-year-old) donors. They invested heavily in year-round marketing and solicitations. They publicly recognized large donations to encourage the same people to give more. They organized ever-fancier fund-raising galas, all the while using serious and depressing campaigns to trigger feelings of guilt. In short, they fought to capture a greater share of the industry's already shrinking demand by focusing on the same customers and factors their

industry had long competed on. This had the decidedly negative effect of raising their costs at the precise moment demand
was going down, annoying existing donors even further.

Comic Relief took a fundamentally different approach. It
created Red Nose Day, a national day of wacky community
fund-raising, together with a star-studded (and entirely pro
bono) comedy telethon, Red Nose Night, which revolutionized
charity fund-raising. Today, Red Nose Day is almost like a
national holiday in the UK, and Comic Relief has built an
amazing 96 percent brand awareness.

To achieve this, Comic Relief redefined the charity industry's problem, from how to get the wealthy to give out of guilt,
to how to get everyone to do something funny for money; in
essence, crowdsourcing fund-raising. Whereas most charities
hold glamorous special events to attract the wealthy, Comic
Relief eliminated or reduced expensive fund-raising galas,
year-round solicitations and the writing of grants, and counseling and care services. Nor does it target wealthy donors.
It refuses to limit itself to such a small segment; it targets
everyone—the poor, the rich, the young, the old, even kinder-
gartners! With some imagination and perhaps a bit of cour-
age, even the poorest person can make a major contribution.
Take the London travel agent with a reputation as a chatter-
box who got her friends to sponsor her to stay silent for 24
hours, raising over £500 in sponsorships; or the hairy "man's
man" from Manchester, who had all his body hair waxed off,
raising £500 as well. Taking part is as cheap and easy as purchasing one of the hard-to-resist little red plastic noses that
are sold everywhere and currently cost £1 apiece. All those
connected to the telethon, including the TV station, donate
their services because they love the cause and generate such
goodwill by participating.

By offering star-studded quality entertainment, community "fun"d-raising where everyone gets the opportunity to
go just a little bit mad, and selling little red noses across the

country, Comic Relief creates a unique, inspiring event that attracts masses of people. And because Red Nose Day happens only once every two years, there is no time for donor fatigue to set in. Comic Relief has fans, not supporters. What's more, unlike other top UK fund-raising charities that can give roughly 87 percent of their income to their charitable purpose, Comic Relief guarantees that 100 percent of donations go directly to the cause. Comic Relief is able to guarantee this Golden Pound Promise, because its costs are low, thanks to all that it eliminated and reduced, and because sponsors and investment income cover its far lower administrative costs. As for marketing costs, they are zero in the UK, as a result of all the free word-of-mouth advertising generated by the Red Nose Day activities held across the country. In 2015 Comic Relief formally brought Red Nose Day to the United States.

Energy Flows Where Your Attention Goes

An inspiring story, no doubt. But what have we learned? Could Comic Relief have been conceived with a red ocean perspective? To find out, let's run through four sets of questions. As we do, ask yourself about your own state of thinking.

One. If Comic Relief had accepted existing industry practices as a given, and let the structure of the UK charity fundraising industry shape its strategy, would the idea for Red Nose Day ever have been conceived? Or is it more than likely that, with competition so intense, demand down, and costs up, it might not even have entered the industry? How about you? What would you have done in this scenario?

Two. If Comic Relief had focused on benchmarking other charities and tried to emulate—and better—their best practices, what would the likely result have been? Would its strategy have been different? Or is it more likely that the more it focused on benchmarking and outpacing the competition, the more its strategy would simply have looked like the competition's? Is this something your organization does all too often, too?

Three. Customer satisfaction and understanding customer needs are hot buttons. Most organizations regularly monitor customer satisfaction scores. But if Comic Relief had focused on better satisfying existing wealthy donors, would those customers have given them the idea to ask everyone—rich and poor alike—to do something funny for money? Or would they have urged them to do what the industry was already doing, only better? Do your existing customers keep you focused on what is, instead of what could be?

Four. If Comic Relief had pursued either differentiation *or* low cost, how would its strategy be different? With a differentiation strategy, wouldn't they simply have been likely to add bells and whistles to the industry's current approach, paying scant heed to what they could eliminate or reduce to simultaneously achieve low cost? If instead they had pursued a low-cost strategy, wouldn't they likely have cut back the industry's existing competing factors without creating anything new to stand apart? How about you? Do you act on the assumption that, to achieve differentiation you need to spend more, while to win through low costs you need to compromise on the distinctive value you can offer?

From Red Noses to Blue Oceans in the B2B Space

Now let's turn to the corporate B2B sector and consider the customer relationship management (CRM) software used to manage organizations' interactions with customers and sales prospects in all areas of their business. CRM software is a growing multibillion-dollar industry. Not surprisingly, it's also highly competitive. Major enterprise resource planning vendors, such as SAP, Oracle, and Microsoft, had long dominated the industry. They have what most start-ups don't have—the deep resources needed to cover the steep R&D costs associated with product development.

And yet, despite these impressive vendors, from the customers' point of view, all the offerings looked pretty much the same. All these firms made highly customized software to match their clients' needs. They all applied the traditional software business model of selling perpetual software licenses, which allow customers to use the software indefinitely. Software was installed, configured, and customized on-site for each client, which required both significant professional services on the part of the vendor and significant internal expertise on the part of the customer. The software also had to be integrated with the client's legacy systems, which could entail substantial changes to their work processes and infrastructure. Overall, CRM software was expensive and time-consuming to install, with a high total cost of ownership. To stand apart in the industry and close a sale, vendors normally pursued one of two strategies: Either they tried to differentiate their product by adding still more features or they offered big discounts in the final stages of negotiation. Either way, everyone in the industry focused on selling CRM software to the businesses that could afford it: large, complex corporations.

The irony of this is that because the software was complex, expensive to purchase and maintain, hard to install, and required considerable middleware and hardware to run, CRM software vendors effectively limited demand for their own industry.

Enter Salesforce.com. Formed in 1999 by four people, former Oracle executive Marc Benioff, Parker Harris, Dave Moellenhoff, and Frank Dominguez, Salesforce.com did not take the existing industry structure as given, nor did it set out to beat the competition. Instead, it strove to make the competition irrelevant by removing all the pain points the industry had traditionally imposed on its clients, pain points companies ironically had come to accept. This last point is worth mulling over, as it happens in all too many industries. If we need a vaccination, we take it for granted that this will usually require a shot, even though most people cringe at the prospect. If we go to the airport, we take it for granted that there will be lines, and we'll feel a measure of stress. And if we fly first class on a domestic US flight, we take it for granted that the first-class seats of US carriers will hardly be roomier or recline much further than those in economy, despite the steep ticket price.

Determined to break out of the red ocean of similar offerings, Salesforce.com launched a market creating strategy that unlocked a blue ocean of new market space. It created a highly reliable, easy-to-use CRM solution accessible over the web, which worked the moment business users signed up for it via a monthly subscription. Not having to purchase a software license or expend resources on infrastructure, deployment, and maintenance reduced the total cost of ownership by roughly 90 percent. Salesforce.com also significantly reduced the risk of deploying its software by allowing subscriptions to be canceled at any time. What's more, by initially offering only one version of CRM software, Salesforce.com dramatically lowered its per-unit development costs. It could also learn which features mattered and which ones didn't based on usage rates, allowing it to focus strategically on what mattered most to users.

The result: In just 10 years since it was founded, Sales force.com earned more than US$1.3 billion in annual revenues. It pulled medium-size and even small businesses into the industry, converting former noncustomers into customers as it grew overall demand. Today, Salesforce.com has over

20,000 employees and annual revenues approaching US$8 billion.

Clearly, the CRM software and the UK charity fundraising industries are worlds apart. Yet, here again, we see striking parallels between the two. First, we see again that players in an industry all too often move in lockstep with one another. They compete in the same way, invest in the same things, and focus on the existing customers of the industry, largely commoditizing and limiting the size of their own industry. Second, we see again that while industry players fight to capture a greater share of existing demand, the market universe of total potential demand is often far greater. And yet, organizations act as though the existing market boundaries define the de facto universe when in reality these boundaries are not fixed but are merely products of our minds. They can be transcended when we apply a new lens to our thinking. Finally, we see again that organizations can redefine the basis of strategy in an industry to open up new market space and achieve differentiation and low cost.

But the question is—how do they do it?

Reframing Your Thinking from Red to Blue

We are now ready to deduce the mindset of blue ocean strategists and the distinctive ways their thinking departs from red ocean logic. The aim here is for you to understand how blue ocean strategists think so that you can embrace this logic as you embark on your own blue ocean shift journey. This mindset acts as a compass to guide your strategic direction. Without getting it right, the market-creating tools, however good, may be misapplied in action and fail to produce your intended shift. As we go through each guiding principle, think about how it allows you to begin to see opportunities where before only constraints were visible.

Blue ocean strategists do not take industry conditions as given. Rather, they set out to reshape them in their favor.

When executives develop strategy, they nearly always begin by analyzing the environment: Is the industry growing, stagnant, or shrinking? Are raw material prices rising or falling? Are competitors building new plants, launching major new product lines, laying off hundreds of employees, or hiring new talent? Is customer demand up or down? Most executives build their strategies on the basis of these assessments. In other words, structure shapes strategy.[1] This view of strategy is deterministic in that: (1) It treats an organization's strategic options as limited by the environment; and (2) it bounds executives' imaginations by the industry's current conditions.

This works fine when industries are attractive. But what if your industry structure is unattractive, and your number-one competitor is barely scraping by or even losing money? What will your strategy be then? To lose less money than everyone else? To pull out? Neither is terribly inspiring, nor is it a path to strong, profitable growth.

What a blue ocean strategist recognizes, and what most of us all too often forget, is that while industry conditions exist, individual firms created them. And just as individual firms created them, individual firms can shape them too, the way Comic Relief and Salesforce.com did. Reflect for a moment on many of the greatest industries. Back at the turn of the 20th century, didn't Ford create a mass market for the auto industry, as Xerox did later in the copier industry, followed by Canon in the personal copier industry? How about McDonald's in fast food? Apple in apps? FedEx in express delivery? Or even DryBar, which launched the "only-blowouts" market space in US hair salons, rather than offering haircuts, coloring, and perms.

Just as single organizations can drive entire industries with powerful ideas, single organizations can shape existing industries and create new ones.² Industry boundaries are not fixed. They are as fluid as your imagination. And one of the greatest ironies is that often it is organizations themselves that contribute to their industry's declining conditions. Think of the US Postal Service that today teeters on the brink as people shift to alternatives like email and express delivery services, which are significantly more expensive. Why is demand for government postal services shrinking? Is it simply because these new, alternative industries are so strong? Partially. But it's also because the total postal experience is so poor. How many times have you entered a US post office and found fast efficient service, with every window open, no lines, and postal workers who actually seem happy to serve you? Was the experience a pleasant one you would want to repeat? Probably not. More likely, you were one of many people standing in line with a dissatisfied look on your face. Or maybe you were one of those people who, after waiting five minutes in line, threw up your hands and walked out, frustrated, with time wasted and nothing accomplished, swearing never to go back.

Organizations contribute to their own downfall more often than they realize, and then blame exogenous market forces they don't control instead. Blue ocean strategists don't. They refuse to take existing industry conditions as givens. Nor do they blame those conditions for their difficulties. They look to themselves for answers, and don't let industry conditions frame their understanding of what is possible and profitable. While shared industry logic may help you make sense of the world, it dramatically restricts your creative thinking. It impels you to leave assumptions unquestioned and ideas unexplored, and to defend the status quo. It also disempowers you. As Steve Jobs put it, "You tend to get told that the world is the way it is...But that's a very limited [view]. Life can be much broader once you discover one simple fact. And that is everything around you that you call life was made up by people that were no smarter than you. And you can change it. You can influence it. You can build your own things that other people can use. And the minute you understand that you can poke life...that you can change it. You can mold it. That's maybe the most important thing—to shake off this erroneous notion that life is there and you're just going to live in it....And once you learn that, you'll never be the same again."[3] Blue ocean strategists act on this insight, which widens their creative palette and drives them to seriously weigh, rather than instantly write off, ideas that set out to shape, not merely accept, industry conditions.

Blue ocean strategists do not seek to beat the competition. Instead they aim to make the competition irrelevant.

Most organizations are stuck in the trap of competing.[4] Having accepted the industry structure as a given, executives proceed to benchmark their rivals and focus on outperforming them to achieve a competitive advantage. Indeed, one can hardly speak of strategy without invoking the idea of building a competitive advantage. But focusing on building a competitive advantage has an unintended and deeply ironic effect, because it leads to imitative, not innovative, approaches to the market. How can this be? This is a critical point to grasp because it's probably affecting your organization and what you do more than you know.

Let's start with the obvious. Every winning organization, by definition, has a competitive advantage. Comic Relief and Salesforce.com certainly do. So having a competitive advantage is good. No one is arguing with that. But that competitive advantage explains what the organization has achieved, the outcome of its strategy. In statistics, this is known as the *dependent variable*. The trouble is that, over time, people have confused the outcome of a winning strategy, namely a competitive advantage, with the process of achieving it or the *independent variable.* So managers have been increasingly urged to build competitive advantages to beat the competition.

At first glance this appears reasonable. If winning organizations have competitive advantages, pursuing a competitive advantage would seem to be the direct path to achieving it. The problem is one of framing. When managers are urged to secure a competitive advantage, what are they likely to do? They automatically look to the competition, assess what their competitors do, and strive to do it better. But, in so doing, their strategic thinking unknowingly regresses toward the competition. The competition becomes the defining variable of strategy, not buyer value. This narrows an organization's view to the competitive factors and shared assumptions held among existing competitors, leading it to improve along the established trajectory.

But should your strategy be driven in this way? Our research suggests not, especially if you are in an increasingly unattractive industry. Focusing on building competitive advantages distracts you from reshaping old industries and creating new ones. It blocks creativity and keeps you locked in the same way of competing as everyone else.

In direct contrast, blue ocean strategists are keenly focused not on building competitive advantages but on how to make the competition irrelevant.[5] They have a quiet disregard for what the competition is doing. They don't assume that just because competitors are doing something it's the right thing to do. The question they obsess about is this: What would it take to win over the mass of buyers, even with no marketing? Why the stipulation? Not because these organizations don't believe in or use marketing just like everyone else. They do. It's just that their aim is to push their organizations to create offerings so compelling that anyone who sees them or tries them can't help but rave about them. As Michael Levie, cofounder of citizenM, which created the new market space of affordable luxury hotels, put it, "Our aim is not to rely on marketing to sell hotel rooms. It is to create a hotel experience that in itself becomes our marketing, because people can't stop recommending it and sharing pictures of it on Facebook and Instagram." That's precisely what drove Steve Jobs's relentless challenge to Apple to create "insanely great" products and services, not products and services that were better than competitors', though, in the end, they were that too.

When organizations frame the strategic challenge this way, the futility of benchmarking the competition becomes clear. It causes managers to fundamentally challenge and rethink all the factors an industry competes on and invests in, and to push for a quantum leap in value. For while an incremental improvement over what competitors do may give you a competitive advantage, nothing short of a quantum leap in value will make the competition irrelevant.

It is this drive to make the competition irrelevant that opens organizations' eyes to the difference between what industries are competing on and what the mass of buyers actually values. Ironically, although blue ocean strategists are not focused on building a competitive advantage, they often achieve the greatest competitive advantage in the end.

Blue ocean strategists focus on creating and capturing new demand, not fighting over existing customers.

Almost every organization of a certain size regularly engages in some form of customer satisfaction survey. Even if you run a small business or nonprofit organization, satisfying existing customers is usually a key priority. So organizations elicit feedback from customers on what they like and don't like, on how they are doing, and on what they need to improve. As organizations garner insights, this often leads to a richer appreciation of the nuances in what current customers value. This, in turn, triggers finer segmentation and greater customization to meet their customers' specialized needs. Improved customer satisfaction almost always follows. "Exactly," you may think. "That's what we do. We're great at that." Or "We have a really creative way to tailor our offerings to best meet our individual customer needs."

For all its strength, however, this drive to improve customers' satisfaction scores also tends to keep organizations anchored in the red ocean of existing market space. In most industries, organizations converge around a common definition of who their customers are: older, wealthy, educated donors for the UK charity industry, for instance, or large complex corporations for enterprise resource planning software. This common definition then defines whom they expend their resources and efforts on. While this focus on existing customers is fine when industries are growing, it starts to impose real limits when demand is stagnant or in decline. It prevents organizations from seeing the wider potential of new demand outside their industry that they could tap into. And as Comic Relief and Salesforce.com show, in many industries, existing customers are just a drop in the bucket, compared with all the noncustomers who can be reached through market-creating strategies.[6]

Moreover, when you ask existing customers, "How can we make you happier?" their insights tend toward the familiar, such as "Offer me more for less." But this focus almost always drives you to merely offer better solutions to your industry's existing problem, keeping you trapped in the red ocean.[7] The US retail industry painfully pays for this focus at the end of every year, when their customers, who have been trained to expect preholiday sales, ask for the sales to start even earlier and for the stores to offer ever-larger discounts. Now holiday decorations can be seen in stores as early as October. As for strong, profitable growth, customers may be happier with the earlier and larger discounts, but retail sales have hardly inched up while profit margins continue to shrink.

Instead of fighting to win a greater percentage of existing

customers, blue ocean strategists seek to create new demand by looking to noncustomers. They recognize that extra demand is out there, waiting to be unlocked. By looking to noncustomers and what turns them off about an industry, they begin to uncover the major pain points—like pity pleas— imposed by their industry that make people choose against it. In this way, they glean critical insight into how to open up new market space.

As you will discover on your blue ocean shift journey, non-customers, not customers, provide the greatest insight into what your industry is doing to limit demand and how you can overcome this. The opportunity here is to create new demand where there is no competition, not to simply get a tad more of a shrinking red ocean.

Blue ocean strategists simultaneously pursue differentiation and low cost. They aim to break, not make, the value-cost trade-off.

As discussed in chapter 1, for a red ocean strategist, strategy requires making a choice between differentiation and low cost. By contrast, blue ocean strategists follow a different path and see market-creating strategy not as an either-or, but as a both-and approach. In short, they pursue differentiation and low cost simultaneously.[8]

Think back to Comic Relief. With its little red noses, its focus on community "fun"d-raising and mayhem, and its shift from year-round solicitations to a unique experience once every two years, Comic Relief is clearly the most differenti-ated fund-raising charity in the industry. At the same time, it has a low cost structure. Unlike traditional charities, Comic Relief doesn't plow time and money into expensive galas, or write grants to solicit funds from governments and founda-tions, or engage in counseling or care services. Instead, it uses high-street retail outlets, from supermarkets to fashion stores, to sell its little red noses. By some estimates, Comic

Relief has stripped away more than 75 percent of traditional fund-raising operations. Comic Relief's staff costs are also very low, with ordinary citizens volunteering to do the bulk of the fund-raising by engaging in silly antics that others sponsor. What's more, thanks to the widespread media attention and free word-of-mouth advertising that Red Nose Day generates, Comic Relief avoids large advertising costs. The result: Comic Relief broke the value-cost trade-off, pioneering a new value-cost frontier.

Organizations that pursue differentiation to stand apart from competitors tend to focus on what to offer more of. Those that pursue cost leadership tend to focus on what to offer less of. While both of these are viable strategic options, which a great many organizations currently pursue, both will keep you stuck in the red ocean, operating on your industry's existing productivity frontier. To offer buyers a quantum leap in value and break the value-cost trade-off, blue ocean strategists focus as much on what to eliminate and reduce as they do on what to raise and create. It is the simultaneous pursuit of differentiation and low cost that allows blue ocean strategists to leapfrog the competition, creating the positive buzz that drives thumbs-up and five-star ratings on websites, and attracting not just new customers but fans, who can't do enough to sing their praises.

Expanding Your Field of Vision

Adopting the perspective of the blue ocean strategist is like looking up at the night sky at the single constellation your industry has long been focused on and then turning your head to see the vast expanse of the universe that hadn't been in your field of vision before. It shifts your thinking from constraints to new opportunities. With it, you will be guided in the right direction to challenge industry structure, break from industry logic, look to noncustomers, and craft strategies that achieve both differentiation and low cost. You can't expect to create a blue ocean if you think like a red ocean strategist.

Now let's dive into the next chapter. There we outline how humanness is systematically built into the blue ocean shift process and how that inspires and builds people's confidence so that they own and drive the process. The chapter also shows how people's creative competence is unlocked in the process and what you can expect at each step.

CHAPTER 4

Humanness, Confidence, and Creative Competence

People are paradoxical. We aspire to make a difference. We want to change the world for the better. That's what makes our energies soar, our hearts beat faster, our adrenaline surge. Yet, simultaneously, most of us fear we can't. We need reassurance.

No matter how tough, confident, or polished we may appear, all of us are tender at our core. When we think about people as people, not as corporate executives, entrepreneurs, or government officials, and certainly not as human resources, we realize that, behind our titles, all of us are incredibly vulnerable. We strive to avert reproach. We want to avoid making fools of ourselves. We steer clear of revealing what we do not know. In our organizations, opening ourselves up and putting ourselves out there all too often trigger fears of losing status, respect, security, and power. So, our penchant is to cling to what is, instead of exploring what could be. This includes people at the top, whose egos are often the most fragile of all.

That is your truth, our truth, and virtually everyone else's truth. That does not make us weak. It's what makes us human. Not addressing these basic human truths, or assuming them away, is why so many change efforts and attempts to drive organizations to become more creative and innovative fail. They have not acknowledged and built what we call *humanness* into the process. The process of conceiving and executing a blue ocean shift does.

Humanness builds psychological understanding into the strategic process so that people are willing to engage fully at every step—even when they're hesitant, may not trust one another, or are skeptical of their ability to succeed on the transformation journey. When we feel genuinely understood and appreciated for who we are as whole people, when we feel respected not because we are brilliant, bold, and perfect, but because we have something to contribute and want to make a difference despite our insecurities and vulnerabilities, we stop feeling like imposters with something to hide. We trust other people. We burn with desire to honor the faith that we feel is placed in us by putting in the extra effort to make success happen.

Humanness, in short, builds our confidence to act by eliciting our emotional engagement. It relaxes us and makes us feel secure enough to reach beyond what we know and explore the as-yet unknown. It inspires us to tap into our curiosity and creativity, which are abundant, powerful, and vastly underutilized by our organizations as well as ourselves. This is critical for reshaping and reimagining industry boundaries.

From Humanness to Creative Competence

While humanness builds our confidence to act, market-creating tools and clear guidance on how to apply them build our creative competence. Market-creating tools and guidance give people the intellectual understanding of the legwork needed to make a blue ocean shift happen.

Think of it like aiming to create your ideal body. Having the right mindset will direct your thoughts away from the kitchen to the gym. The confidence to act will inspire you to actually get in your car, go to the gym, and exercise. But as any athlete will tell you, to transform your body you need to know the specifics of what you have to do: how often to go to the gym, how to stretch, what machines to use in what order with how much weight, how many reps to do, the proper balance between cardio and strength conditioning, and how to eat properly. Without that knowledge, you aren't going to be able to create the strength, resilience, and flexibility to transform your body. That's the power that a systematic process, built on creative frameworks and actionable tools, brings to market-creating strategy. The tools and frameworks provide the specifics of what it takes to create and re-create markets. They transform your ambition into what we call *creative competence* and give you the levers of control you need to reshape market boundaries in your favor.

When confidence to act and creative competence meet, real results are achievable. Don't let anyone ever tell you that one without the other is sufficient when transformation is your goal. An organization that has the confidence to make a blue ocean shift but lacks the knowledge of how to get there is like a gambler. It can expect lots of misdirected efforts and failed attempts. Conversely, an organization that knows everything you can and should do to create a blue ocean but lacks confidence to act will never actually do it. Let's look at how the blue ocean shift process achieves both.

How Humanness Is Built

To help people develop the confidence to act, three elements that address different aspects of our humanness are built into the blue ocean process: atomization, firsthand discovery, and the exercise of fair process. Let's look at each one in turn.

Atomization

While making a blue ocean shift represents a step-change approach to the market, it is purposely designed not to feel that way inside the organization. The process recognizes that the bigness and newness of the goal can be overwhelming. "You want *us* to chart a future beyond the existing market? You count on *us* to think differently and shape industry boundaries? *Are we...am I* even capable of doing this?" That's most people's knee-jerk reaction, and it's natural.

Then how do you get people to make a blue ocean shift? You don't. That is, not with one great leap. Instead, you break the challenge down into small, concrete steps that move people forward in increments that inspire and build their confidence. So, for example, people are asked to identify the factors an industry competes on. Or to pinpoint the biggest obstacles to simplicity in an industry. Or to zoom in on buyer groups that could benefit from your industry's offering but don't currently purchase it. When framed this way, each step pushes the boundaries of our thinking, but no one step overwhelms us. And, at any one stage, none of us can say that what is being asked of us is too big a leap. Yet, the culmination of these small steps leads to a blue ocean shift.

We call this *atomization* after Einstein's reflection that if you deconstruct any challenge into its basic components, or atoms, and focus on solving them one at a time, even the largest challenge shifts from being overwhelming to being intellectually and psychologically solvable.[1] As people register the feasibility of each step, tangible evidence that creating new market space is possible accumulates. People come to appreciate how what once appeared to be a daunting objective is, in fact, within their reach. Fear begins to melt into quiet confidence and pride, as people feel their creative competence expand.

Firsthand discovery

Our ideas about what is possible and what we are capable of are not only a function of the size of the challenge we face. They are also grounded in our past perceptions and experiences. And, in organizations, what most of us see and know to be true is the red ocean of intense competition. This makes it our safe harbor, emotionally and intellectually. So we cling to it, even when we know we shouldn't. Every time a new person is "shown the ropes," it reinforces the organization's existing strategic perspective.

Challenging people's view of the world by asking how the established strategy may need to change goes against this natural tendency. But *natural* does not mean *inevitable*. The question is, if defending the status quo and trying to bend reality to fit within it comprise the organization's default behavior, what can a leader do?

Creating the conditions that will enable people to discover for themselves, firsthand, the need for change, instead of being told, is the answer that emerges from our research. The blue ocean shift process achieves this in two important ways. First, people are handed no predetermined conclusions. Rather, at each step, people are given tools that allow them to arrive at the answers themselves. The tools show them how to think in new ways and allow them to discover for themselves the need—or the lack of need—to make a blue ocean shift. With no predetermined conclusions, people don't feel manipulated. And because the process allows them to reach the conclusions themselves, their creativity and understanding of what matters expand, as does their ownership of the results.

Second, the process changes what people see and experience, leading us to open our minds and change our understanding of what we know to be true because we witnessed it ourselves.[2] The process achieves this by creatively putting you and your team face-to-face with the market, instead of praying for insight, or building it and assuming people will come, or relying on third-party market research. It gets you out of the office and into the field to speak with both customers and noncustomers, to act like buyers and experience products and services as they do, to feel buyers' pain points that were always there but that you'd never seen before, to observe alternative industries and human behavior—in short, to collect visceral insights. In this process, people start to see and feel the need for change and how they might shift the strategic playing field to make it happen.

Seeing truly *is* believing. It moves us from the unsettling, highly vulnerable mindset of "I don't know" to the quietly confident one of "I know," not because we have been briefed by a report or told by a third-party focus group, but because we saw and experienced it for ourselves. People start waking up, thinking, "Why didn't we ever see that before? It's so obvious!" No matter how stubborn people are, they start to see patterns that had escaped them or that they'd written off as anomalies before. Confidence rises. Optimism increases. People's creativity expands.

Fair process

The third element of humanness is fair process. Fair process speaks to the fundamental fabric of who we are as people. It confers the gift of trust, enabling us to relax and inspiring our commitment and voluntary cooperation.

What is fair process? Essentially, it comes down to three principles that we have written about and studied for nearly 30 years: engagement, explanation, and clear expectations.[3] The power of these principles cannot be overstated. They are the foundation on which the blue ocean shift process is built. *Engagement* means actively involving people in strategic decisions that affect them by asking for their input and allowing them to refute and challenge the merits of one another's ideas and assumptions. When managers do that, they communicate their respect for the people who work for them and for their ideas. It builds collective wisdom. Fostering engagement in this way generates better decisions and greater commitment from those involved in executing them.

Explanation means providing people with a clear account of the thinking that underlies the process and the strategic decisions reached at each step. Explanation reassures people that their opinions have been considered, and decisions have been made with the company's overall interests at heart. This fosters people's trust in managers' intentions—even if their own ideas were rejected.

Lastly, *clear expectations* means just that: stating clearly what people can expect, and what their roles and responsibilities are, at each step and in moving forward after the process is complete. Although the expectations may be demanding, when people know what the goals and milestones are, and who is responsible for what, they feel safe and respected.

When we talk about expectations, we mean expectations for the entire organization, not just the blue ocean team, so that everyone who will be affected by the shift is brought along and not surprised at the end by an alarming fait accompli. Just as the team's leader exercises fair process with team members, they, in turn, have to exercise it with their functional cohorts: engaging them in what the team is finding; explaining the process behind it; setting clear expectations about what will come next and why. If you want buy-in, surprises do not tend to go down well in most organizations. Even good surprises may be rejected if the process leaves people feeling discredited and rolled over.[4]

What makes fair process so powerful is that it communicates through its action how much people are valued as individuals and recognized for their intellectual and emotional worth.[5] When we feel valued, we feel emotionally secure and are intrinsically motivated to give our all. We trust, we commit, and we move from being self-protecting to being open to sharing, exploring the new, and giving our best ideas even when we are uncertain as to how they will be received. Anyone who has ever worked in an organization understands how important this is.

The courtesy of the respect that fair process conveys triggers something at the core of the human spirit. Fair process internally civilizes us. It helps us suspend judgment and build trust so that we can listen, learn, weigh others' points of view, and contribute. Otherwise, it's too easy for people to put on a show of acceptance, while intending to do the exact opposite, because they feel internally violated. Fair process takes a huge step to closing that gulf, which is especially important when change is at issue.

By weaving fair process together with atomization and firsthand discovery into the process, humanness and, hence, confidence to act are instilled and reinforced. By doing so, execution is no longer an afterthought. Rather it is built into the process by creating people's buy-in to the outcome of the process itself. What's special about this buy-in is that it persists, even when the resulting decision is at odds with what people had originally hoped for. While we may wish it were otherwise, we also accept that things cannot always go our way, and that short-term personal sacrifices are sometimes needed to advance the success and promote the survival of an organization. This acceptance, however, is conditional on the presence of a humanistic process.

Figure 4-1 captures in one graphic the essence of how humanness is built into the blue ocean shift process. The figure shows how the three elements address different aspects of our humanness and collectively produce the confidence to act and make a blue ocean shift. As shown, atomization breaks the challenge down, so that it is easy to act on; firsthand discovery allows people to see things that they never saw before

Figure 4-1

How Humanness Is Built in the Process

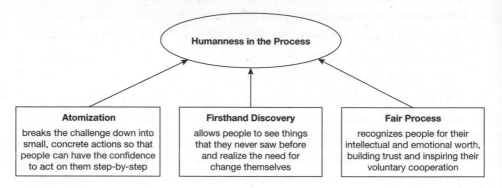

and firmly believe in the need for change; and the exercise of fair process makes people feel valued and respected, inducing their voluntary cooperation.

When strategy implementation is internally driven in this way, instead of externally imposed or manipulated through carrots and sticks, people voluntarily support and enact strategies to make a blue ocean shift. The attitude at the end of the blue ocean shift process is palpable. In two words, it's "We're launching."

The Right Tools with the Right Guidance

Eight to 9 out of 10 entrepreneurs fail. In almost any other context that would be a shocking statistic, but, for some reason, it's something that the entrepreneurial community has long accepted as okay. We were never okay with it. The blue ocean shift process comprises five systematic steps that minimize the randomness and trial and error in creating new markets so you maximize the chances of hitting the bull's-eye. It uses proven market-creating tools and frameworks to build an organization's creative competence to pioneer a new value-cost frontier with a supporting business model that simultaneously achieves differentiation and low cost. And it provides clear guidance on how to apply these tools in action, including what to expect and how to avoid errors and missteps along the way. The tools are visual, which makes them easy to understand and apply. We've used them with equal effectiveness with C-suite executives, people on the front lines, and the owners of small Main Street businesses. People in the arts, government, and education have also used them to unlock blue oceans. So have high school students and religious organizations. We dare to say that no one who goes through the process will ever see and understand their market—or any market—the same way again. Here's the sequence the process follows, and the tools and guidance you'll learn in each step.

Step One: Get Started

Step one tackles how to choose the right place to start your blue ocean initiative so that your zone of transformation is not too ambitious and you focus on areas that are most feasible in light of the organizational constraints you may confront. To achieve this, we introduce the **pioneer-migrator-settler map**, which guides you to target the area where you have the most to gain by the blue ocean journey. Here we discuss how to apply the map, and what the results reveal. We also identify the key traps and pitfalls teams fall into in applying this tool and explain how to avoid them.

Once the scope of your transformation is set, it's time to construct the best team for your journey. How many people should be part of the team? What mix of skills should ideally be brought together, and what levels of functional and hierarchical authority should be represented? How much time can team members and you expect to commit to the process, and how will that affect people's regular work? And what will this look like if you're a small business owner or entrepreneur, a CEO, a product manager, or a government leader?

Step Two: Understand Where You Are Now

Step two tackles how to inspire a natural wake-up call in the team and in the wider organization about the current state of play in your industry. It shows how to collectively build a clear picture of the current competitive landscape. When people see what the strategic reality is, and agree on the need for change, you can create real alignment and a collective will to make the shift.

To achieve this, this step introduces the **strategy canvas** tool. The strategy canvas allows your organization to see in one simple picture all the factors an industry competes on and invests in, what buyers receive, and what the strategic profiles of the major players are. It exposes just how similar the players' strategies look to buyers and reveals how they drive the industry toward the red ocean. Importantly, it creates a commonly owned baseline for change. In this step you will learn how to draw the strategy canvas, what you can expect as people work together on this, how to interpret the completed canvas and build a shared understanding of its strategic implications, and what the potential traps in applying the tool are and how to avoid them. The beauty of this step is that, once you've completed it, you will not need to tell anyone that a blue ocean shift is necessary. Rather, the organization will find this out for itself and tell you. People will viscerally feel it.

Step Three: Imagine Where You Could Be

To make the shift from what is to what could be, step three introduces the **buyer utility map**. This analytic tool helps you discover the specific pain points and points of intimidation that your current or target industry is imposing on buyers throughout their entire experience. More importantly, it helps you identify the unexplored spaces where value is trapped and waiting to be unlocked. In the blue ocean shift process, pain points and boundaries are not constraints. They are blatant opportunities to change the playing field of strategy—opportunities that most industries have become blind to. Here we walk you through how to apply the buyer utility map to your situation, and what to watch out for as you trace and assess buyers' total experience. We discuss how to interpret the results, and highlight the potential pitfalls in working through the tool and how to overcome them. By understanding the ways in which an industry, even an intensely competitive one, blocks buyer value and narrows the basis of its appeal, the seeds for new pathways to unlock innovative value begin to sprout. People gain confidence that blue ocean opportunities are out there, and that they just might have what it takes to create them. Already the organization has benefited from the identification of low-hanging fruit.

Step three then shows you how to break away from conceiving too narrowly of whom an industry's customers are. To achieve this, we introduce the **three tiers of noncustomers**. This analytic framework allows an organization to identify the *total* demand landscape that lies outside the current industry understanding. Here we show you how to apply each of the three tiers to your situation, discuss how to interpret the results, and highlight the questions people are likely to have in working through the framework and how best to address them. In this step, noncustomers that were once invisible to an organization are made visible, so latent demand can be unlocked. With shock, amazement, and sometimes even humor, people wake up to discover that the customers everyone has been fighting over are often only a fraction of the potential total demand. The concept of a blue ocean is no longer a metaphor. People start to see, feel, and define its potential.

Step Four: Find How You Get There

Step four is where organizations learn how to create commercially compelling new market space by redefining the playing field of strategy. This is when you learn how to put random brainstorming aside and apply systematic paths to reconstruct market boundaries and create and re-create markets. The **six paths framework**, the analytic tool introduced in this step, demystifies and provides a structure for blue ocean creation. The paths show you how to look at the market universe anew and to see what others don't see. Here you will learn how to explore each path to extract the insight needed to redefine, reimagine, and shift market boundaries: whom you should interview and observe in the field to gain insight; how to record and synthesize your findings; and how to identify and avoid the common traps that lie along the path to reconstructing market boundaries. The result is firsthand insight into practical ways to reframe and redefine the problem an industry focuses on, identify and solve brand-new problems or seize brand-new opportunities, and create breakthrough solutions to the existing problem of an industry.

Step four then shows you how to make sense of these insights and formulate them into well-constructed strategies. To achieve this, we introduce the **four actions framework**, which drives the team to focus on what they could eliminate, reduce, raise, and create to construct six potentially viable blue ocean strategic moves. What makes this tool so powerful is that it forces everyone to push their thinking to pursue both differentiation and low cost, which is what will break the value-cost trade-off and create blue oceans.

Step Five: Make Your Move

Step five introduces the **blue ocean fair,** where the decision is reached on which blue ocean move to pursue. The fair is

designed to take the politics out of the decision-making process, obtain validation and feedback on the strategic options,
and consolidate people's commitment to and support for the
chosen move. This step addresses the dynamics of the fair,
including who will attend, what should be presented, the
dynamics of the presentations of the strategic moves, and
how the participants vote on the moves' strengths and weak-
nesses. It also illustrates the calibration that occurs as people
voice their opinions and reasoning, and how, ultimately, top
management selects which option to move forward with.

The result is a clear decision, validated by key stakeholders
with a wealth of feedback and insight on how the chosen strategic
move can be further refined and potential gaps in execution can
be efficiently and effectively closed. After the fair, rapid market
tests with the chosen offering's rough prototype are conducted to
cross-check market reactions and refine the idea, as needed.

Step five then elaborates on how to finalize and launch your
blue ocean move. Here we show you how to formalize a big-picture
business model for the move that can deliver a leap in value for
buyers and strong profitable growth for you or, in the case of a
nonprofit, a leap in the net donations available for the cause.
You'll learn how to effectively launch and roll out your new blue
ocean move and how to use the strategy canvas to guide decisions on what to do and what not to do, so the organization has
integrity in its execution. The rollout process also outlines how to
further validate, calibrate, and refine your blue ocean approach
to maximize the size of your new market and hence your success.

How to Make the Process Work for You

Figure 4-2 provides a high-level overview of the process. The
process is a balance of hearts and minds, of humanness, confidence, and creative competence. And when you balance hearts
and minds, you gain hands: People act. *The beauty of the process*

Figure 4-2

Overview of the Blue Ocean Shift Process

Step One:	**Get Started**
	• Choose the right place to start your blue ocean initiative: *The Pioneer-Migrator-Settler Map*
	• Construct the right team for the initiative

Step Two:	**Understand Where You Are Now**
	• Collectively build one simple picture that captures your current state of play: *The Strategy Canvas*
	• See and easily agree on the need for the shift

Step Three:	**Imagine Where You Could Be**
	• Discover the pain points of buyers imposed by the industry: *The Buyer Utility Map*
	• Identify the total demand landscape you can unlock: *The Three Tiers of Noncustomers*

Step Four:	**Find How You Get There**
	• Apply systematic paths to reconstruct market boundaries: *The Six Paths Framework*
	• Develop alternative strategic options that achieve differentiation and low cost: *The Four Actions Framework*

Step Five:	**Make Your Move**
	• Select your move at the blue ocean fair, conduct rapid market tests, and refine the move
	• Finalize the move by formalizing your big-picture business model that delivers a win for both buyers and you
	• Launch and roll out your move

Note: Italics refer to the corresponding analytic tools to be used.

is that each of the five steps with its corresponding analytic tools and guidance has value on its own. This is important because, although the five steps comprise the full process for making a blue ocean shift, not every organization will be at the same starting point. For example, you could be part of a company that was once a market leader and whose profits are still strong, but whose competitors are closing in fast. Buyer reviews suggest your company's offering no longer stands out, but most of management remains in denial. You may not be ready to go through the full process, but you know you need to wake the organization up to the imminent threat, and you don't want the wake-up call to be hitting the wall and entering the valley of death. What to do? Apply step two and the analytic tool of the strategy canvas. It is a highly effective way to change the conversation from one of illusion and denial to one grounded in reality.

Or suppose your organization's offering still stands apart, but the size of your industry is small and you are yearning to grow. Fighting over existing customers will cut your profit margins. Yet you don't have a grip on who the industry's non-customers are. Jump to step three and apply the analytic framework, the three tiers of noncustomers, to gain insight into the latent demand you might be able to tap into.

Are you tired of A/B testing random new business ideas in the hope of someday hitting on one that will create a new market? Do you find your creative pathways blocked? In either case, jump to step four to learn how to apply the six systematic paths to creating commercially compelling new market space.

The principle of atomization that works for individuals also works for organizations. While most organizations today need to break out of the red ocean, we've found that, despite their desire to create a blue ocean, many are not yet ready to embark on the entire journey. That doesn't mean they can afford to stand still, however. *That's why we designed an atomized process so that every organization can get value out of applying a step or steps, as needed, to start moving. In other words, the process is not an all-or-nothing deal.*

As illustrated above, organizations can zoom in on the step that best addresses their current need and apply it independently. Insights on moving from red to blue can be had at each step, whether done in isolation or as part of the overall process. As we discuss each step in the following chapters, the independent value that can be derived from it will become clear. In this way, every organization can start sailing, based on who they are and what they are ready for. Importantly, each step has the three elements of humanness woven in, so your organization's confidence will strengthen as its creative competence grows. In this way, mobilization is built into each step of the process.

With the above understanding of the blue ocean shift process and how each step simultaneously builds confidence and creative competence, let's dive in. The next chapter tackles the first part of step one by showing you how to choose the right place to start your blue ocean initiative.

PART TWO

The Five Steps to Making a Blue Ocean Shift

Step One: Get Started

CHAPTER 5

Choosing the Right Place to Start

At the threshold of every blue ocean initiative is this question: Where do we begin? The answer: We begin by scoping out the initiative, which means working out which business or product/service offering you're going to tackle.

For a start-up or an organization with only one predominant offering, choosing the right scope is straightforward: To ensure that it gets launched in the blue ocean, not the red, a start-up needs to focus on the offering it's setting out to create. Focused organizations and small entrepreneurs—be they owners of a single restaurant, a plumbing service, or a local dental practice—should concentrate on their existing offering.

For existing organizations with multiple offerings, however, choosing the right scope is not at all straightforward. Think about GE, IBM, or Procter & Gamble, whose corporate umbrellas cover many large businesses, each with wide product and service offerings. Even a single division of a large organization can present a multitude of possibilities. The Consumer Lifestyle Division of Dutch electronics giant Philips, for instance, offers products ranging from electric shavers, to electric toothbrushes and air flossers, to blow dryers, curling irons, and women's electric epilation devices.

To help complex organizations like these set the scope of

their blue ocean initiatives, we created a simple, but powerful tool called the pioneer-migrator-settler map. It allows you to assess your current portfolio of businesses or offerings in one simple graphic and hence to see beyond today's performance. With this tool, you will gain a clear picture of your organization's value innovation pipeline, or the lack thereof, and the prospects for growth inherent in your portfolio.

In this chapter you will learn how to create a pioneer-migrator-settler map for your organization. We will show you how to use the map to select the right scope for your blue ocean initiative. We will also show you how the process of creating and using it builds people's confidence in and support of the initiative, and how to avoid the traps in plotting it that can be especially problematic for organizations with histories of success behind them.

Mapping Today to See Tomorrow

Traditionally, leaders have used two measures to assess the strength of an organization's portfolio of offerings: market share and industry attractiveness. The more attractive the market, the thinking goes, and the larger the piece of it you have, the healthier you are, and—here's the important point for strategy—the less need there is to change course.

But is this so?

Market share is important. And most organizations want more of it. But market share is a lagging indicator. It's a reflection of past, not future, performance. Kodak, for example, was the market leader in the photographic film industry at the precise moment digital film was taking off. Its market share was staggeringly large, but its strategic vulnerability was high. On the flip side, Apple's share of the smartphone market was tiny when it launched its iPhone, while BlackBerry's share was commanding. Yet we all know what happened.

Apple's small market share was a product of its recent entry into the industry, not a predictor of its future success, just as BlackBerry's large market share was a product of its history that masked its strategic vulnerability.

A similar argument can be made for industry attractiveness, since today's seductively tempting industry may become singularly unattractive tomorrow if, for example, lots of other organizations decide to jump in and put lots of resources behind their move.

The pioneer-migrator-settler map largely gets around these issues by replacing market share and industry attractiveness with "value" and "innovation." Value is crucial, because it forces you not to rest on your laurels but to assess each of your businesses based on the value they currently deliver to buyers. The value you deliver today drives buyer behavior, which determines your future growth prospects, whereas the value you delivered yesterday determines your current market share.

Innovation, on the other hand, is key because it allows you to overcome existing industry conditions. Without it, companies are stuck in the trap of competitive improvements. With it, even a once-declining industry can be turned into a highly profitable growth market. Think of ActiFry's strategic move, which turned a highly unattractive commodity industry—electric home French fry makers, which had been declining in value 10 percent per year—into a high-growth, high-margin, new market space. Or citizenM Hotels, which is transforming the stagnant low-profit, midrange hotel industry into a high-growth, highly profitable, new market space of affordable luxury accommodations. Industries, in the end, are what we make them. Do exciting things, innovate, and your industry will become vibrant. Do more of the same, and watch the industry's attractiveness decline.

Assessing your product/service offerings according to how much innovative value they offer buyers lets you see how strategically vulnerable or healthy your portfolio really is. What you want to understand is this: which of your offerings or businesses are "me-toos" that offer only imitative value; which are better than competitors' but only marginally so, delivering improved value; and which, if any, are value innovations that deliver a true leap in value. To capture this, the pioneer-migrator-setter map is divided into three segments:

- **Pioneers** are businesses or offerings that represent value innovations. They don't have customers; they have fans. They offer unprecedented value that opens up a new value-cost frontier. These are the businesses or offerings that hold the key to renewing your portfolio. Their strategy breaks away from the competition. Pioneers are poised for strong, profitable growth.
- **Settlers** are the other extreme. These are businesses or offerings that offer value imitation. They compete by making incremental changes to an offering or its price. Their strategy converges with the rest of the industry. Unless the industry itself is growing and profitable, settlers have little or no prospect for growth.
- **Migrators** lie somewhere in between. They represent a value improvement over the competition and may even be best in class. But they do not offer *innovative* value.

Figure 5-1 shows the filled in pioneer-migrator-setter map of a consumer appliance company. While each circle represents a different business, product, or service, for convenience we'll refer to all of these as "offerings." Adding in the current revenues derived from each of the offerings via the size of its circle shows you not only which are poised for growth, or vulnerable to decline based on their position on the map, but also how much is at stake, with a larger circle indicating that more would be at stake.

Figure 5-1

The Pioneer-Migrator-Settler Map of a Consumer Appliance Company

Pioneer-Migrator-Settler Map

Pioneer
Value Innovation

Migrator
Value Improvement

Settler
Value Imitation

Key for plotting:

Larger revenues   Smaller revenues

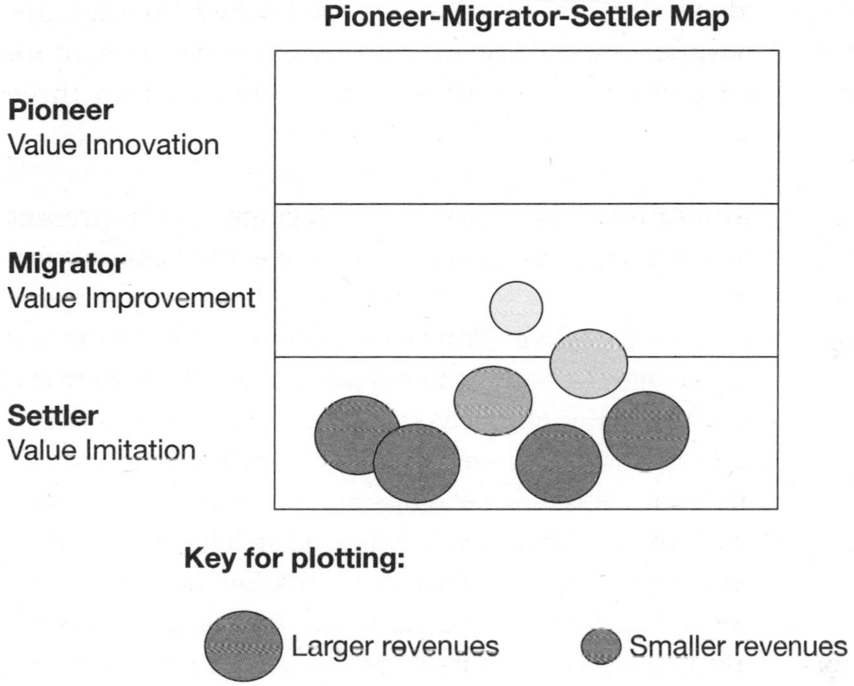

In the case of the consumer appliance company shown in the figure, one thing immediately jumps out: This organization is strategically vulnerable, because it is essentially living off its past success. It may be profitable today, thanks to its commanding market share in several of its units. But it is dominated by settler businesses, which means it is playing off past strategic moves, rather than creating new moves that will become the bread and butter of the future. In organizations with blue ocean offerings, you will see pioneers that are planting the seeds for tomorrow's profit and growth.

Were you to plot Microsoft's portfolio on the pioneer-migrator-settler map, you would see that it is in a similar position. Over the last 10 years or so, Microsoft has earned more than US$100 billion in profits; yet its stock price has remained relatively flat, and it is no longer the talent magnet it once was. Why? Were you to plot its offerings on the map, you see that almost all of its profit comes from just two products—Microsoft Office and Windows—both of which are now decades old and settlers. What the stock market and talent no longer see is the company's next big killer app or any other pioneer. Sure its R&D labs are among the most impressive and well-funded in the world. The trouble is the company is not translating its advances in technology into value innovation offerings.

Microsoft is not alone. When we ask organizations to plot their current portfolios, most resemble the consumer appliance company's we've mapped out here. How about you? If you were to plot your organization's portfolio, how do you think it would stand in value innovation terms? Are you building your blue ocean growth businesses for tomorrow? Or not?

Understanding your company's portfolio in terms of its degree of value innovation is critical for two fundamental reasons. First, it allows you to see beyond today's performance numbers so you can identify whether you are strategically vulnerable and, hence, need to act. Second, having an aerial view of your portfolio, based on value and innovation—the indicators that fundamentally drive buyer behavior—readies you to begin scoping out your initiative. We say *readies* because even if your portfolio is dominated by settlers, as the consumer appliance company's is, the last thing you want to do is embark on a corporate initiative to shift them all. That's simply too broad a scope. And introducing too much change at once will lower people's trust—in you and in the process—and likely exhaust everyone's energy.

A successful blue ocean process is based on what we call an "earn the right to grow" approach. This means selecting one settler offering, applying the blue ocean shift process to it, seeing the results, and then, based on this experience, rolling out the process to other businesses or product/service offerings in your portfolio. In addition to helping size an initiative properly, this approach can build confidence among your people and trigger the feeling that you're being both fair and reasonable, thereby relaxing them and strengthening their willingness to open their minds to new ideas.

How to Plot Your Pioneer-Migrator-Settler Map

Now let's turn to you and your organization's map. Defining the scope of your initiative will allow you to create a shared understanding of your portfolio in value innovation terms, and to see how widespread the need for change and blue ocean initiatives is across your organization. Here are the steps you want to follow.

Identify the key businesses or product/service offerings in your portfolio

Start by identifying your key businesses or product/service offerings and choosing the people who will participate in the process. At a minimum, the group should include the heads of each of the organization's units. Oftentimes, the people selected may wish to bring one or two of their key people into the group. This can be very helpful, as well as feel reassuring, because it means they can calibrate their thinking with others from their unit when it's time to plot their offering.

Identify which offerings are pioneers, migrators, and settlers

Next, provide each manager with the definitions of pioneers, migrators, and settlers, as we have above. Be clear that the goal is to arrive at a reading of where each business or product/

service offering stands in terms of value and innovation and *not* in terms of market share or industry attractiveness. It is also important to remind people that each offering should be assessed from the point of view of buyers, not in terms of your organization's other offerings. That is, how would buyers judge your offering: as a pioneer, a migrator, or a settler, compared to the other offerings available to them in the market? We've seen managers mistakenly plot an offering as a pioneer because it was the most innovative one the company had. But when we asked them to articulate how their offering provided a quantum leap in buyer value, compared to the available alternatives, it became clear that, from the buyers' point of view, it was actually quite similar and should be plotted as a high settler. This kind of myopia is symptomatic of an organization that is too internally focused.

In plotting the businesses or offerings, let everyone know that the size of the circles should be drawn as a function of their revenue, relative to the organization's other businesses (that is, the higher the relative revenue, the larger the circle). If you have a pioneer that does not have a mass following, and therefore is a small circle, place a question mark inside it. When an offering delivers unprecedented value, its revenues should reflect that. When that's not the case, the question is why. It may be because the offering was just launched, which would make sense. But it might be because it's actually not a value pioneer at all, but a technology pioneer that few buyers can see the value of. Be sure to explore this point. Many organizations with significant R&D budgets or that operate in technology-intensive industries fall victim to this misconception. When they plot their pioneer-migrator-settler maps, they show a scattering of pioneers. But the circles are usually small, and that's not because they represent new offerings. As we probe, it becomes clear that, although the managers of these businesses can explain why these offerings represent breakthroughs in technology, they struggle to articulate in simple terms how and why these breakthroughs provide a leap in value for buyers. That's an important point: It almost always signals a strong disconnect between the development people and buyers, which needs to be addressed if the money invested in R&D and technology development is to translate into commercially compelling blue oceans.

Plot your portfolio

Now, using a blank pioneer-migrator-settler map, plot *your group's* assessment of each business or offering. To help you perform this task effectively, relevant materials and templates are provided for your free download and use at www .blueoceanshift.com/ExerciseTemplates. Usually, once a top management team has learned the core concept and workings of the pioneer-migrator-settler map in action, together they can complete their map with relative ease.

The aim is to capture each offering's *current* position on the map. Notice that we said "your group's" assessment and *not* "your" assessment. Why? As we explained in the previous chapter, firsthand discovery and fair process are critical components of the blue ocean shift process. While you may have an instinctive sense of how your organization's portfolio should be plotted, that doesn't mean other key players will agree. Say the manager of a sizable business or product/service offering has an inflated view of his or her unit, even though its offering may have long since become just like everyone else's. If you were to plot that business or product/service offering as a settler, he or she would most likely pull back, resist, and resent you for seeming to downgrade his or her unit.

The best way to avoid this problem is to have the managers of the different units plot their offerings collectively. As a starting point, ask each of the managers to plot their unit's offerings on the map. Then open a discussion so that people can probe one another on why the offerings are plotted as they

are. Working together in this way helps keep everyone honest. As managers hear others' perceptions, everyone's knowledge of the organization's total portfolio is upgraded, creating
a shared understanding. So, in the end, the offerings that get
plotted as settlers or low migrators get plotted as such by the
people running those units. It's their call, not yours, which is
the outcome you want.

While plotting the pioneer-migrator-settler map, your
managers may say they need additional research to assess
their offerings' positions accurately. This seems reasonable.
Yet in our work we've found that when people are brought
together to do the plotting as a group, their perceptions tend
to be close to 80 percent accurate. The aim here is capturing
the relative position of offerings within their industry, not per-
fection. In most cases we've found that quantitative market
research results in slight, but not dramatic, movements on the
map. But that research does not fundamentally change the
relative position of the offerings. For example, with additional
research, what we call a "low migrator" may be found to actually be a "high settler," meaning it falls just below the demar-
cation line, rather than just above it. However, the marginal
difference does not change the ultimate conclusion. So should
this issue arise, try asking questions like these: "If further
research were done, what would you expect?" "Do you think
your current plotting would shift substantially, or would it be
likely to nudge up or down?" "Is it likely that what appears
to be a settler might actually be a pioneer, or vice versa?"
In practice, we've found that nudging is almost always the
answer. This tends to put this issue to rest so that the group's
focus can come back to the big picture.

If disagreements within the group arise about how high or
low an offering should be plotted, get them to challenge one
another's assumptions by asking what is distinctive about
its value and innovativeness. Is the business or product/
service offering really a migrator or a pioneer? What is the

unprecedented value it delivers? Does it capture the target mass of the market? Alternatively, if people think an offering is plotted too low, ask, "Is it really a settler?" Check to make sure that people don't have an inflated view of their unit's offering. Or, conversely, that they're not underrepresenting its accomplishments. Continue to challenge people and keep the discussion going until there is a consensus that every business or product/service offering is properly positioned. This should allow you to agree on a fairly robust assessment of your current portfolio.

Developing the pioneer-migrator-settler map is an interactive process. Although there is often initial dissent about the appropriate assessments, we find that disagreements very soon become minor and that, after some shuffling, everyone agrees with the final picture.

Inside an Electronics Service Company

What are pioneer-migrator-settler map discussions really like? Let's listen in on the dynamics of a top management team for a US electronics service company that we'll call ESC, who were called in by the president to plot their pioneer-migrator-settler map. ESC has built a successful business in field repair for the end customers of electronics corporations and corporate IT and telecommunications infrastructure. Here, we will show how they interact with each other and build their shared understanding as they go through the process of plotting the map. Along with the president, attendees were the business development director, global operations vice president, IT director, strategic planning manager, controller, European operations vice president, Asian operations vice president, and the HR manager.

"As you know, we've been doing very well over the last few years," the president begins. "We are now approaching

US$500 million with over 5,000 employees in more than 10 locations." The president turns to the controller. "And as I can confirm," the controller adds, "we continue to earn operating margins notably higher than our parent company [a multibillion-dollar corporation]." Heads nod. Almost to a fault, people sit straighter in their chairs on hearing this. People visibly feel good about their performance and proud.

"Despite good business results so far," the president continues, "what are our prospects for future profitable growth? There are a number of new challenges emerging in the market."

After receiving an overview of the pioneer-migrator-settler map from a blue ocean expert, the team sets out to plot their portfolio. Upon first blush, it looks like the organization is swimming in a blue ocean. "Those corporate accounts are clearly pioneers," the business development director argues as they begin plotting their portfolio. "The margins here are at the top of our industry." "We agree," the Asian and European operations vice presidents add, nodding their heads. After checking and verifying sales numbers, the controller confirms, "Globally our pioneers account for 35 percent of our total business. Not only are margins high, but so are revenues." High-fives all around. After more discussion, the team plots another 30 percent of their portfolio in migrators, with only 35 percent of their business in settlers. The top team is feeling pretty good.

In presenting the map, the blue ocean expert notes that the team has plotted their portfolio based on corporate accounts, not based on their portfolio of service offerings. From the perspective of corporate accounts, the map looks strong. Only that's not the point of the map, so the expert challenges the team. "In our industry," one member shoots back, "we think and act based on corporate accounts, not service lines. That's how our industry works."

"When you are in a B2B service industry like ours, the dynamics are different," the business development director explains. "It's all about chasing RFPs [requests for proposals] for large corporate clients. That's where the money is." Heads nod in agreement. "When corporate accounts are highly profitable, we're clearly doing something right. To us—and probably to the rest of our industry—that's a pioneer." The temperature in the room is rising slowly.

"All true," the president responds. "Seen from the perspective of corporate accounts, we certainly have done a good job so far. But we all know that competition has been heating up. The question is: Are the services we offer what they need to be to stand apart and win big accounts in the future without significantly reducing our margins? If not, why should we expect strong profitable growth in the coming years?" You could visibly see people register the significance of the president's subtle reframing. The industry may focus on chasing large RFPs and high profit margins, and ESC may have succeeded in doing so with its existing service offerings. But the prospect of ESC's future profit and growth performance needs to be assessed based on how compelling its portfolio of services are from the perspective of customers. Customers will go where they can receive a leap in value.

The team agrees to go back and redraw their portfolio from a service line view of their business. This mapping of their business reveals a very different picture. No matter how much the top team debates and searches for what allows each service line to stand apart, the same answer ultimately comes back. Service line after service line is a me-too settler. "As far as we can tell," the team concludes, "we essentially offer the same services in the same way as everyone else. Roughly the same quality of repairs, same pricing, same level of customer service, same turnaround speed..."

The team goes silent. Their pioneer-migrator-settler map

looks very red. "How can the switch from corporate accounts and profitability to service lines and value innovation paint such a different picture?" one member asks. "We thought we were largely swimming in a blue ocean." As the team probes the discrepancy, a realization hits them. Many of the corporate accounts originally mapped as pioneers are longtime customers, whose contracts date back five to seven years, while the more recent customers of less than two years are the ones the team has plotted in the settler section of the map.

The standard of what truly constituted a pioneer, or even a migrator, begins to take shape in people's minds. The team realizes that they may hold inflated views of their business. Given the multiyear contractual nature of the industry, the higher-margin corporate accounts, in fact, seem to better reflect historical success and customer inertia, rather than innovative value delivered or future performance. More recent RFPs won have taken far longer to secure and have profit margins significantly lower than those of several years back. A new mood has set in. The atmosphere is somber.

The president breaks the atmosphere. "We are not in the valley of death," he reassures the team. "We are still recognized as a leader in the field. We should feel good about that. But nontraditional players are now entering the industry, like major consulting companies intent on chopping the market up. There is also growing talk of some companies keeping field repair processes in-house as a way to build customer intimacy."

"What are our growth expectations for the next five years?" the HR manager asks.

"Ten percent in real terms," the controller responds.

"Does our pioneer-migrator-settler map show we have the horses for that?" the IT head continues.

"I was just thinking along the same lines," the business development director says, as he projects the map the group has just collectively plotted on a wall for everyone to see clearly. The silence in the room speaks volumes. The team realizes that their efforts are focused on benchmarking competitors and making operational improvements. ESC has scant planned investments to rethink and innovate their service line to make it stand apart.

"Well, now. We have our work cut out for us, don't we?" the president concludes.

What Your Plotted Map Reveals

Once your organization's map is complete, you are ready to discuss its strategic implications. Is your portfolio settler-heavy—like ESC's and that of the majority of companies that are stagnant or declining? Has a business that was once a pioneer, generating huge profits and growth, recently become a settler, suggesting that the organization's growth is likely to slow if another pioneer is not launched?

The ideal portfolio to aim for depends, of course, on your industry. In fast-moving industries, for example, you will want and need to have more pioneers than settlers. In industries with large fixed costs for organizations and sunk costs for buyers, a portfolio with a few solid migrators and maybe one pioneer would be the right mix for securing today's success while building for tomorrow.

Stress to the group that the objective is not to create a portfolio dominated by pioneers. It is to create a healthy balance between today's businesses—your settlers that provide cash and a measure of earnings stability—and the pioneers that are the growth engines for tomorrow. This is the path to profitable growth. Figure 5-2 depicts this path for the consumer appliance company, showing how its managers have set out to shift their portfolio's center of gravity from settlers toward a better balance of migrators and pioneers.

Figure 5-2

Creating a Healthy, Balanced Portfolio: The Case of the Consumer Appliance Company

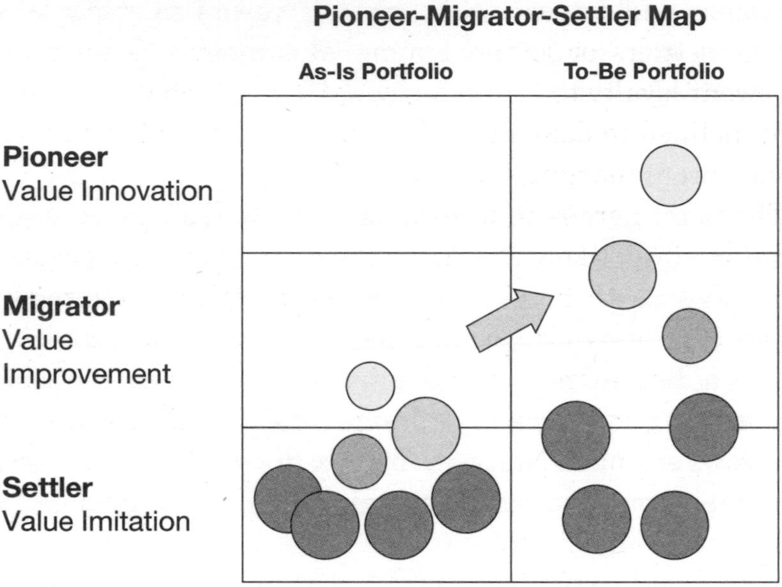

Pioneer-Migrator-Settler Map

| | As-Is Portfolio | To-Be Portfolio |

Pioneer Value Innovation

Migrator Value Improvement

Settler Value Imitation

If, after this exercise, you find that your current map already has a healthy balance across pioneers, migrators, and settlers, your organization is on a solid track to build for the future while seizing the present. In that case, you can hold off on launching a blue ocean initiative. To have a strong growth portfolio, a company needs robust pioneers; but it also needs stable revenues and cash flow to manage market expectations and provide resources. This is where settlers and migrators can add great value.

If, on the other hand, the portfolio you've plotted presents a situation not too far from the portfolio in figure 5-1, help the group to appreciate the strategic implications through questions like these: "What are the prospects for strong profitable growth from our settler and low migrator offerings?" "Are their industries growing so rapidly that we can expect strong profitable growth despite the offerings being settlers and migrators?"

Ask what might happen if you were to share the map with Wall Street analysts. Would they expect a positive earnings surprise from the organization, or would they be likely to rate your stock a hold or downgrade it? And, finally, discuss how customers might react to the map. If buyers saw your offerings as settlers or low migrators, would they be impressed and swear loyalty to your offerings? Or would that make them more inclined to demand price cuts and put further pressure on your profit margins?

The point here is to use the map to build a shared understanding of the likely consequences of inaction. Are the organization's growth ambitions consistent with the aggregated pioneer-migrator-settler map the group has drawn? Or is there is a discrepancy? As the implications sink in, the team's motivation to launch a blue ocean shift initiative takes hold and grows stronger. Now it's time to catch the wave and share your intention to select a single business or product/service offering to launch a blue ocean shift initiative and begin upgrading your overall portfolio.

Defining the Right Scope

As you study the map you've created, you may find that, like ESC and the consumer appliance company in figure 5-1, you still have too many candidates to choose among. In the face of this common dilemma, we have found the following criteria to be particularly helpful. Ideally, the scope of your initiative should be defined by the business or product/service offering that meets all (or the greatest subset) of these four criteria.

First, the business or product/service offering is a settler or a low migrator; that is, it's only slightly above settler status, making it clear that it's currently swimming in a red ocean.

Second, it's headed by a manager who is eager to break out of the red ocean and believes that fundamentally rethinking the strategy is key to doing that. Selecting a unit with such a manager is crucial: The manager's enthusiasm and conviction that change is needed are what people in that unit will feed off during the process. This kind of energy both builds people's confidence and signals that waffling will not be allowed. That goes a long way toward getting everyone on the same page. By contrast, selecting a manager whose unit may desperately need to change, but who offers nonstop excuses as to why things are the way they are, or myriad reasons for why no new idea or approach could possibly work, is to court failure before the process even starts. These kinds of managers project the wrong kind of energy, the kind that signals to those below them that they don't really believe in the initiative. That, in turn, will eat at people's confidence and willingness to give their all. You can lead a horse to water, but you cannot make it drink. So don't try.

Third, ideally, no other major initiatives should be underway in the unit. If the people who support a business or product/service offering are already stretched by a major reorganization, say, or the implementation of a new enterprise resource planning system, this is usually not where you want to start, even if the leader is genuinely interested in undertaking the initiative. People can do only so much beyond their regular jobs and do things well.

Fourth, the business or product/service offering has its back against the wall. While a settler offering may have limited prospects for growth, as discussed above, that doesn't necessarily mean it's losing money. In fact, it could still be quite profitable. When a settler or a low migrator offering is not just swimming in a red ocean of competition, however, but is also operating in the red, or facing an onslaught of all-new competitors that are gaining traction fast, that situation helps create a sense of urgency and a willingness to try new ideas to turn the tide. This natural energy tends to unlock a hunger for a new approach that a blue ocean initiative can leverage.

Over the next week or weeks, if needed, engage the managers of each unit in a series of discussions to assess their readiness—and that of their units. Then select the one that best meets all or the greatest subset of these four key criteria.

With the right scope for your initiative set, and with credibility and positive energy building, you are now ready to put the right team together to make a blue ocean shift happen. That's the subject of the next chapter. So let's get started.

CHAPTER 6

Constructing the Right
Blue Ocean Team

"I THINK THE BOX WITH the wide pink stripe looks best. It really pops. And the bright color gives it a nice edge."

"I couldn't agree more. It will definitely catch women's eyes."

The trouble is the packaging the marketing team decided on wasn't for a women's product. It was for an iron that didn't require ironing, and it was designed principally for men and young adults of both sexes. You simply hang your wrinkled shirt or pants on a clothes hanger or the back of chair, run the small handheld device up and down the garment, and voilà, with the help of a strong burst of steam, the wrinkles fall away—in less than half the time ironing takes. No skill necessary. No ironing board, either.

The trouble had started eight months earlier, when the head of domestic appliances, whom we'll call "Brad," spoke with his counterpart in marketing (let's call him "Joe") about including one of his staff on the team Brad was assembling for a blue ocean initiative. Quickly outlining how busy marketing was with "major" new product launches and campaigns, Joe's attitude was clear: "Just create the new product and don't worry. We'll take it from there. We know the market. That's our forte."

Truth be told, Brad wasn't exactly keen on bringing some-one from marketing onboard the team, either. Within the division, the commonly held belief was that "When it comes to the consumer and the market, marketing never listens to anyone. They don't think anyone else has anything to add or knows better than they do."

To motivate his team, Brad decided not to push it and to forgo getting marketing involved. It just seemed easier and made everyone—both his division and the marketing team—happier. So the business division rolled up its sleeves and set about applying the blue ocean shift process to the humble iron.

The market in Europe for irons couldn't have been blood-ier. The process revealed a range of similar irons at every price point, with the number of special features climbing with each jump in price. Convinced there was most likely no new path to go down, the team was surprised as, step-by-step, that belief was overturned when new insights began to emerge. Like how, despite all the cool features added to irons over the years, no iron addressed the greatest issue of all: People hated ironing. They didn't want ironing made better. They wanted no ironing at all.

What's more, to iron you had to have an ironing board—and a good one, for the iron to work well. This was an unwel-come added cost. Ironing boards were also big, clumsy, hard to store, and a hassle to set up and put away. Those issues had never been addressed, either, since ironing boards were in another industry and, technically, not the iron makers' responsibility.

The team saw a huge opportunity in these unaddressed problems, as well as a growing ocean of noncustomers: men, who, as they married later in life and lived on their own lon-ger, were doing more and more of their own household chores. Men didn't like going out looking sloppy, but they hated the tedious task of ironing even more. And most couldn't afford to have their clothes professionally pressed. Young adults of both sexes were also a largely untapped ocean of noncustomers. Yet the industry generally acted as if it were still the 1950s, and that when it came to domestic chores like ironing, women should be the focus of their efforts. And women, it was also believed, wanted to do a meticulous job.

The ironless iron would change all that.

As agreed, the blue ocean team shared the prototype and the results of the process and rapid market tests with marketing. And, as agreed, the marketing team took the baton. But not having been part of the process, marketing was full of doubts.

"It can't create a crease. Creases are important," said some of the marketers.

"They don't get it. Women buy irons, *not* men, and rarely young adults," added others.

So the marketers decided to do damage control. They knew you had to target customers, not noncustomers. That was just plain common sense. So they put the new "device" in a box with a striking pink stripe to attract existing customers, and they pitched it as a supplemental iron made for those times when creases weren't necessary. Packaged and sold that way, women saw the ironless iron as just one more add-on, another thing to store in their already crowded cupboards. They never thought it could replace ironing. It was never sold as if it could. And men and young adults—the ocean of noncustomers who were the prime targets—never gave the pink-striped box a second glance.

What the marketing team did went against what the blue ocean team found mattered. But what the blue ocean team found mattered went against the accepted wisdom the marketing team had mastered. The lesson: If people are not part of the process and there to discover firsthand the power of the ideas that open up new value-cost frontiers, it's too easy for them to dismiss those ideas as irrelevant, deny their validity, and push to bend them right back to the industry's so-called "best practices," even when those best practices may be outdated or just plain awful.

That's why putting together the right team to carry out a blue ocean initiative is incredibly important. When you are shifting—changing what you are doing and the factors on which your industry has long competed—all the key players who will make that shift need to be involved.

We're going to talk here about how to construct the right team in an established organization or division (be it for-profit, nonprofit, or public) with typical line and staff positions, where executing a new strategy will likely depend on the cooperation of people across various functions, and the usual politics and naysayers will need to be overcome. If you own a small, family-run business or a single store on Main Street, or you're an entrepreneur just starting out, you may well have only a handful of professionals at most in your organization. But while you may not have the depth of talent to draw on that a larger organization can bring to bear, don't worry. Founders and owners almost always have much more control in aligning people around their blue ocean vision. By understanding the dynamics of what makes a team successful, you'll be in the best position to know how to leverage your employees or the people you have access to as you set out on your blue ocean shift journey.

What Does the Right Team Look Like?

Who, then, should be on this team? As our cautionary example about the iron suggests, you want representatives from all the functions and organizational levels that will play a key role in bringing a new offering to market. In a typical corporate setting, that would usually include someone from HR, IT, marketing, finance, manufacturing, R&D, and sales, as well as someone on the front lines, like a call center staff member or someone who works on the store floor. While organizations routinely separate functions and hierarchical levels to achieve efficiencies, these divides create silos, often break trust, and motivate people to suboptimize when what you need is all the parts working together so that ideas get built for execution from the start and everyone owns them.

All in all, you should look to create a team with 10 to 15 people. The lower limit is to make sure all the major functions and areas are represented, have a chance to contribute, and discover firsthand the need for change. The upper limit is to keep the process manageable and the team flexible and fast. More than that tends to become unwieldy and frustrating for those involved, unnecessarily sapping the team's energy and breaking down the integrity of the process.

When setting up the team, we've found that executives can be hesitant to include people from a particular function who might be perceived as more trouble than they're worth, or who could slow the process down as they struggle to get into the blue ocean mindset. Like Brad, they may shy away from marketers or want to leave out HR people, whom they see as benefits administrators with little strategic vision. However, we caution against this. Have you also heard the refrain "Finance trumps strategy"? We certainly have. Over the years, many people have told us how their efforts to innovate were thwarted by finance staffers inclined to support what they knew and could measure, not what could be. Not surprisingly, they worry that the same result will befall their blue ocean shift initiative.

We've found otherwise, however, in our research over the last 10 years.

When finance people are included on the team, and go through the process, just like the other members, they develop firsthand insight into the need for a strategic shift and the power of the blue ocean strategic move they've helped create. Finance staff members become bean counters when they are asked to sign off on strategic imperatives they don't deeply understand. Like all of us, they simply don't feel comfortable putting money behind ideas that are foreign to them. To turn finance into your ally, put a finance representative on the team from the start. The team will gain the power and robustness of this functional discipline, and finance will become your true strategic partner in the investment decision-making process. All sides learn and grow from the process.

While you want a cross section of people on the team, be sure that everyone selected is directly involved in the division or product/service offering you're aiming to shift from red to blue and therefore has skin in the game. This cross section is critical, because it ensures that there's someone from every function who can personally and authentically affirm the credibility of the shift the team is developing. These people will be the conduits to their functions and to the hierarchy at each step of the process, relaying firsthand updates on the team's findings. This is what makes those findings believable and testifies to the robustness of the process.

Contrast the experience of the iron manufacturer with this one from a corporate foreign exchange provider. Before starting the blue ocean shift process, the company was convinced that account executives were one of their key competitive advantages vis-à-vis large banks. Not surprisingly, the account executives agreed, as their swagger and status in the company showed. But as the team went through the process, one truly unexpected finding that emerged was that buyers disdained the account executives' role and hated wasting their time talking with them. They saw the account executives as the people who focused on coming up with creative excuses and smoothing over the problems and frustrations clients had with the company's services. What good was attention from an account executive when wire transfers were frequently executed late, or customers failed to get confirmation that transactions had been executed, or they received scant market knowledge to properly hedge their currency payments. Had the account executives not been on the team and heard this feedback for themselves, rest assured they would have vehemently insisted that the process had not been done correctly, that the team members didn't know what they are talking about, and that—to the contrary—account execs were what set the company apart. But because they were included and heard customers say the same thing time and time again, they couldn't deny it.

More telling, this finding led account executives to a realization about themselves. Yes, they had long been perceived as the company's superstars. But now they could see that all too often they were heroes not because they added real value for clients but because they stopped clients from leaving by being smart in excusing, apologizing, and calming them down. And so, the team made the decision—with the support of the account executives themselves—to phase out the position. Account executives became sales reps for large, high-value accounts, effectively tripling the company's sales force and increasing the company's revenue generation capability significantly with no increase in cost.

In organizations with geographically scattered operations, a common refrain is "Our area is different." In one company that had a poor track record of rolling out virtually any initiative globally, subsidiary managers summed up their take on the head office's view of the world as "Nuts in the field, brains in the center." Not surprisingly the "nuts" took great pride in quietly derailing and slowing down head office initiatives. Having someone from each key geographic region included on the team goes a long way toward remedying this situation. People feel their area is valued and that they are not viewed as brainless doers to command.

What typically happens first on such international teams is that the regional members grouse about how their area is different, and how no new "global" strategy can possibly work there. To which the response we recommend is, "If that's true, the process will reveal it. And if it does, we'll say *sayonara* to the aim of creating and rolling out a blue ocean shift globally." The clarity of that single statement goes a long way toward creating openness and engagement in the process. Then, as the teams get started, what they typically discover is that, if the organization could shoot the lights out on a few key common concerns voiced by customers and targeted noncustomers around the world, people would gladly forgo the majority of their idiosyncratic regional wish lists. This reinforces real buy-in and excitement in the process. While more than one team is needed for multinationals with geographically diversified operations, for the purpose of clarity and simplicity, we will focus on the one-team situation.

What to Look for in Team Members

So far we've been talking about where your team members should come from. In fact, we've equated the individuals with their functions, referring to "marketing" and "finance" as if the people were their jobs. Now we'll shift gears and talk about the individuals themselves.

Human dynamics is something many leaders gloss over. And, true, setting the right human dynamics does take time and thought up front. But the rewards are priceless. That's why, when it comes to whom to select for the team, job title is not the most important factor. Character is. What you are looking for are people who are well respected and already have credibility with others in the organization. That may or may not overlap with their status in the organization. You want to select people who are good listeners, are known to be thoughtful, and are willing to raise questions when others don't. People who not only can dream big but also are noted for their commitment to getting things done. These are the people others will naturally tend to admire and listen to. Such people elevate the credibility of the team within the organization and the respect team members have for one another.

At the same time, you will also want to put one (or potentially two) known naysayers on the team. Though to ensure
that they can't dominate the team's dynamics or undermine
its positive energy, they must be the clear minority. Why have
them there at all, then? For one thing, putting a devil's advocate on the team boosts the credibility of the process and the
team's findings. It signals your confidence that the process
can withstand their doubts and misgivings. It shows that you
intend to scrupulously examine any idea that challenges the
status quo to ensure that potential downsides are fully considered and not simply glossed over, only to come back and bite
you later. In addition, when skeptics go through the process
and see, feel, and experience for themselves the ways your
current strategy fails to excite the market, they tend to stop
complaining. And when *they* are convinced, the momentum
for change is reinforced further.

Back in the day, when Bernie Marcus was still running Home Depot with a viselike grip, the leader of one of
its second-tier suppliers of electric lighting felt his company
needed to make a blue ocean shift to get a bigger slice of Home
Depot's and other major retailers' business. But neither argument nor numbers could convince the naysayers in his company that their products weren't good enough. They claimed it
was the sales force that needed upgrading. Full stop.

Then the leader took a different tack. He put the two key
naysayers on the initiative team to meet the market. The team
started with customer #1, Bernie Marcus himself. And Bernie
let it rip: The product was a me-too. It was too expensive. It
was not reliable. It was a waste of valuable shelf space. After
that naked feedback from Bernie, the naysayers were visibly
ashen. No more urging for a new strategy was needed.

Be prepared for people to be, on the one hand, glad they are
chosen for the team and, on the other, apprehensive about the
extra work that will require. On average, team members will

spend 10 percent of their weekly work time on the initiative, with peak points, when they will need to set aside around 20–25 percent, scattered over the course of the project. This work almost always comes on top of their day jobs. But as they say, "No pain, no gain." Fortunately, we can also say the gain will outweigh the pain.

In the process, team members step up to leadership, gain experience working with people from different functions and hierarchical levels, learn firsthand and up close about the market, and acquire a big picture of the organization and the environment (often for the first time)—all highly valuable exercises for every person involved. Working on a blue ocean initiative team changes the scope of the members' day jobs, shifting their focus away from the routine to more strategic concerns.

People learn to ask future-focused questions about how to create innovative value, what adds cost but no value (like account executives at the corporate foreign exchange provider), what could add a little cost but deliver a leap in value, and who the industry's noncustomers are and how to convert them to customers. This transforms everyone on the team, making them more valuable to the organization and to themselves. You will want to discuss these benefits with team members up front. People appreciate knowing that the extra work they'll take on will be more than repaid by the new skills, team connections, and ideas about future opportunities they will gain by participating.

Appoint a Kingpin Team Leader

Job title isn't everything, but the head of the team, whether it is you or someone you appoint, does need to outrank the other members. That simply makes it easier for them to accept and follow the leader. The disproportionate influence of a strong kingpin, both on the team dynamics and across the company, will help mobilize large swaths of the organization to support the initiative.

The team leader is expected to act as the team's first contact point, maintaining direction and excitement, keeping everyone informed, and helping the team navigate through the organization. The leader also needs to anticipate problems that could hinder the team's ability to complete its tasks and address these issues proactively. Organizations are often tempted to delegate a lot of this work to assistants. However, we strongly advise against this for a number of reasons. When a team leader directly undertakes these tasks, it signals that the initiative is important and not to be taken lightly. It shows respect for team members. And it keeps the fire burning, closing loopholes for procrastination and halfhearted efforts. It's far too easy for people to play games with assistants, telling them, "We'll get back to you soon," only to respond three weeks later, compromising the process and draining energy from the initiative.

For Dysfunctional Organizations: Enlist a Consigliere

Is your organization dysfunctional? Ridiculously bureaucratic? Or highly political so that getting things done feels akin to walking through a minefield? Large, older organizations may feel this way. So can government entities. In these situations, in addition to putting the team together and selecting the right team leader, you also want to think about enlisting a consigliere. This is particularly important for organizations that have operated in the same way for a long time or have a strong institutional culture.

A blue ocean shift initiative can overturn many established industry and organizational conventions. This may have ramifications for how work is currently done, which, in turn, may inspire anxiety in the hearts of the people doing that work now. Where human emotions and behavior are involved, an ounce of prevention is truly worth its weight in gold. So you need to be mindful throughout the process of any potential resistance that may be brewing or poised to arise when it comes time for implementation.

A consigliere can help you anticipate these issues before they become intractable. A consigliere is someone in the organization with an ear to the ground, a master of organizational politics, who knows who the big players and blockers are, and who's hungriest for change and likely to be one of your strongest supporters. As a respected insider, he or she can advise the team and provide air cover from potential detractors, as well as garner support from individuals who might otherwise want to thwart the initiative actively or through passive aggression. The best candidate is someone who is highly influential, can be a quiet advocate, and also has the will to get involved, if necessary, to remove obstacles the team might face.

With the scope of your initiative set and the right team in place, you're ready to move on to the second step of the process. Here we'll discuss how to get a clear understanding of the current state of play in the industry, align everyone on the team, and inspire a natural wake-up call among the team members and the wider organization about the need to make a blue ocean shift.

Step Two: Understand Where You Are Now

CHAPTER 7

Getting Clear About the Current State of Play

Do you have one simple picture that captures your overall strategy, a picture that every manager understands and that puts everyone on the same page? Do you know what factors your industry or target industry competes on and invests in? Do you know what sets your product or service offering apart, and how it diverges from the competition's? In short, do you and your team have an objective view of the current state of play in your industry?

Whether you are about to embark on a blue ocean shift, or simply want to make sure you truly understand your industry's status quo, having a clear and shared picture of the current strategic landscape is critical. First, it ensures that you have a strategy, not merely a collection of tactics that may make sense individually, but that don't add up and may even be contradictory. Second, it ensures that everyone is on the same page. Only when people agree on what the current strategy and strategic landscape are, and see and agree on the clear need for change, will you create real alignment and inspire their willingness to act. You and the team leader you've chosen may appreciate the need to break out of the red ocean and fundamentally rethink your strategy, but that doesn't mean others on the team will share this view, let alone the wider organization.

Beyond this, we've found that while managers typically have a strong sense of how they and their rivals compete on one or two strategic dimensions, few grasp the full picture. They may have slogans, which they confuse with strategy, like "We are the friendliest airline," or "Our strategy is to be the best full-service global bank." But when we probe for specifics, the discussions are typically fuzzy and full of sound bites that competitors could just as equally easily use to describe their products or services.

To address this problem, we developed the strategy canvas, the diagnostic tool that you will use throughout the blue ocean shift journey. Drawing the "as-is" strategy canvas for your offering will give the team—and, through them, the wider organization—an objective picture of current industry dynamics as well as your own and your competitors' strategies. Because there is no foregone conclusion about what the strategy canvas will—or won't—reveal, the team will be able to discover for themselves the relevance, or *irrelevance*, of challenging the status quo and rethinking the strategic profile of your organization's offering in blue ocean terms. This combination of fair process, with firsthand discovery and atomization, is what ensures that people will own, internalize, and have confidence in the results of their work.

The Strategy Canvas

The strategy canvas is a one-page visual analytic that depicts the way an organization configures its offering to buyers in relation to those of its competitors. It crisply communicates the four key elements of strategy: the factors of competition, the offering level buyers receive across these factors, and your own and your competitors' strategic profiles and cost structures. And it tells a story: It allows you to see—and understand—where you and your competitors are currently investing; the product, service, and delivery factors the industry is competing on; and what customers receive from existing competitive offerings. Drawing the strategy canvas of the industry you intend to penetrate is equally critical if you are an entrepreneur intent on creating a new business, or a new nonprofit, because it highlights in one simple picture what you will be up against in strategic terms. It's also a potent visual to use in discussions with potential investors or funders.

Figure 7-1 shows the strategy canvas for the UK charity fund-raising industry before the launch of Comic Relief. The horizontal axis specifies the key factors the industry historically competed on and invested in, which range from pity pleas, to advocacy counseling and care services, to year-round

Figure 7-1

Strategy Canvas of the UK Charity Fund-Raising Industry (Pre–Comic Relief)

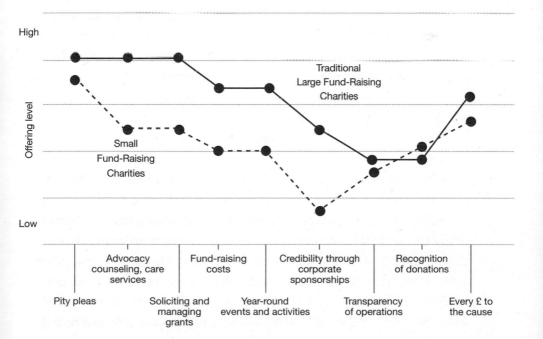

fund-raising events and activities. Note that this axis captures the "key competing factors," not the key value factors for buyers. This is important. Why? Because as you will likely soon discover, there is often a stark difference between the factors organizations compete on and assume deliver value and the factors that buyers actually value. In fact, what companies compete on often not only fails to add value from the buyer's perspective, but can actually detract from it. Think of the year-round fund-raising events and marketing solicitations that charities compete on, which create donor fatigue, rather than inspiring people to give. Think of all the buttons on the average TV remote control, which frustrate and confuse more than they assist. Or think of the vast array of channels you get when you sign up with a cable TV provider, when all you really want are the three or four that carry the shows you love to watch.

As your team focuses on identifying your industry's key competing factors, they will also begin to surface all the areas you and your competitors currently invest in as you attempt to keep up with or surge past one another. These factors increase your cost structure, absorb your organization's time, and can complicate operations. But because they seem to be de rigueur, they are rarely questioned. So as the team expressly identifies these factors, they will also be creating a roster of candidates to consider later, when you're looking for things to eliminate or reduce in order to drop your cost structure while simultaneously offering buyers a leap in value.

The vertical axis of the strategy canvas captures the offering level buyers receive or experience for each of an industry's key competing factors. In the case of the UK charity fund-raising industry or, for that matter, any nonprofit, donors are effectively the buyers of the nonprofit's mission and credibility, which they "pay" for with a donation. A high score on the vertical axis means that an organization offers buyers—here, donors—more, while a relatively low score means that an organization offers less. You now connect the dots to create your strategic profile—a graphic depiction of your organization's relative performance across its industry's factors of competition—and your competitors'. A strategy canvas, as exemplified in figure 7-1, is what we call the as-is strategy canvas because it captures the industry's current as-is state of play. It helps to create a common understanding on industry reality among the team.

What the Strategy Canvas Reveals

Looking at the canvas in figure 7-1, we can literally *see* why the industry had become a red ocean of competition. The industry has essentially commoditized itself. Despite the fact that there are thousands of charities in the UK, from the donors' point of view there is enormous convergence in their strategic profiles. From a donor's perspective, large traditional fund-raising charities all effectively compete in a similar way. The same can be said for small fund-raising charities. What's more, the strategic profiles of both large and small charities essentially follow the same basic shape, only at different offering levels. As both large and small charities try to improve the value of their offerings by providing a little more for a little less, and benchmark industry best practices, the basic shape of their strategic profiles converges. The result, as seen in the figure, is that industry players' strategic profiles become nearly mirror images of one another without challenging the basic shape of their curves. This is not rare. It is commonplace.

Think about major retail banks in São Paulo, New York, Paris, Lagos, or Tokyo. Are there any stark differences in their relative locations, façades, atmosphere, or even tellers? Or, from the buyers' point of view, are almost all of them pretty much the same, except for the language spoken? What about gas stations the world over? Any major differences in what you would expect? Again, the same. Or law firms and management consultancies? Here, too, they're fairly similar, other than potentially being distinguished by a famous high-profile lawyer or a thought-leader consultant. And these are just a few examples. Take a moment and we are sure you will come up with your own long list of organizations whose strategies are driven by one-upping the competition.

The strategy canvas helps you change that. It pushes you to take a step back from the detail you are typically enmeshed in, and clearly see your industry's defining contours—to differentiate the forest from the trees. It allows you to capture and depict a macro picture of the current state of play in your industry, without getting lost in the technical details of small operational differences. Focusing on the basic shape of the industry's strategic profile is essential, because it's impossible to make a blue ocean shift without challenging and altering the industry's basic strategic norms. Depicting the small operational deviations that individual players are making in their offerings will only clutter the big picture that buyers see and be irrelevant for your intended strategic shift.

The Importance of Focus, Divergence, and a Compelling Tagline

To make a blue ocean shift, the basic shape of your strategic profile cannot look like everyone else's. It must distinctively diverge, so that when buyers think about your offering, they do not lump it together with the offerings of other industry players. Specifically, to make a blue ocean shift and stand out to buyers, your strategic profile needs to meet three criteria: First, it should be clear that its basic shape on the strategy canvas diverges from the industry's average profile. It shouldn't simply be a little more, or a little less, than what the competition does. Second, your strategic profile has to be focused. It shouldn't just over-deliver or under-deliver on the same set of factors the rest of the industry competes on. Rather, it should concentrate on the key factors that can offer buyers a leap in value, while eliminating and reducing others. This is what allows your strategy to achieve lower costs at the precise moment you are also offering greater value.

Finally, your strategic profile should have a compelling tagline that speaks to the market and honestly reflects what your offering provides. It must have integrity, not be a wishful marketing slogan. Buyers see through empty slogans fast. A compelling tagline is an important initial litmus test to ensure that the divergence and focus behind your strategic profile are actually linked to a leap in buyer value, and not merely differentiation for differentiation's sake. Consider the strategic profile of Comic Relief, known as Red Nose Day in the United States, which we discussed in depth in chapter 3. Figure 7-2

Figure 7-2

Strategy Canvas of Comic Relief
"Doing Something Funny for Money"

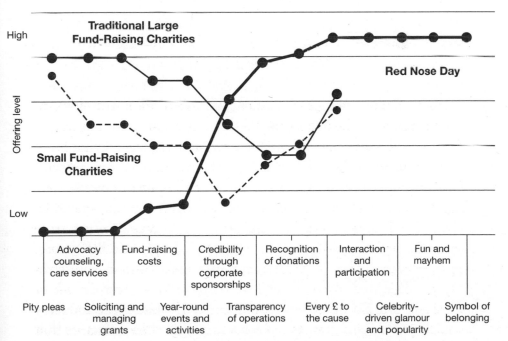

shows how its strategic profile meets all three criteria, opening up a blue ocean of new market space in the UK charity fund-raising industry. Later on, in step four of the process, we will show how this new, or "to-be," strategic profile can be derived.

What does the as-is strategy canvas of your industry or target industry look like? Would it look like that of the UK fund-raising charity industry pre–Comic Relief, where all the major players' strategic profiles followed the same basic shape, and essentially converged, from the buyers' point of view? What does it reveal about your strategic profile? Does it march in lockstep with everyone else's, or does it stand apart, as Comic Relief's does? These are not questions for you to answer yourself. These are the questions you should ask the team to answer through the process of drawing the as-is strategy canvas of your industry.

How to Draw Your Strategy Canvas

The as-is strategy canvas is a self-assessment, not a customer survey. The aim is to understand the team's perspective, what the team members see and register about the current strategic landscape: What do they believe the business or product/service offering you've identified competes on? How much or how little of each key factor does your organization and the competition offer? What is the offering's price point relative to the competition's? What is its relative cost structure? You will likely be amazed by the plethora of insights drawing your as-is strategy canvas can reveal.

Here is how this step unfolds.

Name the industry you are in

Start with a blank as-is strategy canvas, which, along with a supporting explanation, are provided for your free download and use at www.blueoceanshift.com/ExerciseTemplates. Ask the team to name the industry that the business, product, or service you've selected for this initiative competes in or, if you are an aspiring entrepreneur, the industry you desire to enter. The aim is to ensure that everyone on the team has the same reference point and that this reference point is decided by the team, not imposed on them, so that they will fully own the as-is strategy canvas they are about to create. This is typically a straightforward, rapidly accomplished task. However, on rare occasions a team member will start to hypothesize about what industry "we should be in." If this happens, simply remind him or her that at this stage you're focused on defining the industry "as it is," not "as it should be." That will come later in the process.

Identify the key factors your industry competes on

Before the team settles down to address this task, it's important to establish a few parameters:

- Identify no fewer than 5 and no more than 12 key competing factors on the as-is strategy canvas. A minimum of 5 pushes teams who say they only compete on price to challenge their assumptions and to uncover factors that may have become so familiar they no longer register. Basic B2B industries like chemicals and plastics, for example, often fall into this camp, because they take it for granted that the product they sell is a commodity and argue that price is the only distinctive point on which they compete, when, in fact, the competitive factors usually include assessment and technical support services, delivery lead times, inventory availability, and more. Conversely, a maximum of 12 factors pushes teams who come up with overly long lists to focus only on "key" competing factors and not every factor they can name. The aim is to keep the team focused on the big picture and neither oversimplify nor get lost in minutiae. In the case of for-profit companies, price should always be included in the key competing factors.

- Key factors can be related to an offering's product, service, or delivery platforms. So think about all three platforms in coming up with your list. For example, for a turbine engine manufacturer, key competing factors might include customer financing (a service factor), engine power (a product factor), and speed to fulfill orders (a delivery factor).

- Avoid supply-side technical jargon and use words that describe the factor from the buyers' point of view. For example, *speed* instead of *megahertz*.

Before taking up this task as a team, each of the members should develop their own list independently. Beginning this way is key for three reasons. One, it avoids groupthink, which tends to stifle people and to lead to lists that do not fully reflect the range of views within the group. Such self-censorship can engender an unspoken "what if" mindset that may never go away and can discredit the initiative's conclusions. "If I had mentioned this, would the result have changed? Why didn't I speak up?" is not the kind of thinking you want when implementation is the ultimate aim. Two, it challenges everyone on the team to name the factors they believe the industry competes on. You will likely find this is a question that few people have ever given much thought to, even though they often come into the process assuming they have. As they usually soon discover in sitting down to answer this question, it's not easy. Three, it allows the team to appreciate the differences in how each of them interprets what their organization and industry do, and how often people may identify the same factor and yet mean different things (we'll get to that in a minute). People's jobs tend to induce tunnel vision, which this process helps to break down.

Once all the team members have created their lists, the

team should reconvene as a group. At this juncture, have everyone read their list of identified factors and, as they do, record them on a whiteboard so everyone "sees" what others are thinking. When a factor is mentioned more than once, make a check mark next to it, so that the team can also see which factors most members identified and agreed on.

At this point we typically find that roughly 50–60 percent of the factors identified will be the same. We also often hear members comment casually to one another about the time it took for them to come up with their lists, even if they have just completed their organization's annual strategic planning process. "If it's hard for us to identify and agree on the range of factors we compete on, how can we have a clear strategy that is executed with integrity?" is an all-too-common insight. Or, as one executive aptly put it, "Now I know why we never get there. We don't know where we're going." In and of itself, this reckoning opens team members' minds to the realization that they need to think more deeply about their strategy.

Now initiate and lead a discussion focused on the factors where there was no consensus. Asking each member to explain the reasoning behind the factors he or she identified ensures that everyone will appreciate the variety of ways in which their colleagues perceive the industry and enable them to register factors that were always there but were somehow overlooked. At this stage, the team usually finds that another 20–30 percent of the identified factors are actually getting at a similar point, even though members have labeled them differently. They also learn about factors that only one or two members may have identified, but that are quickly recognizable as "key" factors once the proponents have articulated why.

As the team identifies the key competing factors that will appear on the horizontal axis, they may need to be reminded to describe them from the buyers' point of view, not the organization's. *Good people* or *state-of-the-art IT* are examples of organizational factors people often confuse with key competing factors. While these may indeed be strengths of the organization, they need to be translated into factors that speak to buyers, *if they do*. The factors buyers don't see or experience should be scratched. *Good people*, for example, might be *customer responsiveness*, if that's what the good people produce for buyers. And *state-of-the-art IT* might translate into *ease of use*, if that is what it leads to. The point is to continually bring the team around to describing the offering and key competing factors from buyers' point of view, not the supplier's.

Similarly, team members often identify *brand* as a key competing factor. In almost all cases, however, an organization's brand is a direct function of its strategic profile; that is, of what it offers buyers/users. Apple's brand is strong because its offering is strong: leading edge, reliable, easy to use, and stylish. Google's brand is strong because its product works amazingly well, it's quick, it's easy to use, and it delivers reliable results. A brand, in short, is the result of what you do. It's not an isolated, independent factor. To get beyond brand, ask what customers derive from the brand that makes it compelling. For example, what explains Federal Express's brand? That it's reliable, fast, gives peace of mind, and so on. To get to the root of the value the team believes a brand conveys, encourage members to think of the top three reasons buyers would purchase the offerings of the organization to which it belongs.

Decide which key player(s) to compare yourself with

Once the team has whittled down the list of key competing factors, they have to decide on the best player(s) to plot their offering against. We recommend selecting the industry leader, whose strategic profile is usually the benchmark others have focused on keeping up with or beating. If you are the industry leader, select your strongest competitor. You may think, "Hey, how can the as-is strategy canvas capture the industry if only the best player is plotted besides ourselves?" To which we reply, take a moment and think about Pepsi versus Coke or Sotheby's versus Christie's. Or imagine what the strategic profile of every major investment bank, every major haute couture house, every major accounting firm, and every major state university looks like.

Players in these industries may well argue that there are differences across them, and no doubt there are. But, in the big picture, seen from the buyers' (or donors') perspective, they all are pretty much the same. The market leader's strategic profile typically captures the profile others have been converging toward or, in many cases, have already come close to mimicking. Besides, the strategic profile of the best in class is also the gold standard that defines the industry.

If team members feel that an additional player should be plotted for the strategy canvas to be valid, then let them do so. However, we strongly discourage plotting more than three strategic profiles, lest the strategy canvas become cluttered and start to exaggerate inconsequential differences for buyers. For example, a car that accelerates up to 100 miles per hour in 3 seconds versus 15 seconds may matter to car manufacturers and a small segment of auto enthusiasts. But as ordinary car drivers ourselves, our response to such a difference is—sorry, engineers—"no big deal." Remember you are looking to capture the big picture from buyers' perspective, not technical differences from the supplier's perspective that may speak to a relatively small niche.

That said, there are contexts where it does make real sense to plot more than one best player. This typically happens when an organization operates in a market space served by two distinct strategic groups or alternative industries. For example, in the case of the blue ocean initiative team that was headed by Christian Grob at Groupe SEB, at the start of the blue ocean shift journey, the team plotted the strategic profile of its electric home French fry maker not only against its best-in-class traditional competitor's, a global consumer appliance company, but also against a new class of competitors, the best-in-class retailer brand's. With large retailer brands gaining power in the market, Christian's team saw them as important to include on the as-is strategy canvas.

When we worked with a company in the budget hotel industry, the organization plotted its strategic profile against the market leaders in two strategic groups that were relevant from the buyers' point of view: one-star and two-star hotels. In another organization, team members agreed that, although the strategic profile of the market leader was generally representative of what other industry players were doing, there was also a newcomer that appeared to be defying industry logic, growing at a fast clip, and garnering lots of attention. This was not just a new player. This was a new, fast-rising entrant that hadn't started to dominate the industry, but looked like it was on course to do just that. In this case, the team argued that the strategic profile of both the industry leader and this newcomer should be plotted along with its own. These are the types of reasons that make strong strategic sense and that you should look out for.

Rate your offering and the best-in-class player's or players' along the key competing factors

Having chosen the best-in-class player(s) you'll compare yourself with, the team is now ready to rate the offering level for each factor of your business or product or service against theirs. If the team decided that two strategic profiles or groups should be plotted along with your own, rate the offering levels for both of them. For simplicity, however, we'll reference only one strategic profile here in addition to your own.

Using a 5-point Likert-type scale (or some variant thereof), with 1 equal to very low, 3 equal to average, and 5 equal to very high, ask the team to rate your offering level for a given factor and then your reference player's for that same factor, before moving on to the next factor. We have found this approach the most effective way to proceed, because it offers a quick reality check if the ratings tend to be too high or too low. As people challenge one another on just where they and the best-in-class player stand on each factor, and why they feel as they do, a lively discussion usually ensues. What team members often begin to viscerally understand during these discussions is that, in the past, they and their colleagues often had different mental baselines for calibrating their offering, and had essentially talked past one another. As a result, while annual strategic plans were produced, they were more often about tactics to hit performance goals than about the big picture. This is another *aha* moment that seldom gets lost on team members, further opening people's minds.

In plotting price, the team should use the absolute price— the price tag buyers see. So, a high price should be ranked high on the vertical axis and a low price ranked low. While this may sound self-evident, teams often get this wrong and plot a low price high on the vertical axis and a high price low. Why? Because they are incorrectly interpreting price to mean value. But price is not value. Price is price. Just as a low price tag with a dismal product or service offering does not translate into high value, a higher price tag with a compelling offering does not mean low value.

Team members also often ask whether each competing factor should be weighted as part of this step. To this, our answer is no, because it drives you to focus on the wrong thing. The objective of the as-is strategy canvas is to record the factors the industry currently competes on and invests in, and the offering level buyers receive for each factor as objectively as possible. The aim of this step is not to provide a subjective, value-laden assessment of each offering level, but an objective one: Do we absolutely charge a little or a lot, or offer or focus a little or a lot on each factor, and hence invest accordingly?

Later in the process, when team members meet the market, we will drill down into value judgments and shift from what is to what should be.

Draw your as-is strategy canvas

With ratings for the key competitive factors in hand, the team is ready to plot their as-is strategic profile and that of the best-in-class player. The team should begin by putting price as the first competing factor on the horizontal axis, so that it's clear what value is: Value is what is exchanged when the buyer pays. Everything to the right of price on the horizontal axis is what the buyer is gaining. When the strategy canvas is viewed in this way, it is easy to see what buyers get for the price they pay.

Next, the team needs to plot the other key competing factors along the horizontal axis. In plotting, you want to keep your completed as-is strategy canvas from looking like a bowl of spaghetti—a zigzag, where the offering can be described as "low-high-low-high-low-high." With such a drawing, it will be very hard to make sense of and communicate the industry's current state of play. To avoid this, the team needs to plot key competing factors with similar ratings next to each other.

Once this is done, plot the offering level scores the team arrived at for each key factor and then connect the dots to create your as-is strategic profile. The team can then overlay this with the strategic profile of the best-in-class player to arrive at the as-is strategy canvas. Finally, team members are asked to reflect on their as-is strategic profile and see if they can give a compelling tagline that reflects their offering. When they do this exercise, you should make sure the team doesn't develop an advertising slogan, which doesn't really relate to the strategy in any meaningful way. The tagline should authentically reflect the strategic profile they are trying to headline. They will likely struggle to come up with a compelling tagline—one that resonates with integrity—for their as-is strategic profile if its basic shape converges with that of the best-in-class player(s).

What to Expect as You Draw Your Canvas

To appreciate the kind of dynamics that unfold and the insights that emerge as a team draws their strategy canvas, consider this vignette from the experience of a US commercial food service company we'll call School Foods. The company's profitable growth had stalled for some time, and two major players dominated the industry. In this instance, the CEO who took on the project chose to be the team's leader as well.

After discussing their factors of competition, the team began to plot their strategic profile against the two dominant rivals. Given the strength of both, the team argued it couldn't afford to focus on only one. This concern, however, was quickly found to be groundless. The team fast discovered that not only did the strategic profiles of the two rivals converge, but their own strategic profile also followed in lockstep. The strategic profiles of all three converged along the same dimensions of competition: financial accountability, quality of management services, transparency of bidding processes, and the like. The only difference was that the two industry leaders had higher name recognition, whereas School Foods had a high sense of mission, which the team wanted to include on the canvas as a distinguishing key competitive factor. The team was probed: "Do any of your customers know that you value your sense of mission?" "No, not really...I guess not," a team member reluctantly replied. Upon reflection and discussion, the team then agreed: They might be proud of their mission, but customers were clueless about it.

"Do you know what your competitors have to offer in terms of food, quality of service, or ambience?" a blue ocean expert asked. The entire team went quiet. There were blank faces all around. Eventually, a team member responded, "No, we don't really know what they offer, nor do we really know how our food offering is valued versus theirs by our customers." The probing then went deeper: "Why isn't the quality of food or variety in the offering noted as one of your factors of competition? You are a food-service company after all, aren't you?" The group was amused, but ashamed. "I guess we are so focused on winning the bid to provide the service by offering the best financial package desired by the management of the school," one team member confessed.

"Elsewhere at work you always talk a lot about the importance of building relationships in your business. Why isn't that on your strategy canvas?" The team members looked at one another. The head of operations said, "We've always spent a lot of energy on developing and maintaining relationships, but you know it really doesn't add value to customers."

"The industry principally competes on offering an adequate service at the lowest price," one team member chimed in, "but that's only half the picture, isn't it?" "When we really think about it," another team member added, "the factors our industry competes on are contract-related—price, transparency of our costs in bidding, inclusive pricing. It's about giving the customer the best financial deal, not necessarily the best food deal for the end user."

In the span of a 45-minute discussion, the School Foods team realized they were a "me-too" business: Customers didn't see how their offering differed from their competitors'. With their lower name recognition, they now have a good understanding as to why their company's growth has stalled for some time. They did not have a clear sense of how their offering compared to that of their competitors in the core of their product—food. And they competed on factors of little or no value to their *real* customers—the students who eat the food. This was good news. The entire industry was competing on four cylinders. All members of the group could collectively see the wide-open opportunity space to create a blue ocean and now share their willingness and urge to turn on all eight cylinders. They were excited to get started.

Building a Shared Understanding of the Strategic Implications

Now it's time to draw out the strategic implications of your completed canvas. To start, ask all your team members to write down the key insights they gained from drawing the canvas. Tell them that to kick off the group discussion, each one of them will be called on to share their insights. Inviting people to reflect, collect their thoughts, and crystallize the takeaways that jump out at them is a crucial part of building the trust, confidence, and ownership that are at the heart of making a successful blue ocean shift. Setting clear expectations in advance about what will happen during the group session reinforces that this is a fair process, while turning up the heat to encourage everyone to think deeply.

After each of the team members has shared their insights, you'll want to reflect on everyone's observations, using open-ended questions to let people appreciate their collective strategic insights. There are several areas to probe: Does the basic shape of our offering's strategic profile converge with or diverge from that of the best-in-class player(s)? Does our strategic profile merit a compelling tagline that has integrity? Or does our strategic profile confirm that a more honest tagline might be something like "We try hard, but we're hardly different from our rivals?" If potential customers saw the completed as-is strategy canvas, would it give them reason to be our fans and purchase our offering, or would they be largely indifferent to it? And if investors saw it, would this give them cause to upgrade their estimate of our future profitable

growth prospects and sign off on further funding? The strategy canvas is a powerful tool to use in seeking funding, and
in objectively demonstrating to buyers why—when your organization has a compelling strategy—they should, in short, fall
in love with you.

To ensure that important insights revealed in the process
of drawing the strategy canvas don't get lost, the team leader
should also delve into how much agreement, or disagreement,
arose throughout the process. If team members diverged in
their lists of key competing factors, relative offering levels, or
choice of best-in-class competitor(s), probe for the implications
with questions like "How can we consistently sell to the market, when there is no clear strategic vision we all embrace?"
"How can we convince customers to buy our product or service when we, as an organization, can hardly agree on what
we're offering?" And "How can we make consistent investment decisions when we hold different views about what our
strategy is?"

If you are in an established company with a well-known
brand that historically has dominated its industry, but have
seen your profit and growth prospects dwindle, along with
your ability to pull in the best talent, watch out for two things:
In such situations, we have often seen confusion and a high
level of denial as to how serious this trend is and how long it
might continue. In this instance, your as-is strategic profile
may quickly reveal the exact opposite of what it takes to sail
into the blue ocean; namely, that in an attempt to monetize
your well-known brand, you are charging more for your offering than your rivals are, while ironically offering less along
the industry's key competing factors. (This is usually due to
some combination of coasting on your reputation, arrogance,
and the rise of rivals who now play your game better than
you do.) What your as-is strategy canvas may also reveal—
and we've seen this happen numerous times as well—is that
your strategic profile has essentially become a "me-too" with

a high cost structure, because you invest at high levels across the full range of competing factors. Meanwhile, a newcomer that seems to be whizzing by you has a strategic profile that is divergent, focused, and has a compelling tagline. Should either of these scenarios be the case, challenge team members by commenting that "Incremental improvements might buy us time," and adding, "but would they enable us to create strong profitable growth? Would they really enable our offering to break away from the competition and stand apart while having lower costs?" Then go silent. Let the questions sink in and wait for the team members to respond.

When the as-is strategy canvas tool reveals that your organization's strategic profile is a "me-too" or inferior to your competition, it is a powerful mobilization tool to underscore the need to make a blue ocean shift. But don't stop here. There is a maxim that a cup that is full cannot hold any more water. Likewise, when people feel they know it all, they lack thirst. As a result, their room to learn is limited. The challenge is to help team members not only see the need to make a blue ocean shift, but also make room in their mental cups so that they have the space and thirst to look at the world anew, which is at the heart of opening people's minds to new ideas and making a shift.

To encourage a learner's mindset, highlight the unknowns that surfaced during this step by recapping the comments team members themselves made along the way. The kind of comments we often hear and that serve this purpose well include:

- "It was more difficult than I thought to identify our key competing factors. Few of us have a good grasp of the big picture and see the industry through the lens of buyers—although, before we drew the canvas, most of us assumed we did."
- "We and everyone else in the industry tend to reflexively accept the same key competing factors and assume

that, because we compete on them, they deliver buyer value. But is this true? Maybe they're sacred cows or unquestioned orthodoxies that we've simply failed to question."

- "Our strategy tends to be reactive and driven by the competition."
- "If we had drawn the strategic profiles of all the other players in our industry, they would hardly look different than ours or our chief competitor's, plus or minus minor differences in customers' eyes."
- "I see contradictions in our offering, where we offer a high level on one competing factor, while ignoring others that support it—investing heavily in making our online store beautiful, for instance, while not investing in the speed of loading pages."
- "There are strategic inconsistencies between the level of our offering and the price. Basically, we're offering less for more."

Moving Forward

With the as-is strategy canvas drawn, the team now has a one-page picture that captures the current state of play, the assumptions the industry acts on, and the degree of competitive convergence across the existing players. Instead of being told that change is in order, team members have discovered for themselves the need for change. And because they confirm the need for change, they own it. The completed strategy canvas provides not only a compelling, objective case for why a blue ocean shift is in order—or not in order—but also a good baseline against which to evaluate new ideas.

Occasionally (as we saw in the School Foods example), the team will include an executive member who may also serve as the leader of the blue ocean initiative. Obviously, this has major benefits; but it is not always possible. For this reason, be sure to keep the executive team apprised of the main insights being revealed throughout the process. By keeping executive management informed, you set clear expectations and manage their expectations.

Similarly, after this first step, it is key to have team members return to their areas to share the findings and what they've learned from the as-is strategy canvas. Whether with executives or colleagues in their area, they need to walk everyone through the story of what happened in the process of drawing the as-is strategy canvas. This includes explaining how their understanding about the current state of play changed and why, what the as-is strategy canvas reveals, and what the team's plenary discussion brought to light. This builds buy-in and "no surprises" into the process, which are key to implementation and form a powerful way to boost everyone's learning and create a common vocabulary and shared "picture" of the as-is strategic reality the organization faces. As most employees are seldom engaged in the strategic conversation of the organization, this process cultivates a culture of inclusion where people feel they matter.

This brings us to the next step in the process where you begin to imagine what could be. In the next chapter you'll learn to discover all the ways the current industry or your target industry is creating hidden pain points that limit demand for your offering and exclude potential buyers. In the blue ocean shift process, pain points and boundaries are not constraints. They are clear opportunities to change the strategic playing field. So let's start exploring them.

Step Three: Imagine Where You Could Be

CHAPTER 8

Uncovering the Hidden Pain Points That Limit the Size of Your Industry

Wıтн тне as-ıs strategy canvas in hand, everyone can see the big picture—the current state of play in the industry. This gives the team a commonly agreed-upon baseline to assess new ideas against. Now the challenge is to develop an equally clear, big-picture view of the ways in which the underlying assumptions and boundaries that define the industry also limit its appeal and size by causing what we call "pain points."

Pain points are just what the name implies—aspects of a business, product, or service that buyers, knowingly or not, are forced to put up with, and which either diminish its utility in their eyes or are so inconvenient that noncustomers turn to alternatives. While utility captures the satisfaction a business, good, or service provides to buyers, blocks to utility reflect just the opposite—the difficulties an industry imposes on buyers, or pain points. In the blue ocean shift process, pain points—which are often hidden—are not constraints. They are blatant opportunities to change the playing field of strategy. But most industries become blind to them, just as buyers often become numb to them, because they assume that's simply the way things are.

Take the US wine industry. Despite the country's relatively high per-capita alcohol consumption, there are still few wine drinkers. Of all alcohol sales in the United States, wine accounts for a mere 15 percent of the total. If you wonder why, ask yourself how easy it is to choose a wine, given the thousands of wineries, the hundreds of varieties, and the tens of thousands of complicated labels. For that matter, how easy is it even to open a bottle of wine if you're one of the 80 percent of American consumers who don't own a corkscrew? Or to embarrass yourself in front of guests by choosing the wrong wine or chilling it improperly.

To help teams get a snapshot of the practices in their industry that are blocking utility for buyers and narrowing the basis of the industry's appeal, we developed the buyer utility map. This tool gives team members a platform for developing a deep understanding of the ways in which an industry, even an intensely competitive one, limits its demand by creating pain points for current and potential buyers. As team members work with the map, they begin to objectively register that blue ocean opportunities exist, and that they just might have what it takes to create them.

Ensuring that the team really begins to internalize this perspective is critical, because at this juncture the members are typically experiencing two powerful streams of emotion. Having drawn the as-is strategy canvas, they have likely come to understand that maintaining or tweaking the status quo will not put their organization on a strong, profitable, growth trajectory. To get out of head-to-head competition and into the blue ocean, something different will have to be done. Along with this sentiment comes another underlying, but almost always unvoiced, question, namely: If blue ocean opportunities exist, why has everyone in our industry missed them? Which is to say, the team's new awareness goes hand-in-hand with that nagging self-doubt we've spoken about before as to whether they—this team—can actually create a blue ocean.

What the team leader *should not* do is ignore these reservations. Pretending they do not exist simply allows them to fester below the surface. Then even a slight bump in the journey—and there will be bumps—can easily shake the team's confidence further. That said, acknowledging these doubts and asking people to suspend them doesn't work either. They always resurface. What you have to do instead is nip these doubts in the bud and continue building the team's collective confidence by allowing the members to keep on discovering their own capabilities and creativity.

How? The team has already begun to experience the process of firsthand discovery through the work of drawing their industry's as-is strategy canvas. Now they will have the opportunity to deepen it, as they systematically uncover opportunities the industry has left on the table or, more aptly, created via the self-imposed boundaries and assumptions its players act under. This may seem counterintuitive. But by gaining a deep understanding of the accepted "truths" that define their industry, the team begins to see who its pain points are forcing out, and who the noncustomers they never thought were even in the picture might be. The buyer utility map is the tool we've developed to help teams generate these insights.

The Buyer Utility Map

The buyer utility map helps team members see that almost every industry—including theirs—has significant problems worth solving. The map outlines the full range of experiences buyers have in using your industry's offering. In so doing, it reveals the problems the industry has failed to address, creating pain points worth solving and, conversely, the levers that could be pulled to address them and unlock exceptional utility. This lets the team identify not only the full range of ways an industry delivers utility to buyers, but also, importantly, where it blocks utility, producing hidden opportunities to break away from the competition and expand the size of the market. Let's see how this works, by looking at the map's dimensions in detail.

The Six Stages of the Buyer Experience Cycle. The map begins by outlining the full breadth of buyers' experience, which is almost always wider than the view most industries hold. As the horizontal axis in figure 8-1 shows, a customer's experience can be broken down into a cycle with six distinct stages, running more or less sequentially from purchase to delivery, use, supplements (that is, other products or services needed to make yours work), maintenance, and disposal. Each stage encompasses a variety of specific experiences. For a retail store, for example, purchasing may include getting

Figure 8-1

The Buyer Utility Map

	The Six Stages of the Buyer Experience Cycle					
	Purchase	Delivery	Use	Supplements	Maintenance	Disposal
Customer Productivity						
Simplicity						
Convenience						
Risk Reduction						
Fun & Image						
Environmental Friendliness						

(The Six Utility Levers)

to the store, finding what you want when you get there, and checking out when you're ready to pay. While these six stages provide a generic template that forces organizations to think through the complete buyer experience cycle, they can be and often are customized to better fit an industry's particulars. To illustrate, imagine once again that you're a customer of the wine industry. Your buyer experience cycle would be something along the lines of: Search (variety, food pairing, region, etc.) → Purchase → Chill → Opening/Sharing → Drinking → Disposal of bottle.

Interestingly, many industries focus on one or two stages of the experience cycle and overlook all the opportunities the remaining stages afford. This bounded rationality often creates pain points that escape industry players because they simply aren't considering them. By identifying the full range of stages in the buyer experience cycle, the buyer utility map begins to generate insight into the unquestioned assumptions an industry is based on—assumptions that detract from buyer value and can be reversed.

The Six Buyer Utility Levers. The map also displays the major levers organizations can pull (or not) to provide greater utility for buyers. While the six stages of the buyer experience cycle run across the horizontal axis of the map, the six utility levers run down the vertical axis, producing 36 potential "utility spaces." In the case of simplicity, fun and image, and environmental friendliness, the utility these levers offer is clear. The idea that a business, product, or service could reduce a customer's financial, physical, or reputational risk is also fairly straightforward. And a product or service offers convenience simply by being easy to obtain or use. The most commonly used lever is customer productivity, which captures how efficiently an offering can fulfill buyers' needs in each stage of the buyer experience cycle by saving them time, effort, and/or money. Interestingly, just as industries tend to focus on a small subset of stages, they also tend to focus on a small subset of the six potential utility levers, overlooking the expansive opportunities the full set affords.

Where does your industry or target industry concentrate its efforts among these 36 possible spaces? Executives in commoditized red ocean industries typically focus on only a few, leaving the rest virtually wide-open for blue ocean possibilities where today only inadvertent pain points reside. As you will see below, that's precisely what Christian Grob's team at Groupe SEB found when they filled in the buyer utility map for the European electric French fry appliance industry discussed in chapter 1. This is not an anomaly, either: Few industries or organizations realize the breadth of utility spaces they could explore or, on the flip side, the narrowness of their current focus. And simply asking people to imagine, without any help, that new utility can be created seldom helps them expand their field of vision.

When people can *see* how few spaces their industry focuses on, however, and *see* and name the range of utility spaces there are to explore, they literally *see* where trapped value may be hidden. That's certainly what also happened to Kimberly-Clark Brazil when the company's initiative team applied the map to toilet paper. "What could we do with simple toilet paper?" was the initial question everybody had in mind, since they all knew the industry was highly commoditized, swimming in a bloody red ocean. They couldn't imagine what could be done beyond producing toilet paper more cost-effectively than the competition. But as you will discover in a subsequent chapter, the map helped them see ample untapped utility spaces they could exploit to create a blue ocean in the industry.

To drill down and get clear on exactly what these pain points are and where on the map they are hiding, the buyer utility map provides a straightforward, structured method for systematically thinking through all the possibilities. As shown in exhibit 8-1, team members are guided to consider the biggest blocks to each utility lever and the factors that give rise to them at each stage of the buyer experience cycle. As pain points become visible that no one had ever noticed before, or that the industry knowingly ignored—as players

Exhibit 8-1

Uncovering the Blocks to Buyer Utility

Purchase	Delivery	Use	Supplements	Maintenance	Disposal
Customer Productivity:	What is the biggest block to customer productivity in each stage? What are the key reasons for this block?				
Simplicity:	What is the biggest block to simplicity in each stage? What are the key reasons for this block?				
Convenience:	What is the biggest block to convenience in each stage? What are the key reasons for this block?				
Risk Reduction:	What is the biggest block to risk reduction in each stage? What are the key reasons for this block?				
Fun and Image:	What is the biggest block to fun and image in each stage? What are the key reasons for this block?				
Environmental Friendliness:	What is the biggest block to environmental friendliness in each stage? What are the key reasons for this block?				

focused on beating one another in the current game—more *aha*s emerge.

Plotting Your Buyer Utility Map

How do you plot a buyer utility map for your offering? Here are the steps.

Start with the buyer experience cycle

Walk the team through the generic buyer experience cycle shown in figure 8-1, making sure everyone is clear on what it captures. To help you effectively perform the tasks discussed in this chapter, relevant materials and templates are provided for your free download and use at www.blueoceanshift .com/ExerciseTemplates. Then, using this as a baseline, ask them to put themselves in the shoes of buyers, and imagine their total experience from purchase through disposal. While the buyer experience cycle for many industries generally follows the generic pattern shown in the figure, the team can also customize theirs for their business, product, or service offering, renaming some of the stages, for example, or adding or deleting stages to fit the specifics of their industry. In the case of personal computers, for example, a typical buyer's experience would include *setup* as a stage after delivery and before use.

Next, challenge the team to identify the specific activities that fall within each stage of the cycle. This will help everyone begin to get a rich, full understanding of what buyers actually experience over the life of the offering. Going back to the PC industry, for example, setup would include getting the PC out of its big, tightly packed box; reading and making sense of the setup instructions; connecting the PC's wires to all your other devices; climbing under furniture (which is when many of us hit our heads) to plug the PC in; and throwing away the box and all the protective casing inside it.

Explore the six buyer utility levers

Once the full buyer experience cycle is laid out, the team can turn to the six utility levers. To ensure that everyone understands what each buyer utility lever means, the team leader should post the summary definitions presented in exhibit 8-2. Then move methodically from stage to stage, posing the same two questions about each, as shown in exhibit 8-1, namely: "What is the biggest block to [insert utility lever here, e.g.,

Exhibit 8-2

What Each Utility Lever Means

To ensure that everyone is clear on what each buyer utility lever means, below is a summary for your easy reference:

Productivity: Anything to do with efficiency—less time, effort, and/or money—in fulfilling buyers' needs.

Simplicity: Anything that eliminates or minimizes complexity or mental hassle.

Convenience: When and where I want something— like 24/7, 365.

Risk Reduction: This may be financial, physical, and emotional, including reputation.

Fun and Image: This is the tangible and intangible aesthetic look, feel, attitude, and style an offering conveys.

Environmental Friendliness: This utility lever is about "green" matters. Is your offering environmentally friendly? Or do buyers prefer your offering because of your organization's strong reputation for environmental friendliness?

customer productivity] in this stage?" and "What are the key reasons for this block?" While both questions aim to uncover the same problems, we've found that the richest answers come from exploring both perspectives.

To illustrate how dramatic the insights can be, consider the experience of a company in the Mexican retail furniture industry. The industry historically thought about delivery in terms of delivering new furniture to the buyer's apartment complex, which in Mexico City meant depositing it in the building lobby. In fleshing out what delivery means from the buyer's perspective, however, the team quickly realized how narrow this definition was and the pain points the industry unknowingly imposed. Delivery for buyers was not only about getting the furniture to the apartment building. It also encompassed getting the furniture from the lobby up to the customer's apartment. Many on the team recounted horror stories about people struggling with family and friends to get their new furniture up to their apartments after a tiring day at work. Yet, somehow, even executives in the industry had simply assumed that hassle goes with getting a beautiful new room of furniture.

Such assumptions are not uncommon. Don't most of us assume that dealing with an insurance company will entail getting the runaround, that getting gas for our car is a drag, that bottled water will be hard to carry and store, or that buying an iron also requires that we have a large, clumsy, hard-to-store ironing board? As you flesh out the blocks to utility that fall in each stage of the buyer experience cycle, even executives who consider themselves market savvy are typically surprised by all they've never thoroughly thought through.

Fill in the buyer utility map

As the blocks to utility surface, you should put an "X" in each space where a pain point was revealed. Figure 8-2 shows a

Figure 8-2

The Buyer Utility Map of Electric Home French Fry Makers: Pre–Groupe SEB's ActiFry

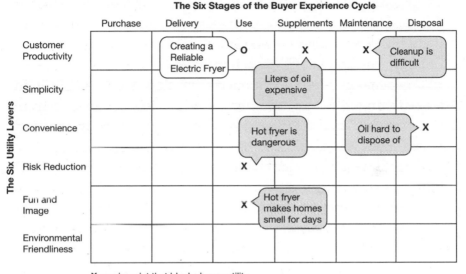

The Six Stages of the Buyer Experience Cycle

	Purchase	Delivery	Use	Supplements	Maintenance	Disposal
Customer Productivity		Creating a Reliable Electric Fryer	O	X	X	Cleanup is difficult
Simplicity			Liters of oil expensive			
Convenience			Hot fryer is dangerous		Oil hard to dispose of	X
Risk Reduction			X			
Fun and Image			X Hot fryer makes homes smell for days			
Environmental Friendliness						

The Six Utility Levers

X = pain point that blocks buyer utility

O = utility space the industry currently focuses on

completed buyer utility map, in this case for electric home French fry makers that Groupe SEB found when the team applied the map. As shown on the map, make sure to capture the reasons for each "X," whether in speech bubbles, as we've done here, or on a separate sheet of paper. Cataloguing the reasons behind each pain point is important, because the team doesn't want to lose any of the work or insight gained here.

Finally, use an "O" to mark the utility spaces the industry currently focuses on. To do this effectively and avoid putting "Os" all over the map just because the industry minimally touches on a space, you should get the team to distill the industry's *core* utility. Once again, the aim is the big picture. Go back to the as-is strategy canvas to provide the baseline:

What is the industry fundamentally offering from the buyers' perspective? Boil down the central utility buyers experience by using your product or service. Christian Grob's team at Groupe SEB found, for example, that despite the intensity of competition, the industry essentially focused on only 1 of the 36 potential utility spaces—*productivity in use*, that is, creating a reasonably priced electric French fry maker that worked reliably. That is the "O" shown in figure 8-2.

As the team works to complete their map, you should remind them that today's negatives could become positives in tomorrow's strategy, and that the pain points they've identified reflect buyers' perspective. When the negatives of their industry are unearthed, people in established organizations can feel uncomfortable or get defensive. Your role is to remind them about the potential opportunities that lie behind these pain points. Let them know that what your organization and the industry have focused on, as revealed by the map, may have been enough to succeed in the past. The point here is not to look back and it's certainly not to cast blame. It's to build a compelling future together and pain points provide strong clues on how to do just that.

One last observation about this stage of the plotting process: In some cases, after completing the map, one or more members of the team may question the results. And, indeed, as the team goes through the rest of the blue ocean shift process and meets with and interviews both customers and noncustomers, these insights may well be refined and altered. Hassles the team did not perceive in this initial step may make themselves known and be found to be significant. Others the team identified may be found to be less important than they had originally thought. At this point, though, you should immediately follow up by asking the team member or members who've expressed concern what percentage of conceivable inaccuracy they're worried about: 100 percent? Or 20–25 percent?

In our experience, the far lower range is almost always the answer. That's your opportunity to stress the strength of the results: Even assuming 20–25 percent of the utility blocks the team identified are inaccurate or incomplete, it doesn't invalidate the other 75 percent uncovered through this one step. In short, blocks to utility still exist, and the flip side represents opportunities to redefine the strategic playing field. Then go on to assure the team that as the initiative continues, they will have ample opportunity to systematically meet customers and noncustomers, validate or disprove their insights, and learn how to look at the market in new ways. This type of honest, direct discussion eases people's anxieties and strengthens collective confidence. In the case of Groupe SEB, for example, not only did the team confirm the pain points noted in figure 8-2, but the next steps of the process led the team to discover other important pain points that had long slipped under the radar, such as how the high calories in French fries discouraged noncustomers from patronizing the industry.

As an aside: We have seen the above concern come up often in organizations that have a culture of analysis paralysis, where data tends to be used not to help people take action, but rather to postpone and even invalidate actions that move away from the status quo. Should this happen, it's an important signal to take note of as you move forward with the process, because it means that additional handholding will likely be required as the team learns to step back and see the big picture, atomized step by atomized step.

Is What You See What Buyers See and Experience?

With the completed buyer utility map in hand, the team can bring the insight it contains to life. To initiate the discussion, ask the team members to juxtapose the insights gleaned from the as-is strategy canvas with those revealed through the buyer utility map. Have them first recap what they learned and the conclusions they reached from the as-is strategy canvas. Provide prompts as necessary: That competition is intense? That the strategic profiles of the industry's players have largely converged? That the room for future profitable growth is viewed as limited? That it is hard to find opportunities to break away from the competition? Jotting down the key takeaways to these questions creates an additional opportunity for team members to internalize the lessons from drawing the as-is strategy canvas.

With that done, shift to the completed buyer utility map, asking: "What, by contrast, does the map we collectively created reveal?" "Is the industry, knowingly or unknowingly, imposing pain points on buyers across their total experience?" "Could these pain points be limiting current customers' use of our industry's product or service?" "Would existing customers jump ship and champion an organization that eliminated these blocks to utility, and even use more of its offering?" "Could these blocks to utility also be discouraging or intimidating other people—noncustomers—from patronizing our industry?" "How many of the 36 utility spaces does our industry genuinely focus on?" As one executive put it, while answering this last question, "We are here [pointing to two utility spaces on the map], when there's all that out there [dragging his finger across all the "Xs" on the rest of the map]." That's when the team first begins to appreciate and see the real possibility of creating blue oceans.

As the discussion above suggests, creating the buyer utility map for their offering enables the team to see that red oceans need not be inevitable, and that insights into new opportunity spaces begin to be revealed just by applying this one analytic tool. Completing the map can be tough, however, in industries where, over the years, management has seemingly become disconnected from market reality and buyers' experience. We have been called into industries fraught with hassles and inconveniences where, at the same time, management stares almost blankly at the buyer utility map. Understanding the obstacles that buyers experience in using their industry's products or services, or even their own product or service, is hard for them to get their heads around.

In some cases, organizations are so close to their industry that they fail to see what hassles still exist. In others, the players have historically held unique positions, which gave them little or no incentive to focus on buyers' experience and the blocks to utility they themselves created. In still other situations, the organization itself has unwittingly put rose-tinted glasses on management's eyes, creating a gulf between the way they see and experience their industry and the way ordinary people do. One of the top three US automakers, for example, was known to have employees systematically take care of management's cars while the executives were at work—making all the necessary tune-ups and repairs, filling their tanks, and washing their cars. And when dealerships heard that management would be dropping by, they rolled out the red carpet. When you don't have to experience any of the hassles of buying, owning, and maintaining a car, or suffering breakdowns and waiting and paying for repairs, and when dealerships couldn't be more accommodating and sparkling, it's no wonder you'd lose touch with the pain points imposed by your company and industry.

When any of the above is the case, our response is "Stop. Go no further." Likewise, if the answers coming back are thin, or lack conviction, or are loosey-goosey in any way, or if there isn't a deep level of agreement among the team members, you need to take a different tack. Have all of them get up, go out, and see with their own eyes what it means to experience your industry's offering across the entire buyer experience cycle in the same way that ordinary people do. You'd be surprised how many organizations lack a wide-angle understanding of their buyers' total experience and all the pain points they encounter along the way. This is why we stress, time and time again, that seeing is believing and that you should never, ever outsource your eyes or ears. In fact, even organizations that don't struggle with the map are often keen to do this for added learning.

To see how this process works, and how, in executing it, the scales fall from people's eyes with a speed no market research report we have ever seen was able to achieve, let's look at the experience of a team that went into the field to learn.

Learning to Look Through Buyers' Eyes

On a cold, snowy, late-winter morning, the senior executive team of one of America's largest pharmacy chains gathered in a hotel conference room to work on their buyer utility map. The company was growing like gangbusters; yet this growth was largely through acquisitions. Their main rival in the US$250 billion US pharmacy market was following suit.

8:00 a.m.

"OK. I need a volunteer." The nine C-level executives look at the team leader with mild anxiety. "I need a volunteer." Heads turn, faces contort, and at last the vice president for IT says, "OK, I'll do it."

"You're all sick," the team leader says. "Not a life-threatening illness, but a serious one: an earache, a sore throat, a bad cold, the flu. What would you do?"

"Go to work!" the executives unanimously respond.

"OK. Let's say you have a sore throat that won't go away. Maybe it's a strep infection. How's your productivity?"

"Rotten," they once again unanimously respond.

"How do your coworkers feel about you?"

"Not happy. You're sick and infecting them," they say.

"Great. So our productivity is low, we may be infecting our colleagues, and none of us uses the pharmacies in our own stores for the most common illnesses. Thank goodness others do."

"Let's start the day over," the team leader then says. "I'd like you [pointing to the VP of IT] to go home. Get back in bed. Don't push through the pain of your sore throat. We'll go home with you. Let's go!"

Back at the executive's home, about 20 miles outside a midwestern city, the team gathers around his bed. They have a video camera with them to capture the buyer experience.

9:30 a.m.

"Now instead of going to work, call a doctor. You may have strep throat. You don't want to get anyone else infected, do you?"

The VP calls his doctor. It's 9:30 a.m. The earliest he can be seen is 11:30 a.m. The team waits. Video is rolling. The executive is told to stay in bed. He can only communicate on the phone or by email (preferable, as his fake strep barely allows him to speak).

10:30 a.m.

With his doctor's office more than 30 minutes away when the roads are clear, the team sets out. Between the snow and the stop-and-go traffic, it takes 45 minutes to get there. All ten members sit or stand in the crowded waiting room, which looks more like an emergency room: children with hacking cough, adults sniffling in their sleeves, a few infants spitting up. After 30 minutes of waiting—appointments are running behind schedule—the team is let in to see the doctor.

11:45 a.m.

A nurse takes the "patient's" weight and height. He sits down and is told to strip down to his underwear. Hysterics aside, everyone on the executive team feels bad for the VP as he goes to the bathroom and emerges in his tighty-whities, or shorts.

12:15 p.m.

After, what seems like forever (particularly for the VP sitting up on the examination table in his skivvies), the doctor arrives. He takes the patient's blood pressure, tests his reflexes, asks about his dietary habits, probes why he's overweight, asks how much he drinks, and if he's thinking about having children. Very intrusive.

After a throat swab, a few more minutes of waiting, and

getting the results from the nurse, the team is done. At this point, the team is several hours into the buyer experience cycle. While the VP actually had a clean bill of health (it was a fake strep throat, after all), the team improvises that he has received a prescription for antibiotics and analgesic medications. So they get back in their cars and drive to the pharmacy. As most people do, the IT executive chooses the location nearest to his house.

Another 45 minutes of driving and they're at the store. As at many American suburban pharmacies, the team finds ample parking. But as the doors open, it is like walking into a grocery store. Aisles of merchandise: chewing gum, toys, magazines, soft drinks, diapers, and finally, some 50 yards later, the pharmacist. The team goes over to the prescription counter and realizes that after handing in their prescriptions, customers are told to wait. Fifteen minutes is the average wait time recorded—a small eternity for people who don't feel well, many with children climbing on their laps.

That is the buyer experience cycle of the person who does the right thing and doesn't expose colleagues to contagion.

3:30 p.m.

The team reconvenes at the hotel meeting room. They now map the buyer experience cycle with relative ease. As they start to assess the utility blocks they experienced that day, the executives are flabbergasted. One executive blurts out, "Who wants to spend their day doing that? It's so much easier being sick. There are just too many pain points." Another executive chimes in, "Think of all the people suffering needlessly just to avoid all the hassles we experienced. Didn't we even joke this morning about going to work sick, even if our productivity is down, and others don't like it? We don't even patronize our own industry when it comes to a common, serious, but non–life-threatening illness!" Silence. Then energy builds as possibilities to eliminate this pain point, break away from the competition, and unlock new demand start to come into view.

"What if we put a doctor in the pharmacy?" suggests one team member. "Too expensive," replies another. "What about a nurse-practitioner? They're one-third the cost, and they can write prescriptions for most of the common ailments we're looking to treat." "You walk in, you see a 'doctor,' and you're out within minutes! Hours and hours of boredom and pain are gone." "Sales grow." "And people feel better." Quiet grins. Team members sit noticeably taller. Electricity runs through the room as the red ocean parts and blue ocean possibilities begin to open before them.

The First Rule of Fieldwork: Experience What Buyers Experience

As the example above reveals, when insights are lacking at this step, there is no substitute for going into the field to discover them firsthand. Asking the marketing department to come in and walk a team through the buyer experience cycle, or provide research reports to fill in the blanks, will not work. There are no shortcuts. We cannot emphasize enough the danger of allowing a team to outsource their eyes and ears, even to their subordinates. It will ensure that the members learn almost nothing, and that what they do learn will be nonvisceral—data points that seldom register and are rarely engraved on people's hearts and minds.

In going out in the field, we strongly recommend that, wherever possible, the team assume the role of ordinary buyers, or observe existing buyers in their professional environments or homes, being careful to document the difficulties these individuals encounter across the full buyer experience cycle. Do not confuse this with holding a focus group. Focus groups are artificial forums. While they are fine for gathering input on how to incrementally improve a product or service, they will provide neither the rich insights nor the conviction you and your team need and will only get by going into the field.

Teams who observed buyers at the point of sale alone have gained insights into pain points that had eluded their industry for years. Similar wake-up calls have occurred for teams who watched how their offerings were explained, stored, set up, used, and disposed of. To document the difficulties buyers experience, you may want to ask the team to take pictures or to video what they see and experience to support their findings.

Note that we have rarely met a team that wasn't initially somewhat reluctant to go out in the field, with some members even questioning what they could possibly learn. However, we have also never observed a team that didn't come back glad they had done it and with a visceral, grounded understanding of what buyers experience and the blocks to utility they face. Such knowledge is immensely worthwhile.

In the end, one of the biggest obstacles to implementing a blue ocean shift can be the executive team, even if they sanctioned the project. Many executives become blind to the hassles and grievances that buyers and users of their industry's offerings face day-to-day. They may realize they are stuck in a red ocean, and they may aspire to sail into the blue ocean, but to build both their understanding of what this will mean in practical strategic terms and their confidence in the team's work, you need to follow the principle of "No surprises— EVER." This means thoroughly debriefing senior executives about what the team has found after this and every step, and having them hear it directly from the team members themselves. Even if they say this isn't necessary, it is necessary. In fact, it's more than necessary. It's indispensable, because it means that any doubts executives may have can be caught early and addressed up front.

If the executive team seems to be discounting what the blue ocean team has found, make sure to invite the doubters to see the pain points ordinary buyers experience for themselves. When this has happened, we have never witnessed executives be other than profoundly influenced. The experience not only shifted their thinking, but renewed their confidence in the initiative. Their status and involvement also did wonders to garner support for the project across the organization, providing yet another illustration of how mobilization is built into every step of the blue ocean shift process.

With the buyer utility map assessed, collective confidence created, and the executive team apprised of the results, the team is now ready to move on to the next task—understanding the three tiers of noncustomers they can unlock to create all new demand and expand the size of the economic pie.

CHAPTER 9

Discovering an Ocean of Noncustomers

For the past 25 years, the business mantra has been "customer first." The blue ocean strategist's mantra is "noncustomers first." The aim of making a blue ocean shift, remember, is not to compete for existing customers but to create new demand and grow your industry. That's done by unlocking new utility for your noncustomers. Yet, few organizations have a sound grasp of who their noncustomers are or why they continue to remain just that—noncustomers.

This brings us to the next task: understanding precisely who your noncustomers are and why they don't patronize your industry. The buyer utility map gave the team initial insight into the pain points and blocks to utility the industry imposes on its existing customers that may potentially also turn noncustomers away. Now you will begin to widen the lens so the team can see the total demand landscape. Doing this offers insight into two of the questions executives raise most often: "Is the concept of noncustomers relevant to our industry?" And "With a compelling blue ocean offering, how much new demand could we unlock?" After working through this step, no executive ever looks at demand in the same way.

Think of Square versus Visa, MasterCard, and American

Express. All three rank among the world's top 100 brands. Yet despite their global reach, strong brand recognition, and deep pockets, all three compete head-to-head, essentially striving to win a greater share of the wallets of the same group of customers: established merchants and their customers. This is particularly true in America, which accounts for the greatest share of all three companies' card circulation, and where nearly 75 percent of all adult Americans already have more than one credit card.

The way the industry saw it, the US credit card market was saturated, with scant room for profitable growth, especially given the tighter regulations on interest rates and fees that followed the 2008 global financial crisis. But was it? That wasn't the way Square saw it. To the contrary, Square, founded in 2009 by Jack Dorsey, who also cofounded Twitter, and Jim McKelvey, saw an ocean of noncustomers.

Yes, most Americans have a credit card, and almost all medium-sized and large merchants accept them. But could Americans use their credit cards to pay the pizza delivery person, the gardener, the electrician who visits their home, the piano teacher, or the ice cream truck at the beach? Could they use credit cards or debit cards to pay the babysitter or the housekeeper, or to pay back the friend they borrowed $50 from? No. Every person who wanted to make a person-to-person payment was a noncustomer of the credit and debit card industry, and so were many new businesses and microbusinesses, like farmers' market vendors, food trucks, and pop-up shops.

Of America's 27 million small businesses, roughly 55 percent don't accept credit cards. Yet research shows that more than 55 percent of customers wish they did. Moreover, other studies show that when people are given payment options in addition to cash, they are likely to spend more per purchase, which helps small businesses grow. In other words, there were lots of entrepreneurs, small business owners, and newly started businesses that didn't offer customers the option of

credit or debit card payment, but would benefit handsomely
if they did. And there were lots of person-to-person transactions, typically handled by cash or check, that people would
be thrilled to use credit or debit cards for. This is the ocean of
noncustomers Square saw in 2009 and has been rapidly capturing with its mobile payment system, which allows individuals, small businesses, and even large organizations to accept
credit or debit card payments on their iPhones, Androids,
or iPads, simply by attaching a free Square reader, a small
plastic device that's literally a snap to use. Today many other
followers have joined in and, like Square, are unlocking this
ocean of noncustomers, which continues to grow, while the
industry itself is constantly evolving.

As Square, Comic Relief, Salesforce.com, and many others
understood, the universe of noncustomers not only exists, but
provides expanding growth opportunities. Yet most organizations are so focused on their industries' existing customers
that they cannot see beyond this narrow frame. To be fair, it
is always easier to talk with existing customers, the ones who
have already crossed your threshold. And, of course, their
opinions matter. But, to grow, you have to bring new people
into the industry.

The Three Tiers of Noncustomers

To help organizations broaden their vision, we developed a
framework that defines and identifies three tiers of noncustomers, as the graphic in figure 9-1 shows. The three tiers
provide successively wider lenses with which teams can view
the ocean of noncustomers they could tap into to unlock new
demand. We have found that without such an organizing
framework, the notion of noncustomers, though seductive,
becomes too broad a catchall to use to systematically analyze
and understand—and hence capture—potential demand. In

Figure 9-1

The Three Tiers of Noncustomers

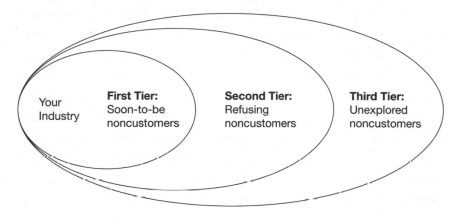

First-tier "soon-to-be" noncustomers are on the edge of your industry, waiting to jump ship.
Second-tier "refusing" noncustomers consider your industry and then consciously choose against it.
Third-tier "unexplored" noncustomers are currently in seemingly distant markets.

this context, we present two formulas that are key to making a blue ocean shift and, we would argue, are increasingly tied to your organization's ability to grow.

First, contrary to common practice,

Total demand potential ≠ function (existing industry customers)

Rather,

Total demand potential = function (existing industry customers + first-tier noncustomers + second-tier noncustomers + third-tier noncustomers)

Let's consider the definitions of the three tiers, how they differ, and why they are often closer to an industry than most organizations imagine.

First-tier noncustomers are all the soon-to-be noncustomers of your industry. These buyers patronize your industry not because they want to, but because they have to. They use current market offerings minimally, to get by, as they search for or simply wait for something better. Upon discovering a superior alternative, they will eagerly jump ship. In this sense, they sit on the edge of your market. Go back to the US credit card industry. Of the small and midsize merchants who accept credit card payments and debit transactions, many do so reluctantly. They have tolerated the cost of installing point-of-sale technology, the fees for processing transactions, and the often hidden costs they may be charged (especially those that don't have the bargaining power to negotiate fees), because they knew customers expected to be able to pay with their cards. But these noncustomers would willingly make a switch if an easier, less cumbersome, and less expensive alternative to the current system existed.

Just think for a moment about how many industries you patronize only because you have to, not because you want to, are proud to, or enjoy the experience. And think about how you might love to jump ship if a compelling alternative came along. If you are like most people, you will quickly realize how many industries and organizations you are a first-tier noncustomer of. First-tier noncustomers are not only highly vulnerable to being poached, but if an alternative could eliminate their pain points, it's likely the rate and frequency of their use would multiply. Do you know who your industry's first-tier noncustomers are?

Second-tier noncustomers are refusing noncustomers—people or organizations that have consciously thought about using your industry's offering, but then rejected it, either because another industry's offering better meets their needs or because yours is beyond their means, in which case their needs are either dealt with by another industry or ignored. For the credit and debit card industry, second-tier noncustomers are all the new businesses, microbusinesses, and self-employed individuals who thought about offering credit and debit card payment but in the end chose against it. Even though they knew customers would probably appreciate it, their small annual sales, the fragility of their new enterprise, or the perceived complication of setting up and paying for the point-of-sale system made them reject the industry. Cash and checks tend to be the standard payment options for this broad swath of organizations.

Think about how often you or your organization has been a second-tier noncustomer. For example, did you recently choose to paint your living room after contemplating the pros and cons of using wallpaper instead? If yes, you were a second-tier noncustomer of the wallpaper industry. Or did your management decide to use stone flooring in the new head office after contemplating wood as an alternative? If yes, your organization was a second-tier noncustomer of the wood-flooring industry. You see, being a second-tier noncustomer is as easy as that, and happens far more frequently than most people or organizations ever assume, imagine, or give much systematic thought to. And yet, think of how close second-tier noncustomers actually are to patronizing the industry they chose against. The simple fact that they contemplated and weighed the pros and cons tells you that the industry they rejected is still far closer to capturing their wallets than most of its players ever realize. Do you know who the second-tier noncustomers of your industry are? And why, after considering your offering, they dismissed it?

Third-tier noncustomers are the furthest away from an industry's existing customers. Commonly, these unexplored noncustomers have never been thought of as potential customers, nor targeted by any of the industry's players, because their needs and the business opportunities associated with them have always been assumed to belong to other industries. Go back to credit cards. Before Square, the industry always assumed that a merchant was half of the transaction equation. All the transactions that occur between individuals were left off the table and unexplored, because they were assumed to belong to another industry—cash and checks. After all, who would install a point-of-sale credit/debit card system at home? Yet, we would wager that most of us have opened our wallets to pay someone, only to discover that we've run out of cash and wished we could use a credit card instead. But since we can't, what do we do? We reluctantly but hastily go to the nearest ATM. Those are the third-tier noncustomers that Square set out to unlock through its simple, easy-to-use, easy-to-carry, pay-only-when-you-use-it Square reader.

Do you, like Square, know who the third-tier noncustomers of your industry are? Have you or your organization ever given much thought to this tier? You should, because this can be the largest catchment of noncustomers an organization can unlock. Quick caution, though: Do not be tricked into thinking third-tier noncustomers are "everyone else." They are not. They are people or organizations that would ideally like to use, or who could benefit from, what your industry fundamentally offers, but who have never seriously considered doing so because your industry has made this somehow unfeasible, unattractive, or unimaginable.

Identifying the Three Tiers of Noncustomers in Your Industry

When teams are introduced to the three-tiers framework, a natural first reaction from some members is to question whether the concept of noncustomers applies to their industry. The concept is typically easy for executives to grasp when their organization operates in or intends to enter a nascent industry. In those circumstances, most teams get the applicability right away, even if they struggle initially to identify who the dominant noncustomer categories in each tier are. Take, for example, the MP3 player. As Apple was designing the first iPod, the number of noncustomers of MP3 players was huge and far overshadowed existing industry customers.

Noncustomers abound in every industry, however, not just new ones. Think for a moment about orchestras or museums. Significant noncustomers? Absolutely. How about credit cards? Square highlighted just how many noncustomers there were. CRM software? Think of Salesforce.com. Flying? Think about US aviation pre–Southwest Airlines. Coffee drinking? You bet—Starbucks grew that industry. And the list goes on and on.

The purpose of this exercise—and what you should aim for—is to move the discussion of the three tiers from a theoretical concept to a pragmatic reality. Identifying the three tiers of noncustomers in your own industry allows you to make this happen.

Begin with the basic concept

Start by laying out the definitions of the three tiers of noncustomers using the descriptions and graphic from the previous section. To deepen the team's understanding, and to show how the tiers apply in various industries, walk the team through several examples from outside their own field. Table 9-1 shows the three tiers of several red ocean industries: the credit/debit card industry discussed above, the UK charity fund-raising industry examined before, the language translation industry, and the orchestra industry. Ask the team questions like these: "If these red ocean industries all had oceans of noncustomers could the same be true in our industry?" And "If we were to zoom out, and apply a wider-angle lens, would we see our own noncustomers?" You should pose these questions to the team explicitly to ensure they are seeing the connection between the noncustomer insights of these industries and your own industry setting. As your team discusses these examples and answers these questions, the meaning and relevance of the three tiers will begin to sink in. This is typically a sit-up-in-your-chair moment for team members, when their emotions start to shift

from denial—"Nah, this doesn't really apply to our industry"—
to wonder—"Could it be in our industry, too? It might just be."

Table 9-1 Noncustomers in Various Industries

	First Tier of Noncustomers	Second Tier of Noncustomers	Third Tier of Noncustomers
The Credit Card/ Debit Card Industry	Small and midsize merchants that reluctantly accept credit and debit cards for payment	New business, microbusinesses, and self-employed individuals who do not accept credit or debit cards	Individuals needing to make payments to other individuals
The UK Charity Fund-raising Industry	Older wealthy individuals who feel frustrated with year-round solicitations for funds	Young professionals who choose not to donate, due to the lack of transparency in percentage of funds that go to the cause	Children and low-income individuals who never thought of donating
The Language Translation Industry	Large corporations frustrated by the time, expense, and fractured nature of securing language translation of business materials, including website copy, brochures, product documentation, etc.	Midsize organizations that don't use translation services for the vast majority of languages, even though, with the Internet, people from virtually every country can be their potential customers	Individuals with blogs and small organizations, who never thought of using language translation, even though it could open a far wider global audience and customer base for them
The Orchestra Industry	Individuals who attend concerts once a season or every few years, as it's seen more as something they should do than something they want to do	Individuals who can afford to attend but choose not to, as they find the experience boring, outdated, or too pretentious	Individuals who never considered going to the orchestra, as they have no real knowledge of classical music and feel the orchestra experience is essentially for the educated elite, not ordinary people

Shift to your industry and offering

Realizing that noncustomers probably abound in their industry doesn't always make it immediately obvious who those noncustomers are. So rather than ask your team to identify them now, start by discussing who typically buys and uses the industry's current offering. Everyone working on the team (and in the organization) should have a good feel for this information already. It's also information that's generally available in considerable detail, so it provides a good reference point for the team as they start thinking about the total demand landscape. The objective, however, is not to engage in a deep analysis of fine-grained demographic differences within the existing market, as marketers often do. Rather, it is to see whether a major variable, such as age, sex, income, family structure, or, for a B2B business, organization size is a reasonable predictor of who the industry's existing customers are. For video games pre–Nintendo's Wii, for example, the dominant customer demographic was young males between the ages of 14 and 26. Likewise, higher-income, older, educated individuals were the predominant donor group for the UK charity fund-raising industry pre–Comic Relief. As for CRM software, before Salesforce.com entered the scene, the dominant customer group was Fortune 500 and 1,000 firms.

Throughout this discussion, it's important for you to keep the team focused on the big picture, and not to let people get bogged down or lost in minute details, like what proportion of young male video game users are black, white, and Hispanic. Such a discussion and analysis may be the path to refining an offering, but it will prevent the team from seeing the major defining contours of the industry's current customers. In our experience, too many organizations that have analyzed their customers in granular detail fail to see the big picture and the commonalities that unite the largest group of them.

If team members identify several groups of existing customers, challenge them to see whether they can identify a broader category that would encompass most, if not all, of them. The point here is not to duplicate what marketing departments are generally good at doing, which is developing a refined understanding of the differences across existing customer segments. Rather, the purpose is to seek a higher-level understanding of the macro contours and commonalities that cut across and unite existing customers so you'll be able to see the forest for the trees.

Identify the three tiers of noncustomers in your industry

Now we turn from current customers to noncustomers. Using the three-tiers graphic, shown in figure 9-1, as a guide, ask each of the team members to think through and write down their thoughts about who might be in each tier. To help you perform this task effectively, relevant materials and templates are provided for your free download and use at www.blueoceanshift.com/ExerciseTemplates. Here are the questions you want to ask:

1. Who sits on the edge of our industry and uses its offering reluctantly and/or minimally?
2. Who considers our industry and then consciously rejects it, satisfying their needs through another industry's offering or not at all?
3. Who could strongly benefit from the utility our industry offers, but doesn't even consider it, because the way it is currently being delivered makes the industry seem irrelevant or out of their financial reach?

For many people, this will be the first time they've ever been asked to systematically think through the issue of noncustomers. As we have witnessed, if an organization has given thought to noncustomers, it's usually in terms of their competitors' customers, not the noncustomers of their overall industry. They ask, "Who are our competitors' customers, and how can we win a greater share of those who patronize other players?" But this is not the meaning of noncustomers in blue ocean terms. What is key at this stage is getting team members thinking deeply about noncustomers and, critically, letting them discover for themselves how little they may know or have thought about the wider opportunity landscape that exists beyond the current industry's horizon.

Organizations often become comfortable commissioning and outsourcing large, formal market studies. Hence, it is not surprising that, at this juncture, we've often been asked, "Don't we need to be supported by formal market research so we will know, concretely, who the three tiers of noncustomers are?" In response, remind them that the blue ocean shift process is built on firsthand discovery that will be done when the team goes out in the field. The purpose here is to maximize the team's firsthand learning and confidence in what they see for themselves in the field. With firsthand discovery, the resulting strategy is likely to be executed strongly, as the confidence that emanates from the team reverberates throughout the larger organization.

Much to their surprise, team members generally find that, by struggling through this exercise independently, they flesh out a rich list of noncustomer groups and are really pushed to broaden their thinking. Equally important, they see how tightly focused on existing customers their strategic lens has been. When people are spoon-fed answers by having reports commissioned up front, they seldom realize what they don't know, and too often easily conclude that they "got it, knew it, no big deal," when, in fact, they didn't have or know it, and it *is* a big deal. People seldom realize what they don't know or appreciate the value of what they've learned if they haven't struggled to obtain it themselves. Making people discover firsthand that what they know—and don't know—is key to getting them to internalize and value what they learn.

After each of the team members has compiled their list of noncustomers, ask them to share their thoughts about whom they put where and why. The objective now is for the team to identify and select the people or organizations they collectively see as the dominant noncustomer group or groups in each tier. Note that team members may continue to feel a bit uneasy, because they're being asked not only to move away from what they know, but also to share their thoughts in front of their colleagues. Some unease is good, however, because it means that team members are being pushed to broaden their current understanding. As each of the team members contributes their thoughts on each of the three tiers, you should record and post them in front of the group. This allows everyone to see the whole team's thoughts, which in itself is eye-opening, as they get to appreciate the differences and similarities in how each of them views the same market reality.

As people share and debate their selections and the thought processes behind them, team members' understanding of who potentially belongs in each tier starts to deepen. So does their confidence that opportunity exists in the untapped demand that lies beyond the boundaries of their industry as it's currently defined. Typically, as members discuss the validity of one another's reasoning, a number of customer groups are crossed off, and different sets of customers get grouped together, producing fairly solid agreement among team members as to whom they see as the main noncustomer groups in each tier. With this, a good understanding of the industry's total demand landscape starts to come into focus.

Determine the rough size of the new demand landscape

In this age of Google, where search is simple and easy, and a significant amount of industry information is available online, the team can now proceed to get a good sense of the new demand that a reconstructed offering could potentially unlock. Break the team into subteams, and ask them to Google basic statistics on the rough size of each of the non-customer groups. What are the relative proportions of the groups? Just how big is their respective potential demand, based on their per-capita or, for B2B players, per-organization spending? Have each team do this for all three tiers.

The objective here is not to nail down specific numbers for each tier, but to get a rough sense of how potentially important each tier could be to the organization, if it were unlocked. For example, if a noncustomer group is currently small and only growing in single digits, it's likely this tier will remain small for the foreseeable future. On the other hand, if a non-customer group is growing at a fairly consistent clip of, say, 30 percent a year, the team can reasonably surmise that even if the group is relatively small today, this tier has the potential to become a significant source of noncustomers within a meaningful time frame.

By the end of this step, teams have usually surprised themselves by how much they agree on who the key groups of noncustomers in each tier are and the relative demand potential for each. In the next stage of the process, these answers may be revised: The relative proportions of potential demand across the three tiers may shift, for example, or a new group of noncustomers may be identified. Nonetheless, these insights allow the team to see both that there is clear scope for creating new demand and how limited their understanding of the unlocked demand beyond their industry's conventional boundaries has been. The power of this step lies not only in the insights and confidence gained, but also in the speed with which team members achieved and internalized these insights. This can usually be accomplished in a half- or full-day off-site meeting.

To see how the three-tier exercise can transform a team's understanding of the potential demand for their offering, let's listen to a group of educators discover their noncustomers.

Discovering an Ocean of Potential Undergraduates

A private, four-year, US university that we'll call CU faced a mounting challenge. With a student body composed primarily of first-generation, college-bound youth from families in the bottom 25 percent of the country's income distribution, CU had a vital mission. But the school's retention rates were falling and operational costs were rising. The president of CU not only wanted to turn this situation around, he wanted to grow CU and make it a model urban university for youth.

The CU blue ocean initiative team, comprising faculty and administrators, had just completed the buyer utility map exercise. As the team leader summed it up, "There are a lot of pain points in our industry, based on outdated, misguided, or wrong assumptions." "Exactly!" said a team member. "We believe we provide a quality education because our hearts are in it, we work long hours, and we charge a premium. But none of that really matters. Quality is what students get out of school and what they can afford. And the competition is getting tougher."

"The question is," the team leader continued, "Will surveying our current students give us the answers we need to create a blue ocean and break away from the pack?" Team members quickly agreed that existing students were likely to request the same things their peers at other schools did: better dormitories, a more lively campus, better teachers, greater course selection, better school food. "What we're saying," the team leader concluded, "is that if we start looking for solutions by asking our students what they want, *at best*, we'll achieve incremental gains at an even higher cost. And we won't grow. To do that we'll have to look outside our market, at our noncustomers. We know who our customers are, but who are our noncustomers? Maybe we can discover some answers by focusing first on what our ultimate purpose really is."

After some spirited discussion, the team reached a unanimous conclusion about what constituted their purpose: providing a step change in the lives of young people in terms of their economic prospects, self-confidence, and ability to thrive in the world. "If that is really the case," said the team leader, "and we all heartily believe it is, then let's use that to be more specific about who the dominant noncustomer groups in our three tiers are."

"First tier are bright students who enrolled in CU but now are insufficiently challenged by their classes and classmates," one professor observed. "They are increasingly tempted to transfer to other schools for a greater intellectual challenge."

"An even bigger group are students who attend with the help of financial aid, parent PLUS loans, and Pell grants," added another. "But as soon as those supplemental funds run out, typically in the third year or so, they depart. And neither we nor our peers have strong work-study programs to help them close that gap, nor have we challenged ourselves on how we could dramatically bring costs down to make our education more affordable. Essentially, we try to offer and match everything your standard four-year private college offers with a small fraction of the resources. So, our costs are high while quality is compromised. It's not even clear that what these students need from CU to make a step change in their lives is what your standard college offers." Silence.

Once the discussion on the first tier wound down, and everyone felt heard, the team leader shifted to the second tier. "Who are the refusing noncustomers of private four-year universites?"

"This tier is huge," noted one team member. "It's all the students who choose to go to state universities, over private colleges like ours." Heads nodded. The noncustomer demand landscape was growing.

The conversation did not stop here, however. "What about all the students who choose to go to junior colleges?" a faculty member asked. "That's another large group of second-tier noncustomers. Those are students who may want a four-year school but ultimately choose a junior college—maybe because it's more practical, given their professional aspirations and personal lives, or because they have more confidence that they can succeed in that environment, or maybe they just don't have the funds. Whatever the reason, it's still a big catchment of second-tier noncustomers." Without any analysis or debate, everyone in the room agreed that second-tier noncustomers represented a larger tier of potential demand than the existing market.

The team leader then shifted the discussion to the third tier, the noncustomers who could benefit from higher education's ultimate purpose, but who never thought about the industry's offerings as an option. "What are your ideas on who this would be?" asked the team leader. After a little while, a sober answer came back: These noncustomers are the peers of our students who chose another route entirely. Many of CU's undergraduates come from poor public school districts where K-12 education itself is weak. Students in economically impoverished districts typically are discouraged from considering higher education, and those who do seldom receive the kind of counseling they need and that is routinely provided for their peers in better-off districts. And yet for these young people, higher education could be the most powerful path out of poverty.

Where could these noncustomers be found? The team members were full of ideas: "The military." "Blue-collar work." "Missionaries." "Store personnel." "Maybe entrepreneurs?" This tier, the team agreed, was the largest of all. "Look at our competition locally," said the team leader. "Are they trying to understand these three tiers of noncustomers?" "No! Not at all," responded team members. "That's why all colleges look the same." The eagerness in the room to look beyond their usual customer base was palpable, as was the team members' impatience to get started.

Understanding the Strategic Implications of Your Three Tiers

Before beginning to discuss the overall implications of this exercise, have team members again collect their thoughts individually and write down the takeaways that jump out at them. Then, as with all the steps in the blue ocean shift process, ask each of the team members to share the insights they recorded to ensure that all points are put on the table and to create collective ownership of the discussion. This precludes the most articulate from drowning out the opinions of members who may be more reserved but no less perceptive. More than that, the simple act of having each member record and voice their key takeaways ensures a deeper level of internalized learning, even before you start to calibrate the points the team has made.

In our work with teams, we find they tend to get the most out of this discussion when you structure the group discussion via a set of systematic questions:

- What did we learn? Who are the first-tier, second-tier, and third-tier noncustomers of our industry or target industry?
- What is the approximate magnitude of each tier of noncustomers, relative to the industry's existing customer base?
- Is each of the three tiers small, suggesting scant room to create a blue ocean? Or are one, two, or all three of

the tiers noteworthy in terms of the magnitude of their potential demand?

- Which tier, if any, has the largest group of noncustomers that could potentially be unlocked with a reconstructed offering?
- Do we see a link between the blocks to utility revealed in the buyer utility map and any of the three tiers?
- Might these blocks to utility be causing the noncustomer groups to patronize another industry to fulfill their ultimate purpose?
- If yes, do we imagine that this tier of noncustomers might be unlocked by systematically exploring what it would take to convert them into customers?

As team members review what they have discovered, they may become eager to probe deeper into the hurdles or attitudes that are keeping the industry's noncustomers noncustomers: "What's missing from the industry's offerings, which, if we included it, would start to unlock new demand?" they may ask. This is a sign that they're intellectually engaged and eager to take their learning to the next step. You should let them know that in the next step of the process they will do precisely that. That said, if the energy generated by this topic is high, allow the team to hypothesize about what could be different, while at the same time reminding them that, right now, the points being made are just that: hypotheses. This allows people to feel heard, while also signaling that developing blue ocean offerings demands grounded live field research and a structured method, not simply brainstorming in a conference room. Team members usually respect this reminder tremendously.

As they discuss the broad context of the industry and the available demand opportunity, the team's understanding of the relative proportions of the market for existing buyers and users and the three types of noncustomers will start to crystallize. As it does, their perception of potential demand will shift from existing industry customers to the far larger total demand landscape.

End Strong

At the end of this step, to ensure that everyone is on the same page, and to create another opportunity for team members to internalize key lessons, you should recap the steps the team has taken to date. Specifically, you want to remind the team that, as they applied the as-is strategy canvas tool, they became clear on the current state of play in the industry, the factors the industry competes on, and the degree of convergence between their organization's current strategic profile and that of its competitors—convergence that has likely thrown the organization into the red ocean. The subsequent step, where they applied the buyer utility map, revealed both the subset of utility spaces in which the industry currently competes and, at the same time, the pain points and points of intimidation imposed by the industry that potentially limit usage by existing customers and turn noncustomers away. By doing so, the team has already been able to benefit by identifying low-hanging fruit that the organization could act on and fix, even if it decided not to go any further. Last, by applying the three-tiers framework, the team gained a good grasp of the potential new demand that could be unlocked with a reconstructed offering. Noncustomers who were once invisible to the team and to the industry have now been made visible.

At this juncture, the team's confidence and competence are usually another notch higher. Team members start to think, "Yes, there is a way out of the red ocean, and just maybe there are real opportunities that we could unlock to create a blue ocean." The team dynamic will also have started to shift quite noticeably, as team members now begin to push to get on to the next step, rather than wait for the team leader or top management to push them to move forward. This is the emotional state you want to achieve, and it brings us to the next step where the process shifts from broadening perspectives and imagining what could be, to generating practical, real-world, blue ocean options. Here the team will meet the market and explore the six systematic ways to reconstruct market boundaries to unlock new demand and create new market space. Let's get started.

Step Four:
Find How You
Get There

CHAPTER 10

Reconstructing Market Boundaries—*Systematically*

How can you reconstruct market boundaries and change the conversations you have about where opportunities reside so as to conceive and open up a new value-cost frontier? Every organization, even the most innovative, must face this question sooner or later. If you have embarked on a blue ocean shift initiative, it is the question your team is now primed to take on.

Through their work together, team members have come to have a visceral understanding of how the blue ocean shift process and tools enable them to see what they haven't seen before, to build their collective confidence, and to develop a new level of awareness and openness. People feel how their participation in the process is increasing their personal understanding of the market and, with it, their commitment to the process. They are likely clear about the red ocean the industry is immersed in and the need to shift out of it. They have seen how a focus on benchmarking and beating the competition has not only blinded the industry's players to a wealth of unexplored opportunity spaces, but also created pain points that limit its size. They have identified the contours of new

demand that could potentially be unlocked by thinking differently and offering noncustomers, as well as current buyers, a
leap in value. Now they are ready for the process to shift, from
broadening perspectives and imagining what could be, to generating practical, real-world, blue ocean options.

To this end, we developed the six paths framework to
demystify and structure the work of seeing opportunities
where others see only red oceans of competition. This stage
of the process is where team members dive head-on into the
market, get their hands dirty, and do the kind of grounded,
field-based research that can generate actionable insights
for changing the strategic playing field. Simply getting out
into the field, however, is not enough. If you want different
answers, you need to ask different questions and listen to different people. People are as insightful (or not) as the questions
you ask them. Ask standard questions and you'll get standard
responses that keep you anchored in the red ocean. Ask questions that force people to think in fresh and innovative ways,
and you'll gain insights into new market creation. As you will
see, each of the six paths guides you to look at the market universe in a new way by shifting the questions you ask and the
people you listen to.

Imagine a one-way street you've gone down a thousand
times in your car and you think you know by heart. Then
one day you walk up that very same street but in the reverse
direction. Suddenly you're jolted. You notice a house that you
never observed before, or a tall tree in someone's yard you'd
never taken notice of, or a stunning view of a distant lake that
was hidden from your sight when you traveled in the old one-
way direction. That's what the six paths do. They show you
how to travel down roads in new ways so you see new things
that were always there but had been blocked from your view.
And just as it's awe-inspiring in life when we see new things
we hadn't seen before that had been in front of us all along,
people feel enlightened in the process when they, with the

help of the six paths, learn to see the same reality differently and discover blue ocean opportunities.

How was this analytic tool developed? When we analyzed strategic moves that created commercially compelling blue oceans by reconstructing market boundaries, we found the six systematic patterns depicted in this framework repeated across multiple industries. Does this mean there aren't other ways to create new market space? Of course not. However, in our role as advisors, working side by side with organizations across diverse industry sectors, we have seen firsthand how effective this framework can be.

The Six Paths Framework: How It Works to Open Up a New Value-Cost Frontier

Most organizations follow a similar pattern in developing their strategies: They start by analyzing their industry: Have new competitors entered? Is demand flat, rising, or declining? Have raw materials prices gone up? Next, they focus on the players in their particular strategic group: the companies or organizations in the industry that pursue a similar strategy or approach to the market. Luxury hotels will tend to assess what other luxury hotels are up to, for example, while budget hotels will do the same versus their strategic competitors. But since they operate in different strategic groups, neither one tends to pay much attention to the other. Then, the strategic lens narrows once again, to focus on current customers—their own and those of their competitors—and how the distinctive needs of those customers can best be served. Not surprisingly, therefore, budget hotels don't pay much heed to the wealthy, nor do luxury hotels focus on lower- and middle-income individuals. Both sets of hotels will concentrate on making the best hotel they can, however. In other words, they will define the scope of their offering as the industry has long defined it. With this will go a focus on features that align with their strategic group's customary orientation. For budget hotels, this will mean providing functional, low-priced rooms, while luxury hotels will prioritize sophistication and refinement to enhance their image and prestige. Finally, they will consider the impact of external forces, such as environmental or safety concerns, which are affecting the industry and to which they have to adapt.

In sum, executives tend to define their strategic playing field—and limit their opportunity horizon—on the basis of six conventional boundaries: industry, strategic group, buyer group, scope of the product or service offering, nature of the offering's appeal, and time. Nonprofit leaders, government decision makers, entrepreneurs, and even one-off Main Street storeowners and professional firms typically do the same.

Yet boundaries do not define what must be or should be. They merely define what is. None of them is a law of nature. All of them are the product of people's minds, and, as such, they are open to change. But over time this fact tends to be forgotten, and people come to take them as eternal truths. They become a conceptual cage that organizations lock themselves into, even though every one of these boundaries was created by an individual organization. And just as people and individual organizations created them, so they can change them *if* they are prepared to think in a different way. The six paths framework, shown in figure 10-1, provides six systematic ways to shift the lens you use in looking at the market universe and open up a new value-cost frontier. Path by path, the framework explains how to uncover plausible blue ocean opportunities by looking across an industry's self-imposed boundaries, instead of remaining stuck within them. It also incorporates seasoned advice on what to look and listen for as you pursue each path. Let's explore the six paths in turn.

Figure 10-1

The Six Paths to Open Up a New Value-Cost Frontier

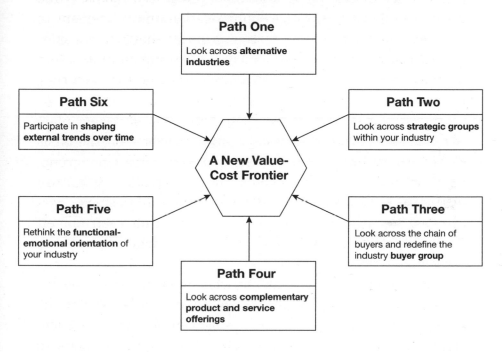

Path One: Look Across Alternative Industries

Red Ocean Lens:		Blue Ocean Lens:
Focus on rivals in your industry	➡	Look across *alternative industries*

   Organizations compete within their own industry and with industries that offer alternative products or services. In making their decisions, buyers often weigh alternative industries and make trade-offs, explicitly or implicitly: Want to put your best foot forward with neat, wrinkle-free shirts—do you iron them at home, send them to the dry cleaner, or only buy shirts made with wrinkle-free material? Going from New York to

Washington, D.C., do you take a plane, a train, drive your car, or take a bus? This thought process is intuitive for consumers. Yet, the tight strategic lens that most organizations use drives them to focus on beating rivals within their existing industry, keeping them trapped in the red ocean. To open up a new value-cost frontier, you have to look across alternative industries and understand why buyers choose one over the other.

The objective in this path is to identify the problems or needs your offering currently solves, and then to generate a list of other solutions or industries noncustomers use to address the same problems or satisfy the same needs. Remember that the focus is *not* on alternatives within your industry—why people choose to fly on one airline over another, for example—but on alternative *industries* that serve the same function or solve the same problem, but that have a different form. What are the decisive sources of value and the detractors of value that make people gravitate to and choose one alternative over another?

Although there may be several alternative industries to the industry you're in or targeting, you should focus on the one(s) that has (have) the largest catchment(s) of demand. These noncustomers hold the key to the greatest number of potential new buyers, and they are the ones you want to interview.

Having identified the relevant alternatives, you need to ask people why they choose one over the other. This question shifts the discussion from all the factors an industry competes on—factors that buyers have been trained to expect and organizations love to marginally improve on, typically for little overall gain—to the factors that decisively create or detract from value. By probing in this way, buyers reveal not the branches of an industry but the fundamental trunk or basic utility that justifies the industry's very existence and size.

What most teams quickly discover is that, despite the wide set of factors alternative industries compete on, one or two usually determine whether people patronize them. For example, why do people hire electricians instead of going to a hardware store to do it themselves, or vice versa? More than anything else, two factors drive people to hire an electrician—expertise and having no time to do it themselves. And only one factor drives most people to patronize a hardware store—cost. The aim here is to drill down to the factors that cause buyers to choose other industry offerings than yours, find a way to combine these decisive factors, and then reduce or eliminate everything else, thereby unlocking new market space that will be commercially viable because it focuses on precisely what potential buyers value.

Remember, asking people why they trade across industries is not the same as asking what makes an alternative industry different, which can reveal a whole host of factors that may indeed be "clever" or different, but that also may have very little value. To avoid getting distracted by "clever ideas," stay focused on why people choose for and against your industry or the alternative. Their answers will signal the decisive value factors to create and eliminate in order to develop a blue ocean offering that is both differentiated and low cost. Exhibit 10-1 outlines the action steps of path one.

Exhibit 10-1

Path One: Action Steps

1. Identify the major problems or needs that your industry's offering or your target industry's offering solves or addresses from the buyers' point of view.
2. Next ask, What alternative *industries* solve the same problems or address similar needs for buyers? Here we encourage people to role-play and ask, "If I were the buyer, what other alternative industries would I consider before even deciding to patronize our industry?" That helps people shift from a supply to a demand perspective.

3. Among these alternative industries, which capture the greatest catchment of customers? Focus here. Interview buyers from each relevant alternative industry.

4. Probe why buyers traded across your industry or target industry and this (these) alternative(s), including what they see as the chief negatives of the industry they rejected and the chief positives of the alternative industry they choose.

5. Record all the key insights gained. A recording template for each path can be downloaded for free at www.blueoceanshift.com/ExerciseTemplates.

Path Two: Look Across Strategic Groups Within Your Industry

Red Ocean Lens:		Blue Ocean Lens:
Focus on your competitive position within a strategic group		Look across strategic groups within your industry or target industry

Most companies focus on outcompeting their rivals to improve their position within their strategic group or market segment. In the hotel industry, for example, five-star hotels tend to focus on outdoing other five-star hotels, three-star hotels focus on outcompeting other three-star hotels, and so on. But this only keeps them doggy-paddling in a red ocean. The key to a blue ocean shift is to understand what factors determine buyers' decision to trade up or down from one strategic group to another. This allows you to distinguish between the range of factors on which strategic groups compete, and the decisive few that drive buyers' decisions to choose one over the other. Again, the focus here is *not* on why buyers choose one particular organization over another, but on why they trade up or down across strategic groups. This will allow you to understand the trade-offs the customers of a strategic group are making when they choose across strategic groups. Understanding the factors that are decisive for noncustomers as well as customers lets you emphasize those factors while eliminating and reducing everything else.

Take the health management industry, a B2B industry that provides large corporations and insurance companies with health management services for employees' health. Health-Media, a player in the industry, was on the brink of collapse in this red ocean. After being forced to take 85 employees down to 18 to stabilize the company, in 2006 its new CEO, Ted Dacko, set the goal to grow it from US$5 million in revenues to US$100 million in four years by using the blue ocean approach. At the time the industry had two strategic groups— one offering telephonic counseling, predominantly for severe medical conditions like disease management; the other offering generic digitalized content, like WebMD.

As HealthMedia explored why buyers traded across these strategic groups, it found that, despite all the factors players competed on, buyers traded up to telephonic counseling for one overriding reason—high efficacy—while they traded down to digitalized content for low cost. In essence, companies competing in telephonic counseling were following a classic differentiation strategy, offering high efficacy through specialized counseling mainly for severe health challenges, but at a high cost. By contrast, those competing in digitalized content followed a classic low-cost strategy of offering generic health information at a low price but with low efficacy. These trade-offs limited employees' use of both strategic groups' offerings, creating an ocean of noncustomers.

The focus of telephonic counseling on severe health challenges meant that most employees' use for it is limited, since what the majority of employees primarily need coaching in is their chronic health issues, like high blood pressure, high cholesterol, stress, depression, insomnia, binge eating, and the like. Besides, its high cost meant that companies could not afford to offer it widely. Regarding generic digitalized content, due to its low efficacy, it did not inspire high employee participation, either.

Instead of competing in either strategic group, Health-Media set out to break these trade-offs. The result was opening up a new value-cost frontier in the industry by creating a new market space called digital health coaching, which combined the far lower cost of digitalized content with a leap in efficacy through interactive online questionnaires that digitally matched people's self-reported challenges with a health plan that would work best for them. And the best part was that HealthMedia offered digital health coaching for the most prevalent health challenges people face, so the offering was relevant to nearly all employees. The result was a leap in value for companies who could now offer digitalized health coaching to a broad swath of employees with high efficacy at a low price. Within just two years, HealthMedia's blue ocean was so compelling that Johnson & Johnson swooped in and purchased the company for US$185 million, an amount far higher than its already ambitious four-year revenue goal of US$100 million.

For your analysis of this path, choose the largest two strategic groups to explore. Typically, we recommend that you zoom in on the one that captures the largest share of customers, and the one that has the largest share of profitable growth, if they are different. If there is a small but very fast-growing strategic group, you should zoom in on that one as well.

As organizations start exploring this path, one of the most common and startling realizations is how many strategic groups have emerged in their industry in recent years, and how much the key players have tended to focus on the old guard that once monopolized their industry. Whatever the industry—from TV (reality programs, new producers from Netflix, to Amazon), to publishing (self-publishing, traditional publishing houses, e-books), the music industry (traditional labels, YouTube self-made stars, young kids rerecording), and the auto industry (Tesla, electric cars, self-driving cars), consumers' options are exploding. Hence, just laying out the strategic groups within their industry wakes people up and lifts the scales from their eyes. Value gained already.

This path tends to be relatively easy for people to get their heads around and apply. Organizations that are big on segmentation, however, often have a tougher time distinguishing the forest from the trees. They tend to list a plethora of groups based on tiny differences in competitive offerings. They frequently fall into the segmentation trap. Should this situation arise, you need to push the team to take a step back and look for strategic commonalities that could enable them to cluster the long list of groups they've identified. In the case of the health management industry, for example, some telephonic counseling companies focused on wellness, others on behavioral health, and still many others on disease management. However, by stepping back HealthMedia saw that, at their core, all these players shared three overriding strategic commonalities—a focus on telephonic counseling, addressing severe—not chronic—health conditions, at a high cost. By understanding the defining contours that united these players that focused on different market segments, HealthMedia did not get distracted by segmentation differences. The point of this path, like all the others, is not to get lost in minutiae, but to identify the decisive value and cost contours that separate distinct strategic groups, as HealthMedia did. Exhibit 10-2 outlines the action steps of path two.

Exhibit 10-2

Path Two: Action Steps

1. Identify the strategic groups in your industry or target industry.
2. Focus on the two largest strategic groups.
3. Interview buyers from each group. Probe why buyers traded up for one strategic group or traded down for the other. Focus on identifying the distinguishing factor(s) that led users of each strategic group to patronize it over the others. Ask the same people what they saw as the dominant negative or turn-off of the strategic group they rejected.
4. Record all the key insights gained, noting specifically the reasons buyers offer to explain their decisions.

Path Three: Look Across the Chain of Buyers

Red Ocean Lens:		**Blue Ocean Lens:**
Focus on better serving the existing buyer group of the industry		Look across the chain of buyers and redefine the industry buyer group

Most industries converge around a common definition of their target customer. In reality, however, the purchasing decision usually involves, directly or indirectly, a chain of buyers: the users of the product or service; the purchasers who pay for it; and, in some cases, the influencers whose opinions can make the difference in a decision to purchase—or not. So for preteen girls' clothing, the purchaser or payer is typically a parent, the users are the teens themselves, and the key influence group might be pop stars.

In thinking about who's in the chain of buyers, it's also worth considering potential influencers, people who could be brought into the decision-making process but currently aren't. Retailers are a good example of an often "untargeted" buyer group for complicated purchase decisions. Just think about buying computer or stereo equipment, or wine or major household furniture—decisions that make most of us nervous. Many, if not most, of the companies that sell products in these categories spend most of their effort focused on each other and the ultimate user, the purchaser. But they have largely ignored thinking creatively about the retailers who sell their products. One of the results is relatively indifferent retail staff who could easily persuade many, if not most, people to go in one direction or another, but instead offer ho-hum knowledge, little passion, and no distinctive services to buyers of one manufacturer's product over another. What if, instead, you offered a leap in innovative value to retailers' staff that made them advocates for your products and services? Would your products start flying out the door?

While the three groups of buyers may overlap, they are often distinct, as are their value preferences. Remember the school lunch provider we listened in on in chapter 7? The purchaser's primary objective was getting the best terms and prices, whereas having the best-tasting lunch was what the users, the students, valued most. Shifting the focus from better serving the industry's traditional buyer group to other groups the industry has historically ignored can be the key to uncovering hidden sources of utility and opening up new market space.

Think of the commercial fluorescent lighting you see in major retailers, supermarket chains, and corporate offices. When Philips Electronics set out to create a blue ocean, it shifted its focus from the industry's red ocean target—corporate purchasers—to a key influence group, chief financial officers (CFOs). In speaking with CFOs, Philips learned that the price of fluorescent lighting that corporate purchasers focused on was a small fraction of the total cost. An even larger component was the cost of disposal because of the high mercury content in fluorescent bulbs. Corporate purchasers never saw that cost, but CFOs did. This gave Philips the insight to create an environmentally friendly fluorescent bulb that could eliminate 100 percent of corporate disposal costs, because it could be thrown in the garbage, instead of having to be carted off to a special dump site. Philips then made the case for buying the new bulbs, which had a higher price and margin but a lower total cost overall, to the CFOs who wielded their power to influence the purchase decision in favor of Philips's environmentally friendly bulbs.

When interviewing people in the "untargeted" buyer groups, conduct the interviews in each interviewee's natural setting. If retailers are an untargeted buyer group, for example, conduct the interviews on the retail floor to get a sense of the store, the layout challenges, the retail staff's issues, the way customers wander around and talk to sales staff, and the speed of checkout. This gives you the benefit of seeing what the retailers themselves may not be able to articulate or even realize. Oftentimes, an outsider observing with fresh eyes sees the challenges, opportunities, and potential solutions far better than the players themselves. Exhibit 10-3 outlines the action steps of path three.

Exhibit 10-3

Path Three: Action Steps

1. Identify the chain of buyers—users, purchasers, and influencers—in your industry or target industry.
2. Identify the main buyer group your industry or target industry currently focuses on. Then shift your focus to those the industry has largely ignored.

3. Interview buyers from the "untargeted" buyer groups. Probe for their different definitions of value. Drill down to the biggest blocks to utility and costs the industry currently imposes on them.
4. Record the insights from each "untargeted" buyer group and group like-minded responses together.

Path Four: Look Across Complementary Product and Service Offerings

Red Ocean Lens:	**Blue Ocean Lens:**
Focus on maximizing the value of the product or service offering as defined by your industry	Look across the total solution buyers seek to understand the complementary products and services that enhance or detract from your offering's value

Few products or services are used in a vacuum; in most cases, other products or services affect their value. But in most industries, rivals converge within the conventional boundaries of their industry's product or service offering and focus their efforts solely on maximizing its value. The key to value innovation is to define the total solution buyers seek when they choose a product or service, and then to eliminate the pain points and points of intimidation across the total solution. A simple way to do this is to think about what happens before, during, and after your product and service is used.

By broadening your understanding of the total solution buyers need or seek, you can often discover new sources of trapped value. Take the electric kettle industry in the UK. Although the electric kettle is central to the British public's love of afternoon tea, the industry had become a veritable red ocean with low profit margins and little growth. While the industry had long competed on price and aesthetic design, Philips Electronics shifted its focus to understanding the total buyer experience. In the process, Philips discovered that the central challenge British tea drinkers faced had nothing to do with the kettle itself; it was the lime scale in municipal water. Before the tea drinkers could enjoy their freshly brewed tea, they often had to fish out the lime scale floating in it with a spoon. Kettle companies never thought to address the problem because it had nothing to do with their industry's offering. But by looking across the buyer's experience and thinking about the whole range of complementary products and services buyers needed, Philips saw this block to utility and created a teakettle with a changeable charcoal filter that removed the scale when the tea was poured. The result: Philips's teakettle turned a slow-growth industry into a fast-growth one, lifted its price point, and created a new repeat revenue stream in changeable charcoal filters.

As this example indicates, it is critical to visit users to see firsthand what happens before, during, and after the use of your product or service. Why? Because only then can you experience the full context and see the range of unvoiced steps and challenges. When people were asked what they did with their electric teakettles, the answer was: Plug it in, turn it on, boil water, pour, and drink. But when Philips visited people's homes and watched how people used their teakettles, the lime scale problem quickly jumped out. From the users' point of view, lime scale had nothing to do with the kettle, so they never thought to voice the problem. Others had become so accustomed to fishing for lime scale that they didn't even consciously register doing it. Lesson: When you ask people about an offering, they tend to focus on the offering and, as a result, their answers rarely stray far from what the industry currently does.

In visiting users, the point is not to sit in their homes,

offices, or factories and batter them with questions. It is to observe them actually using the product or service, so the unvoiced, taken-for-granted assumptions they make and the steps they take can be revealed. Here you want to watch for the processes or circumstances that trigger the need or desire to use the product or service. Are there inconveniences? Are the triggers too costly or intimidating, curbing demand for your product or service? What happens before your customers use your product? What happens during (or around) its use? And what happens afterward?

The buyer utility map, explored in chapter 8, provides a helpful tool for thinking about these observations, because it provides a structure that ensures that you, yourself, don't remain trapped within the narrow confines of your industry. Learning how to observe insightfully and see unvoiced, trapped value is a nonobvious skill for many. But by thinking in terms of the six utility levers and the six stages of the buyers' experience cycle, you are primed to observe more broadly and insightfully. The primary objective is to uncover all the blocks to utility, even if those blocks are not related to your industry as it currently defines itself—be it lime scale for electric teakettles, securing a babysitter for parental moviegoers, getting to the airport for airlines, or opening a ream of paper for your home copier.

You should also probe the largest tier of noncustomers. When major television manufacturers wished to enter the South African market, for example, discussions with rural residents revealed that the key block to purchasing a television for them had nothing to do with the television itself. It was the fact that only a small fraction of the population had access to electricity. Selling car batteries with televisions unlocked an ocean of new demand. This type of insight can only be gained by interviewing and directly observing the challenges faced by noncustomers. Exhibit 10-4 outlines the action steps of path four.

Exhibit 10-4

Path Four: Action Steps

1. Look at the real context in which your offering is used by identifying *what happens before, during,* and *after* its use.
2. Observe buyers as they actually use your product or service. In recording the insights gained, group insights you uncovered so that patterns in the frequency or criticality of observed blocks to utility can be discerned.
3. Use the buyer utility map and the noncustomer tool to guide your observations.
4. Record all insights gained.

Path Five: Rethink the Functional-Emotional Orientation of Your Industry

Red Ocean Lens:	**Blue Ocean Lens:**
Focus on improving price-performance within the functional-emotional orientation of your industry	Rethink the functional-emotional orientation of your industry or target industry

Competition in a given industry or strategic group tends to converge, not only around an accepted view of the scope of an offering, but also around the bases of its appeal. Some industries and groups compete principally on price and functionality: Their appeal is functional. Others compete on generating positive feelings: Their appeal is emotional. A new value-cost frontier can often be opened up by shifting the appeal of a product or service from one basis to another, or by blending the sources of its appeal.

To uncover these opportunities, you first need to get clear on the orientation of your industry. Sometimes this is easy. High-end fashion, for example, has a clear emotional orientation aimed at making people feel both beautiful and elite. But other times industry players are so accustomed to its orientation that they no longer "see" it; they simply take it for granted. To get clarity, ask customers and noncustomers to describe your industry's offering in their words, not yours. Doing this will give you a grounded understanding of whether it is functional or emotional, and what those adjectives mean in a given industry context.

Take the legal industry. When we query customers, the overriding response is that the industry has a functional orientation. It does not aim to generate positive emotions. But what does *functional* mean in this context? It gets the job done—no more, no less. For many people, however, the way the legal industry functionally "gets the job done" simultaneously triggers negative emotions. The top three responses that come back repeatedly are: intimidating (Who can read legal documents anyway?), complex, and overpriced (What industry charges by the minute and then rounds minutes up to a quarter hour?). Now think about the possibilities that could open up if the industry's orientation were shifted to a positive emotional one. How does a legal product or service that is welcoming, simple, with price based on value delivered, not minutes spent, sound? To us, it sounds pretty great.

Or think about supermarkets. Again, the most common orientation is functional. Three descriptors that spring to mind are nuisance, necessary evil, and inefficient (think long checkout lines, slow service at the meat and fish counter, etc.). What could a supermarket be if it set out to shift this orientation to a positive emotional one instead? Think fun outing, stylish, and super-fast. That's the gist of this path: getting you to reimagine your industry by shifting its orientation, which opens the floodgates to completely reconceiving your product or service offering.

To probe customers' and noncustomers' overall impressions of an industry, ask what they would say if they had to choose—functional or emotional. Then drill down to understand what their answer means in that context by asking for the three to five adjectives or characteristics that come to mind to describe it. Their responses can then point you toward the many factors that support and reinforce their impressions of how the industry presents itself. As you flesh this out, you may find that the way people actually see and experience how your industry competes may be very different than the way you see your industry. Then flip the question and probe interviewees (and your team members) on what the opposite characteristics would look like in your industry. This will provide insight into how to shift the appeal of an industry. Overall, this is a path most teams have a lot of fun applying. Exhibit 10-5 outlines the action steps of path five.

Exhibit 10-5

Path Five: Action Steps

1. Identify the industry's current orientation. Is it predominantly functional or emotional?
2. Listen to customers and noncustomers characterize your industry or target industry. Probe the top characteristics that reflect why they see it as functional or emotional.
3. Look for commonalities across their responses and group like-minded comments.
4. Explore what the offering would look like if you flipped the orientation.
5. Record all insights gained.

Path Six: Participate in Shaping External Trends Over Time

Red Ocean Lens:		Blue Ocean Lens:
Focus on adapting to external trends as they occur		Participate in shaping external trends that decisively impact your industry or target industry

External trends affect every industry over time. Nowadays there is hardly a business, nonprofit, or government agency whose world is not being reshaped by external forces. Think of the rise of social media, the growing obesity crisis, the global environmental movement, or aging populations in many developed countries.

Many companies try to project external trends themselves, and they pace their actions to keep up with the trends they're tracking, adapting to them as events unfold. Projecting trends seldom provides insight into opening up new value-cost frontiers, however. Looking at how a trend will change what customers value, and how it might impact a company's business model over time can. As Netflix saw Internet broadband explode, for example, it realized that fast, real-time streaming of full-length films would soon be able to take off. That meant the possibility of instant viewing gratification and complete viewing flexibility. You could change what you watched on a whim. It also meant convenience and ease. No need to preorder DVDs, wait for their arrival, and then mail them back. In other words, no need for Netflix's original business model. This insight inspired Netflix to create a leap in value for buyers, via on-demand viewing, and a new blue ocean for itself. By looking across time— from the value a market delivers today to the value it might deliver tomorrow—companies like Netflix can more actively shape their future and lay claim to opening up a new value-cost frontier.

The aim of this final path is to help organizations go beyond adapting to external trends to participating in shaping them. Learning which trends to focus on is crucial, however. So is knowing the right questions to ask. The first thing you need to get clear on therefore is which trends *decisively* impact your industry. The fact that a trend is having a major impact on other industries or society does not mean it is necessarily relevant to yours. In one organization, for example, the team identified the growing power of the millennial generation with its very different wants and needs. True, the implications of this trend are enormous for many industries; but not, within a meaningful time frame, for theirs—real estate for retirees. Understanding and detailing the implications of each trend specifically on your industry, not the world in general, are key.

Not every trend, even if it's relevant, is one on which a blue ocean can be built in an opportunity-maximizing, risk-minimizing way, however. This brings us to the other two questions you need to ask: Is the trend irreversible? And is it evolving down a clear trajectory? Oil prices decisively impact many industries, for example, and if they have been dropping significantly for many months that may be a seductive trend. But if you can reasonably imagine the price going up in another 6 to 12 months, and industry experts agree with that hypothesis, building on the trend would be unwise. Moving forward with a blue ocean initiative will be highly risky if, as in the case of oil prices, there is a high level of uncertainty about how the trend on which it was based is likely to evolve, or if the trend can be easily reversed.

For trends that satisfy all three criteria, ask, If this trend were taken to its logical conclusion, how would it impact the value we can deliver to buyers? And what would the implications be for our industry and organization? As Groupe SEB applied this path to electric home French fry makers, for instance, the key trends of rising obesity and healthy eating jumped out. The team then realized that existing customers of electric home French fry makers had never voiced this concern in customer surveys, as they had simply taken for granted that fresh French fries meant high calories and high fat. With this new understanding, the team explored the identified trends with noncustomers. This is the time when the team could clearly see the opportunity of unlocking an ocean of new demand by making a fryer with no frying.

Insight on how decisive trends will impact an industry can often be found by looking at other industries that have been, or are being, impacted by the trend. Disintermediation, deregulation, and the emergence of two-sided markets are all examples of trends that many industries have already been swept by. Their experiences can provide compelling insights into what might become possible for your organization, and how you might capitalize on this trend by changing the definition of value in your industry.

The question we hear most often about this path is: "How far into the future should we be looking?" The relevant question back is: "How long would it take you to tool up to produce and launch a completely new offering that will offer buyers a leap in value?" Your answer to this question will indicate how far forward you should be thinking if you want to leverage a decisive trend. The period most often used is three to five years.

The most difficult aspect of this path is getting clear about how a particular trend will affect the value of an industry's current offering, or what a future offering will need to take into account. While the path itself is easy to grasp conceptually, the solutions are not as obvious as they are in the other paths, where the work usually yields a robust initial list of factors that could be changed. To address this problem, the team should consider each relevant trend in turn and ask, "If this trend continues as it has begun, what about our current offering will no longer make sense and might even detract from buyer value, and therefore should be eliminated or reduced?" And "What in our offering will we need to create or raise to deliver a leap in value to buyers?" Exhibit 10-6 outlines the action steps of path six.

Exhibit 10-6

Path Six: Action Steps

1. Identify the three to five trends that are seen as having a decisive impact on your industry or target industry. Give people the option of doing secondary research online to complete this.
2. Discuss and assess the relevance of these trends to your industry. Focus on those that are commonly seen to decisively impact your industry or target industry.
3. Discuss and assess the extent to which each trend is irreversible.
4. Discuss and assess whether each of the trends is evolving along a clear trajectory.
5. List the implications of all the trends that are decisive to your industry, irreversible, and evolving in a clear direction. Detail how each will change what buyers value and how that would impact your business model over time.
6. Record all insights gained.

Applying the Six Paths Framework

Athletes often remind themselves that there is no gain without pain. The same is true when it comes to using the six paths framework. The results are eye-opening and often revelatory. But be prepared: Generating those results takes time and effort in the form of multiple one-on-one interviews and observational fieldwork. While this is the most time-consuming part of the blue ocean shift journey, this is work that team members cannot delegate to anyone else—inside the organization or outside it. There is no outsourcing the team's ears or eyes. Because the insights gleaned from the paths come from the team's own fieldwork, these insights are empowering and build conviction. So don't be tempted to short-circuit the process. If you do, you will undermine the initiative, and shortcut yourself and the insights gained, as well as the potential for successful execution, which is the aim of the entire initiative. Here is how this step unfolds.

Start with the big picture

Begin by explaining that the objective at this stage remains the big picture: The team is looking for insights that will provide clues as to how they might reconstruct their industry's boundaries and open up a new value-cost frontier. They are not yet looking for final answers. The six paths will guide them on the type of insights they need to search for.

This reminder is important, because if team members feel the objective is to straight out search for solutions, many will easily be discouraged when answers do not jump out at them and become frozen by the sheer weight of what is being asked. Remember, this process is very different from what most organizations do to develop strategy. If people feel frozen or discouraged as they meet the market, they will tend to go through the process perfunctorily, instead of being inspired and inquisitive. So you need to make this fun, and let everyone know that now is the time to be a detective and uncover clues. Reassure them that feeling a bit uncomfortable is to be expected and they're not alone in feeling that way.

Divide the team into two subteams

Exploring each path takes time. Asking the entire team to explore each of the six paths is typically asking for a time commitment few can make unless their schedules have been significantly cleared for this initiative. By having each subteam explore only three paths, this step becomes much more doable. It creates a healthy sense of competition, as to which subteam will do the best job, which contributes to fun and the quality of insights garnered. It also mitigates complaints that the assignment is unfair and not feasible in light of team members' regular responsibilities. Explain this reasoning to the team up front, as the subteams are being set up. That way they can appreciate that you understand what is being asked of them; that you expect high-quality work; and that you have also taken practical measures to make this step feasible and motivating by creating the subteams. Silence *is not* golden. Explain the concept behind the subteams.

Walk the team through the entire framework

Now walk everyone through the full framework and explain what the subteams will be exploring along each path. It's key for everyone to have a good overview so that they can respond intelligently to others in the organization who ask about what's happening. Knowing what both subteams are working on will short-circuit the fear and anxiety that can easily get sparked if someone answers, "I don't know. The team leader hasn't shared that with us." Subteam members will also appreciate being treated as equal partners whose understanding matters. The result: more commitment, less fear, with subteam members naturally able to keep the rest of the organization in the loop.

Explain how the process will unfold

Once everyone understands the logic of all six paths, the subteams can get their assignments. You can make these yourself or, and this is often preferable, you can let the teams select the paths they'll work on randomly, via a draw. This way, they choose their own paths, and the process feels fair. Subteam members should agree on which path they will tackle first, and move on to the next path only after that one has been completed.

Members of each subteam should then develop work plans for their assigned paths, beginning with the one they will tackle first. Start by reviewing the logic of each path and the associated action steps, as outlined in exhibits 10-1 through 10-6. To help you effectively perform this task, the relevant materials and templates are provided for your free download and use at www.blueoceanshift.com/ExerciseTemplates. The templates will provide direction on the right questions to probe, as the subteam members go into the field to interview noncustomers and customers. The templates will also help them organize the insights gained in a meaningful way.

To explore each path, team members should begin working individually, then come together to synthesize their insights, then work individually again to gather a broader range of insights that they will subsequently pull together as a team. This sequence allows for the richest array of independent insights to emerge, via the individual work, while at the same time enabling the members to work together to uncover key patterns and identify interesting anomalies across their insights.

For path one, for example, subteam members will first develop their own list of key alternative industries and only then get together as a team to agree on the most relevant one(s) to explore, based on the criteria given for that path. Then each of them will individually interview customers and noncustomers, as prescribed in the path's steps, before coming together to compile the findings. In this way groupthink is avoided and collective wisdom is achieved. A variation of this work pattern applies across the other five paths as well.

As part of the work plan, subteams should get clear on which noncustomers and customers to observe and interview in the field. You don't want subteam members interviewing and observing the same people. Going back to path one, for example, suppose long-haul carriers was the alternative industry the subteam had chosen to analyze. Then you want to ensure that members of the subteam speak to the customers of different carriers by deciding which members will speak to the customers of which long-haul carrier. (These people are effectively the noncustomers of the focal industry.) As part of the fieldwork, take photos, video what you observe, and visit shops. In other words, get real in the field. Going back to long-haul carriers, for example, we'd recommend going to the airport, and speaking directly to people after they've checked in for long-haul flights. We'd also recommend speaking to airport staff involved in check-in and getting their views on why people choose to fly long haul over whatever alternative you are comparing it to. Think of yourselves as detectives. Have fun, and stay focused on the task at hand.

How many people should each subteam member interview per path? Typically, the number is 10 to 12, though some subteams do as many as 15 interviews each, because they find the learning so rich and inspiring. The first interviews for the first path a subteam tackles are usually the toughest, as most team members will be learning a new skill set. So remind them not to get discouraged and just to carry on. By the end of the interview process for a given path, each member should have started to hear some themes in people's responses, as well as a few idiosyncratic responses, which often prove useful as they come together to share their results. So be sure to record these outliers and not pooh-pooh them. The six paths interview work can make people feel awkward, or even squeamish at first, if they're accustomed to understanding customers via large-scale surveys. Let them know you appreciate that, but ask them to persevere. We have never encountered people who were not soon rejuvenated and awed by what they learned by doing this fieldwork.

To maximize the insights gained, remind team members not to "sell." Observe, follow, and ask with due humility. It's imperative that members stay open, and not get defensive as noncustomers and customers start to convey honest responses to their questions. If negative comments come back, probe deeper to extract the most learning. Stress to the team that negatives are opportunities in disguise. So they want to get super-clear on what they are and why they arise. Remind members to record and capture all the insights and answers for every person met, observed, and interviewed *in real time*, not later, when memories can become cloudy. The objective is to see the world with new eyes. No observation is too small, as many seemingly small observations can later add up to the big insight that creates a blue ocean. Think of how the small and repeated observation of lime scale in the UK's municipal water led Philips Electronics to create a blue ocean by creating replaceable charcoal filters.

Paths one, two, and three indicate the relevant noncustomer groups to interview and observe—those in alternative industries, strategic groups, or buyer groups, respectively. For paths four to six, subteams should interview people in the largest tier or the largest two tiers of noncustomers identified in step three of the process (see chapter 9). Whether one or two tiers are chosen depends on the relative size of the tiers. When one tier clearly looms far larger than the other two, we recommend focusing on that tier alone. When that isn't the case, focusing on two tiers works well.

What's Next

After completing their live-action market explorations, the
subteams will be armed with a wealth of new insights on how
value can be unlocked in innovative ways. Inspired by what
they've learned in the field, most of the members will also be
intellectually energized by the new ways of thinking they've
just been exposed to. This brings us to the second part of step
four, where we'll show you how the team will use the insights
they've gathered to craft concrete, alternative blue ocean
moves. Here we will introduce the eliminate-reduce-raise-
create grid, which is key in breaking the value-cost trade-off
and opening up a new value-cost frontier. Let's keep moving.

CHAPTER 11

Developing Alternative Blue Ocean Opportunities

AFTER THEIR SIX PATH market explorations, the blue ocean initiative team members are typically tired but on a high. Factors the industry has long competed on have been shown to be over-delivered or no longer relevant. Market segmentations that had long been taken for granted have now been called into question, as powerful commonalities that cut across strategic groups are revealed. Complementary products and services the industry had never paid much heed to are now recognized as potentially powerful levers for unlocking innovative value. In sum, the team's energy and feeling of empowerment are palpable and, in one way or another, the rest of the organization will feel it too.

What is especially noticeable is the way people engaged in the initiative speak. Instead of quoting reports and facts when they discuss what the blue ocean process is revealing, they recount stories. Stories that have color, names, and places, and draw on specific observations that cause others in the organization to reflect on and question industry practices and to feel viscerally connected to the findings.

Now it's time to distill the team's insights and observations into well-formulated blue ocean strategic options. To this end, we introduce the four actions framework, a tool that will enable you to translate the findings from the team's market exploration into concrete, actionable, strategic options that pursue both differentiation and low cost.

The Four Actions Framework

As figure 11-1 illustrates, the four actions framework is built on four key questions. The questions help you to challenge an industry's strategic logic and business model to arrive at blue ocean moves that break the trade-off between differentiation and low cost. Let's quickly run through them.

Which factors that the industry takes for granted should be *eliminated*? This question forces you to consider

Figure 11-1

The Four Actions Framework

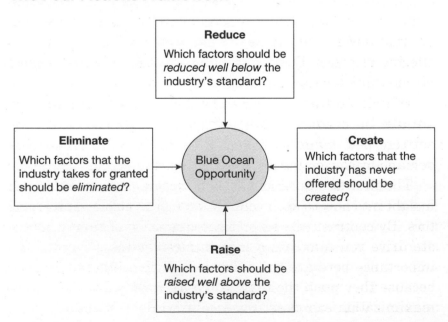

eliminating factors that the industry has long competed on, but which your team found to be irrelevant through the six paths market exploration in the field. Even though these factors no longer add value, or may even decrease it, they are rarely questioned because of long-held industry practice. Other times, organizations are so focused on benchmarking one another that they do not act on, or even perceive fundamental changes in what buyers value. Because these factors buttress an organization's cost structure for little to no gain, substantial cost savings can be made by eliminating them.

Which factors should be *reduced well below* the industry's standard? This question pushes you to determine whether products or services have been overdesigned in the race to match and beat the competition. Here organizations over-serve customers, increasing their cost structure for no gain. By reducing these factors, your costs can be lowered further.

Which factors should be *raised well above* the industry's standard? This question pushes you to uncover and eliminate the compromises buyers are forced to make. These compromises are usually caused by an industry's failure to see that buyers want more of some factors than the standard offering provides. But because the standard is *the standard*, no one thinks to challenge it.

Which factors that the industry has never offered should be *created*? This last question drives you to offer entirely new *kinds* of value for buyers and to create new demand by converting once noncustomers into customers.

The first two questions of eliminate and reduce give you insight into how to drop your cost structure vis-à-vis competitors. By contrast, the second two questions of raise and create drive you to create a leap in buyer value. Of particular importance here are the actions of *eliminating* and *creating* because they push the team to go beyond traditional, value-maximization exercises, which aim to deliver greater value mainly by *reducing* and *raising* levels of the *existing* factors of competition. If *reducing* and *raising* are all that you focus on, you may produce a higher *degree* of buyer value and might even build an advantage over the competition in your existing industry space. But you won't make the existing rules of competition irrelevant, because they don't change the key factors on which everyone else is competing. To open up a new value-cost frontier and leave the competition behind, new *kinds* of buyer value need to be offered through the elimination of existing factors and the creation of new ones.

To ensure that blue ocean teams pursue differentiation and low cost simultaneously, we created the eliminate-reduce-raise-create (ERRC) grid, which complements the four actions framework. Together, these two tools allow you to translate team members' insights and observations gleaned from the field into the concrete, strategic actions needed to make a blue ocean shift. If the team is focused on only a subset of the four actions—not on all four—the grid visually flags the issue and warns the team by showing the blank space(s). Let's walk through this process so you can see how it works.

How One Company Developed Its Blue Ocean Move

"If there ever were a red ocean," observed Michael Levie, co-founder of citizenM Hotels, "the hotel industry would be it. It's redder than red." Four-star hotels offer roughly four-fifths of what five-star hotels offer. Three-star hotels offer roughly three-quarters of what four-star hotels provide and so on down to one-star hotels that offer roughly half of what two-star hotels provide. That is, they all compete on essentially the same set of factors, just more or less of them. "In this industry," noted Michael, "people think they've innovated if they change the paint color on the walls or switch the type of chocolate on the pillow." Against this backdrop, Michael and Rattan Chadha, the CEO, cofounder, and lead investor of citizenM, set out in 2007 to open up a new value-cost frontier that would capture the growing mass of frequent travelers, *mobile citizens*, whether they were traveling for business, on a weekend shopping excursion, or to explore a new locale. As new entrants to the hotel industry, these two entrepreneurs wanted to create a blue ocean with a new kind of hotel chain.

When it came to mobile citizens, Rattan, Michael, and their team noticed that many were frequenting either three-star or luxury hotels. Having sensed that a blue ocean opportunity could exist across these two strategic groups (path two), they wanted to understand why frequent travelers chose luxury hotels over three-star hotels and vice versa. As they did, a host of insights began to emerge.

Here's a glimpse.

"Why do you choose a five-star hotel over a three-star hotel? For the price?"

"Price? No. Who likes paying more?"

"So, is it because of the bellhops and doormen? They're usually much nicer at five-star hotels."

"That may be true. But that's not why I choose five-star hotels over three stars. For me, bellhops tend to take too long to bring your luggage up, and then I always feel the need to fork over a tip. Bellhops are certainly helpful if you have a lot of luggage. But as a frequent traveler, I travel light. For convenience and simplicity, I prefer to carry my own bag. Same for doormen. They may be nice to have, but I don't choose a five-star hotel because of them."

"So, is the front desk a factor?"

"No. Even in a five-star hotel, you usually have to wait. And then, when you do check in, you can get the feeling that the person checking you in is sort of checking you out, judging you. I hate that."

"What about the concierge? Does that influence your decision?"

"No. With Google maps and restaurant and travel apps, it's usually faster and easier for me to figure things out myself than to ask a concierge. Besides, most concierges use these services too nowadays."

"Is it because you prefer the restaurants in five-star hotels to those in three-stars'?"

"No. It's nice that they have them. But I tend to eat out, since five-star hotels are in great locations."

"So location matters?"

"Yes, great locations are important in my decision. Five-star hotels usually are in prime locations, which is what I'm after."

"Room service?"

"Room service is usually expensive and slow. I only use it when I have to."

"What about Internet and phone?"

"That's a real pet peeve of mine. When you stay in a luxury hotel, you're already paying a lot. And then many of them take you for a ride by charging you for Internet and phone services at sky-high rates."

"What matters to me isn't the size of the room. It's a great bed, great sheets, quietness, and a great shower. Water pressure, please!"

"What's the biggest turnoff of three-star hotels that makes you decide not to stay there?"

"They're just not inspiring. They feel so institutional and mediocre. That feeling of luxury, of beauty, of quality, is central to why I choose five-star hotels."

In short, despite all the factors the hotel industry competes and ranks itself on, it turned out that only three factors stood out as *decisive* in determining why frequent travelers traded up to five-star hotels over those rated three stars: the meta-feeling of luxury and beauty they experience there, the more luxurious sleeping environment, and the hotels' prime location.

Conversely, as the team probed why people choose a three-star hotel over a five-star, price jumped out as the most common factor, followed by one other: Five-star hotels often felt too formal and pretentious. "They feel too uptight. Like you have to dress a certain way and act a certain way to fit in. They feel too rarified, not relaxed enough, for me."

To turn these insights into clear actions and a concrete strategy, the team challenged itself to translate them into specific factors to eliminate, reduce, raise, and create. As they did, they started to realize several interesting patterns. For example, the customers of neither five-star nor three-star hotels saw the front desk, concierge service, bellhops, or door-men as key to their purchase decision. The team realized that the front desk does not bring value to customers; it exists for the benefit of hotels to register and process people and payments. Similarly, for frequent travelers, who almost always travel light, bellhops were also seen as unnecessary, and often even as a nuisance. As for the concierge, frequent travelers were for the most part tech-savvy and preferred finding directions and locating restaurants and sights themselves.

"We could potentially *eliminate* these factors," the team reasoned, "and there would be no real impact on value for most frequent travelers—whether they are five-star or three-star hotel goers today, while also lowering our cost structure."

Room size could also be *reduced* without a real impact on value, as people rarely stayed in their rooms much. It didn't escape the team that smaller rooms also meant being able to have more rooms per square foot of real estate space, creating greater yield. "Luxury is a great sleeping environment not room size," the team realized. "Given the high cost of space, significant cost savings can be realized from building smaller rooms. Instead, if we *raise* the quality of the sleeping environment by furnishing rooms with king-size beds, fine linens, good sound insulation, big fluffy towels, and amazing showers," the team reckoned, "we'd delight guests while keeping our cost per room much lower than the industry average."

As team members continued to work through and interpret the market insights they'd gathered, they also recognized
new *kinds* of value they could *create*. "If we eliminate the front
desk, couldn't we adapt and use self check-in kiosks so guests
could check in with no lines? And we could complement them by
replacing scripted front desk staff with multitasking "ambassadors," who are ready to explain how the kiosks work and in
what ways they might be of help in a warm and friendly way."

"If we don't have a front desk, concierge, or bellhop, why
would we need a traditional lobby, which is pretty much empty,
wasted space? Couldn't we create a communal living space
instead, where guests can eat, drink, meet, work, and play
freely anytime they want, 24/7, as they can at home? If the
living space is comfortable and relaxed, but also surprisingly

Figure 11-2

The Eliminate-Reduce-Raise-Create (ERRC) Grid: The Case of citizenM

Eliminate	Raise
Front desk and concierge service Bellhops and doormen Full-service restaurants and room service Lobby	Sleeping environment—extra-large bed, luxurious linens, quietness, shower power Prime location Free movies on demand, phone calls at VoIP rates, free instant high-speed Internet, and lots of plugs for guests' gadgets
Reduce	**Create**
Guestroom types Room size Price vis-à-vis luxury hotels'	Kiosks for one-to-three-minute self check-ins Communal living environment with 24/7 bar and pantry and iMacs for guest use Multitasking "ambassadors" hired for warmth and a can-do attitude; no scripted staff

beautiful, luxury customers' need for beauty and inspiration would be immediately met on entering the hotel and so would three-star customers' need for less formality and pretension." Figure 11-2 shows the results of the team's probing.

In 2008, with the launch of its first hotel in Amsterdam's Schiphol Airport, citizenM opened up a new value-cost frontier of affordable luxury for frequent travelers. Soon after, citizenM began opening hotels in major cities, like London, Paris, and New York. Consider these facts: Its hotels earn the highest *guest rankings* in the hospitality industry, placing them in the "fabulous" and "superb" categories, right alongside five-star hotels. Yet, they're priced to be affordable to three-star customers. The result is an average occupancy rate of 90 percent across its hotels—a whopping 80 percent higher than the industry average. As for costs, its total costs per room are roughly 40 percent lower than the average four-star hotel's, while its cost of staff is a staggering 50 percent lower than the industry's. citizenM outperforms all traditional players, its profitability per square meter being about twice that of comparable upscale hotels. Today citizenM hotels are further expanding across the major cities of the world. "Stylish, high-tech, and cheap," "an overnight revolution," and "a form of religion" are among the accolades the media has showered on citizenM's blue ocean move.

Generating Your Blue Ocean Strategic Options

The citizenM example illustrates how the insights and observations generated from one of the six paths, in this case path two (looking across strategic groups), were translated into a clear and concrete set of actions that formed the basis of its blue ocean strategic move. As citizenM was a start-up, only a small group of people, including the two entrepreneurial cofounders, were involved in developing its blue ocean move.

For organizations that had separate subteams doing the six paths market exploration, only the members who did the field-work for a given path should develop the corresponding move. Because the translation process for each of the six paths is the same, we'll continue using the citizenM example to show how the process works for a path. As we lay out the action steps involved in the process, for the sake of simplicity, we won't use the phrase *the subteam* and will just refer to *the team*. Here is how the action steps unfold.

Extract the key insights revealed by the path

First, get clear on the key insights revealed by exploring the path. Team members should carefully read and review the completed recording templates with all the comments they received and observations they made during the fieldwork. If the team has not yet grouped like-minded comments across the completed recording sheets for a given path, now is the time to do so.

As they work through the comments, the team should pay special attention to the most common factors cited—both positive and negative. Those will be their key factors. Then team members need to push themselves to consider what each factor really means by providing a short, cogent description of the elements that make it up. In the case of citizenM, for example, the team could see that, when it came to room qual-ity, the factor frequent travelers most commonly cited was the sleeping environment. Then when they pushed themselves to identify exactly what in the sleeping environment mattered, they were able to define *sleeping environment* concretely as "bed size, quality sheets and towels, quietness (or sound insu-lation), and water pressure in the shower." Reaching agree-ment on what the salient factors are and exactly what they encompass not only puts everyone on the same page when they talk about their results, but also forces the team to ground insights in specific factors that can later get acted on and are relatively easy to cost.

One of the reasons the first path you work on to create a blue ocean option is typically the hardest is that translating comments into practically framed factors calls on people to think in a way few have ever been asked to do. As a result, anxiety may build, and team members may start to second-guess their ability "to do it correctly." Reassure them that this is natural and that as they work through the path together, and share their results and learn from one another, they'll find that they will do just fine.

Drill down into which factors to eliminate, reduce, raise, and create

Next, you need to decide if the factors you've identified should be eliminated, reduced, raised, or created. Use the four actions framework and the ERRC grid to help organize your answers. These materials are provided for your free download and use at www.blueoceanshift.com/ExerciseTemplates.

To ensure that everyone fully understands how to apply the framework and complete the grid, let's go back to the citizenM example. Because their prime location and more luxurious sleeping environment were decisive in causing frequent travelers to trade up to five-star hotels, the citizenM team deemed it essential to *raise* these two factors to an unexpected height. At the same time, because people choose three-star hotels for their lower price, the team saw the need to offer a price point that was markedly *reduced* from that of luxury hotels. Since customers of neither strategic group valued the front desk experience, the team judged the front desk as *eliminate*. This, in turn, prompted the team's insight about creating self check-in kiosks, so that guests could access their keys and go straight to their rooms with the same kind of time savings an ATM provides over a teller's line at a bank. This is a glimpse into how the process of drilling down works to arrive at a completed ERRC grid.

In completing the ERRC grid for a given path, remember to focus on using *concrete* factors that you can act on and can get a good sense of their cost implications. For example, people often list "inconvenience" as a key factor to eliminate. However, inconvenience is not a concrete factor and it doesn't indicate how it will be eliminated. So, it's important to push the team to get more specific by asking, "What precise actions will be taken or things changed to eliminate buyers' inconvenience?" Likewise, when people list "convenience" as a key factor to create, the word says nothing about how that will be done. So here, too, you would need to probe for a concrete action that will create convenience for buyers. It is critical to understand the difference between concrete factors that describe actions and investments as opposed to desired outcomes, which are the result of your strategic actions. Concrete factors, not outcomes, are what you need to list in the ERRC grid. As you do, also start to think about how you might be able to creatively deliver the factors you raise and create so the cost of delivering them can be lowered. You want to be thinking about lowering cost as you raise value all along.

Occasionally, team members may want to go back to the field and reinterview a select group of people they had previously interviewed to seek further clarification and to test their ideas about what to eliminate, reduce, raise, or create. If a team feels this need, you should let them. But be sure to cap the time for doing so to a month to prevent the team from falling into analysis paralysis.

Check that you are pursuing both differentiation and low costs

The simultaneous pursuit of differentiation and low costs via value innovation is key to opening up a new value-cost frontier and hence making a blue ocean shift. In practice, however, we've often found that groups tasked with coming up with something new tend to focus predominantly on raising and creating. When they do, they end up conceiving of potentially costly offerings that reflect red ocean differentiation, not blue ocean strategic moves. To ensure that this does not happen, remind people that they need to put as much effort into what to eliminate and reduce as well as what to raise and create. In practical terms, that means stressing to team members that for each path they should aim to show concrete factors in the eliminate and reduce quadrants of the completed ERRC grid, as well as in the raise and create ones.

Sometimes a team will argue that there is nothing they can eliminate or reduce. If they do, push back and ask them to think harder about factors they may be taking for granted because that's simply the way things have always been done, but that no longer add value or significantly over-deliver on what buyers need. To inspire them, point to what citizenM eliminated and reduced that had long been sacrosanct in the hotel industry or to what Comic Relief eliminated and reduced, like advocacy counseling, grant solicitation, and year-round solicitations. To spark their thinking, try flipping the question and asking, "What are the stupidest things our industry does?" Then ask them to zoom in there. That's when lightbulbs often start to go off.

People can also fall into the trap of listing factors to "create" that are new to their organization's offering but not to the industry. Remind the team that the only factors that qualify here are those that are largely new to the industry or market space they are focusing on—factors that are beyond the industry's conventional boundaries. A team at one of the largest European gas service station providers, for example, initially put having clean bathrooms and the ability to purchase a fun selection of food in their "create" quadrant. But while these two factors may have been new to the company, which

had a terrible reputation in both areas, they were hardly new
to the industry, which was light-years ahead of the company
in this regard.

Draw your blue ocean alternatives

The team is now ready to draw a "to-be" strategy canvas
for the offering, based on the completed ERRC grid for the
path. The to-be strategy canvas allows you to visualize how
the blue ocean alternative for a given path breaks away from
the existing red ocean reality. To accomplish this, the team
should begin by rating the key factors in the completed ERRC
grid, just as they did when they drew the industry's existing
strategy canvas (see chapter 7). Now, however, all the factors
listed as eliminates should get a score of 0. For the others,
the team should use the same 5-point Likert-type scale (or
variant thereof) they used earlier. As before, when it comes to
price, a high price should be rated as "high" and a low price
should be rated as "low."

Next, plot all the factors along the horizontal axis. So that
the strategic profile of your proposed new move can be easily
appreciated and communicated, list price first, followed by all
the factors that were eliminated, then reduced, then raised,
and finally created. That will give you an easy-to-read strategic profile. Lastly, overlay the strategic profiles of the competition on that of your proposed new move.

Blue ocean moves seldom involve lots of bells and whistles,
nor are the ideas usually fancy and shiny. In fact, once they're
completed, they often look remarkably simple and clear and
have the ring of common sense. Be sure to remind the team of
this, so that they don't begin to doubt the power of their "simple" idea and start adding extraneous or clever factors that
merely complicate it and seriously diminish its blue ocean
potential.

Figure 11-3

Strategy Canvas of citizenM at the Time of Its Launch, 2008

"Affordable Luxury for the People"

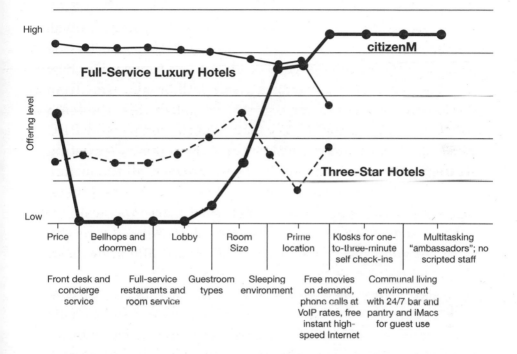

Figure 11-3 shows the strategic profile of citizenM's blue ocean move in contrast to those of the competition. As you can see, citizenM's strategic profile meets the initial litmus test of a blue ocean offering in that it diverges from the competition; it is focused; and it has a compelling tagline that is true to the offering, namely, "affordable luxury for the people."

Now reflect on the strategic profile of your blue ocean option and develop a tagline that is both true to its strategic profile *and* is compelling from the buyers' point of view.

One without the other is not sufficient. To develop the tagline, really dig into how the proposed offering creates a leap in value for customers and how you can best communicate that. In developing these taglines, it's important to avoid falling into the trap of creating catchy but meaningless phrases. Should that happen, you need to redouble the team's efforts to communicate the essence of the offering in a way that will highlight its compelling benefit and immediately speak to the market.

Outline the offerings' economic benefits to the organization

Most industries have a fair idea of how costs generally break down across their value chain. The airline industry, for example, has a good understanding of the relative costs associated with airport fees, fuel, staff, maintenance, food and beverages, marketing, loyalty programs, and so on. Likewise, for luxury and three-star hotels, hotel industry experts like Michael Levie have a good idea of the relative costs associated with land, rooms, staff, full-service restaurants, and so on.

Based on these relative costs, the citizenM team developed a rough idea of how much cost savings would be realized by eliminating and reducing the existing features of these hotels. For those features that the citizenM team was looking to create, but luxury and three-star hotels didn't offer— like self check-in kiosks or communal living space—the team looked outside the hotel industry to get an idea of the magnitude of cost additions. By putting cost savings and additions together, the team was able to outline how the economics of the offering would work. The aim here was to create a win not only for *mobile citizens* through a leap in value but also for the organization through a tidy profit.

As in the case of citizenM, here teams need to provide preliminary indicators of the economic benefits of their proposed offerings and make their business cases, however rough they may be. The blue ocean offering that ultimately gets selected would then have its economics further fleshed out with all needed operational expertise available in the organization to ensure a winning business model.

The outputs of these action steps are: a to-be strategy canvas with a compelling tagline that powerfully conveys its essence, and a completed ERRC grid that highlights how costs will be brought down, while differentiation will be driven up to create a leap in buyer value. With these inputs, rough indicators of the offering's economic benefits, like profit and growth, are developed.

As this process gets completed for each path, what we typically find is that two or three of the paths will yield stronger and more compelling insights to create a new value-cost frontier than the others, while the rest reveal a compelling factor or two to eliminate or create, but fall short of providing enough insights to unlock a new value-cost frontier. If this happens, do not be alarmed. It's normal. That said, you should still go through the entire exercise. Why? For one, it generates tremendous learning for everyone. Moreover, some of the insights from the "weaker" paths can become low-hanging fruit to be acted upon at a later time. So don't short-circuit the process and lose the learning.

Move to the Final Step

With viable alternative blue ocean opportunities created, you are now ready to move to the final step of the blue ocean shift journey. The final step is where you'll learn how to select your blue ocean move, rapidly test it in the market, and tighten and refine it to maximize its market potential. The final step ends with formalizing a big-picture business model for the chosen move and launching it. This ensures that the move you roll out generates not only a leap in value for buyers but, importantly, a tidy profit for your organization.

The team's energy is high. Team members are proud of what they have created, but also understandably nervous, because they are on the cusp of hearing objective feedback and the market's judgment on the proposed blue ocean moves they've generated from their hands-on explorations.

Step Five:
Make Your Move

CHAPTER 12

Selecting Your Blue Ocean Move and Conducting Rapid Market Tests

You ARE NOW READY to select your blue ocean move. The team has developed up to six potentially viable blue ocean opportunities, each captured on a one-page, to-be strategy canvas. It has created a compelling tagline for each that is true to the offering and speaks to the market. And it has completed a single-page, eliminate-reduce-raise-create grid as well as an outline of the economic benefits offered by each strategic option. Collectively, these materials show how each alternative could deliver a leap in value for buyers (or donors if a nonprofit or the public if the government) and a win for the organization.

How will you chose which strategic option to pursue? By hosting a blue ocean fair, an eye-opening but high-pressure event. Here the strategic options the team has developed are opened up for transparent feedback and calibration, so that a decision can be reached on which is the best to move forward with and what aspects of it may still need to be refined and worked through to open up a new value-cost frontier.

In our work with organizations, we often hear complaints that senior management is too conservative and that whatever innovative ideas do get put forth are usually neither championed nor taken seriously. Entrepreneurs often voice the same complaints about the investors to whom they pitch their ideas. But when we ask people to share examples of the innovative ideas that were rejected, we see two common problems. On the one hand, otherwise good ideas are couched in such complex and incoherent language that it's impossible to judge their merits. On the other hand, seemingly good ideas are either all about being different for the sake of differentiation and don't actually offer buyers a leap in value, or they lack a robust profit proposition. Understandably, investors and executives push these ideas aside.

By contrast, we've never seen teams encounter these issues when they make their presentations at a blue ocean fair. Without exception, among the first comments we hear are how professional and easy to grasp the strategic offerings are, and how clearly the presentations lay out the benefits for buyers and for the organization.

Let's look at how a blue ocean fair works.

The Dynamics of the Blue Ocean Fair

A blue ocean fair brings together the organization's senior leadership and all the members of the blue ocean initiative team. Who should be in the room? In addition to the head of the focal unit, the attendees should include his or her top team as well as the heads of marketing, manufacturing, HR, finance, IT, and logistics. Not only are these executives likely to be called upon to provide specialized support once execution is underway, but they may also be asked to remove obstacles within their functional areas as execution begins. So accord them the intellectual and emotional respect they're due, and make sure they understand the full range of blue ocean options you're presenting. By bringing together this cross section of respected corporate community members and influential functional heads, the blue ocean fair creates a natural cadre of ambassadors who can speak from firsthand knowledge about why a shift is imperative and, crucially, the merits of the move that is ultimately chosen.

Customers are also often invited to the fair, as are the noncustomers whom you hope will swell the ranks of your new market space. Suppose, for example, you're looking at options in the B2B environment for new types of sophisticated hospital equipment. You would want to include both your current key buyers and users (which is typically a small group of people, as the industry is quite consolidated), and some potential customers from smaller hospitals that don't currently use such equipment. Similarly, when your success is highly dependent on a broader ecosystem, bringing in select supply chain or ecosystem partners is wise. While these are the kinds of people the team typically met during their six paths market exploration, they can add an additional layer of real-time market feedback to the discussion. For the same reason, some organizations invite players, such as industry analysts, that have a naturally broad overview of the industry's landscape.

For start-ups or small Main Street organizations that don't have the breadth and depth of talent that large, established corporations do, members of the blue ocean initiative team and their top leaders are often the only internal participants. In that case, it is especially important to populate the event with relevant external guests.

The fair begins with the team's presentation of all the strategic options they created. (From here on in, we'll assume for the sake of simplicity that the team has brought all six options to the fair.) Once the presentations are over, the initiative team splits up, and its members go to one of six stations set up around the room. Each station displays a large, poster-sized version of one of the to-be strategy canvases, along with

the eliminate-reduce-raise-create grid and the economic benefits to the organization. The attendees are then invited to visit
the stations to ask for further clarification, share their comments and suggestions, and raise possible concerns. Finally,
they vote for the move or moves they find most compelling,
using stickers or Post-it notes to indicate their choices.

After the voting is all done, the top team asks the attendees why they chose for or against specific strategies, adding
yet another layer of feedback to the process. Simply seeing
the accumulation of Post-it notes or stickers on a blue ocean
option—or the absence thereof—and then hearing people's
comments firsthand, helps team members begin to let go of
ideas that lack compelling traction and rally around those
that garner strong support.

While all the attendees except the blue ocean initiative team
members get to vote, the final decision is made by the organization's executive team. Occasionally, the move these executives
choose is not the one that received the most votes. In that case,
they absolutely must provide explicit reasons for their choice;
but it's a wise practice to follow in any case—even if the choice
seems obvious. A clear and cogent explanation is critical to
reinforcing the fair process built into the initiative and keeping
everyone committed to the outcome.

Holding Your Blue Ocean Fair

Here are the guidelines for conducting a successful blue ocean
fair.

Start with an overview of your industry's red ocean reality and the need to make a blue ocean shift

Begin by presenting the as-is strategy canvas, which shows
the red ocean the industry is confronting and, hence, why a

blue ocean shift is imperative. Then walk through both the completed buyer utility map, which reveals the pain points customers experience and, as a result, the potent opportunities to unlock trapped value, and the three tiers of non-customers, which show the buyers the industry is currently shutting out and who could potentially be tapped to create new demand. This gives the attendees the background they need and helps get everyone on the same page.

It is imperative that senior management attend the fair from start to finish. Without their committed presence, both the blue ocean team and everyone else will assume that they either don't think the initiative is important or they lack the will to see it through. And guaranteed—if senior management skips part of the fair, the initiative team will be demoralized. To get to this point, they have done an enormous amount of work of which they're rightly proud. More than anything else, this is their moment to shine—to show what they've produced despite their initial doubts and trepidation. The organization's leaders must accord the team members the respect they deserve; and the best way to do that is through their eager listening presence. This also sends a strong signal throughout the organization that the initiative is to be taken seriously, which will reinforce everyone's commitment to execution while discouraging game playing. Last but not least, attending the entire fair is the only way the top management team can learn enough to choose the best blue ocean move to pursue.

Have the team present their blue ocean strategic options

Next, each blue ocean option should be presented by a team member who worked on its development. Give him or her *no more* than five minutes for the entire presentation. We set a tight time limit here, because we've found that any strategy that takes longer than this to communicate effectively is probably too complicated, or not well enough thought through, or too undistinguished to be any good. Knowing they must work within such a tight time frame helps all the blue ocean team members really think through, sharpen, and refine the offerings and business case for each alternative as they prepare for its presentation.

It is vital for everyone on the team to use the same format for their presentations. Otherwise, voting and comparison will become very difficult to do well in the short time of the fair. While there are many ways to do this, we've found that the following content and flow serve this purpose well.

- **Describe the offering:** Start by presenting the offering's tagline. Follow this with a short, bullet-point description. This should be very easy to understand, so that the attendees can immediately grasp the gist of the offering and why it is compelling.
- **Present the to-be strategy canvas:** The to-be strategy canvas should show both the strategic profile of the proposed blue ocean offering and the as-is strategic profile of the current industry. In this way, attendees can see for themselves precisely how the proposed move stands apart, diverges from current industry practices, and delivers a leap in value for buyers. It also immediately reveals whether the offering is focused, instead of simply offering more of everything the competition already does, by highlighting what has been reduced and eliminated to lower the offering's cost as well as raised and created to offer a leap in value.
- **Walk through the ERRC grid:** Summarize the factors that the blue ocean option eliminates, reduces, raises, and creates. Because the team has already done the hard work of describing each of the factors in concrete, actionable terms when it built the to-be strategy canvas (see chapter 11), this summary will reaffirm

how the offering breaks from current industry practice, and how it both creates higher value and drives down costs. In established organizations, walking through the ERRC grid will also give people an indication of how much of a stretch the option is likely to require in contrast with the organization's current business model.

- **Summarize the benefits for buyers (or donors for nonprofits or the public for a government entity):** Although the offering's benefits may already have become obvious, it is worth briefly summarizing the leap in value buyers—including the noncustomers who would find the new offering compelling—will gain. For citizenM hotels, for example, this might be, "For a price approaching that of a three-star hotel, customers will enjoy a five-star location, a vastly superior night's sleep, great Wi-Fi, and an experience that's luxurious but not snobby."

- **Outline the economic benefits to the organization:** Using the industry's general breakdown of relative costs across the value chain, size up the magnitude of the cost savings from the factors that have been eliminated and reduced. Then outline the additional costs that will likely be incurred because of the factors you've raised and created. As discussed in chapter 11, the above exercise provides rough indicators of the option's economic benefits to the organization.

If the proposed move might face any potentially significant external hurdles, like government regulations, the team should note them in their presentation as well. With this additional input, the assessment of alternative options can be more complete. It may also be the case that someone at the fair will have overcome a similar challenge, or knows someone in another industry who has. In our experience, being forthcoming about potential difficulties is often the route to finding a solution quickly.

Before moving on to the next presentation, give the attendees five minutes to note their thoughts about what they've just heard on recording sheets. These recording sheets, as well as a summary of the contents to be presented at the fair, are provided for your free download and use at www.blueoceanshift .com/ExerciseTemplates. This will allow you to capture people's immediate, instinctive reactions to each alternative, and help to ensure that everyone in attendance is listening keenly.

Ask the attendees to visit all the stations and then cast their votes

Once all the presentations have been made, encourage the attendees to circulate, think deeply about each option, ask clarifying questions, offer suggestions, and really take in and weigh the instinctive appeal for buyers as well as the economics of each option. One member of the team that developed the option should be at each station to answer questions. Be sure to capture people's feedback just as it happens.

Then give each attendee a few stickers or Post-it notes and ask them to place from one to all of these on their preferred strategic option(s), depending on how compelling they found it. While there is no fixed rule on how many stickers to hand out, in our experience, distributing three to five works well.

Alternatively, if you're worried that attendees might influence one another's selections, you can provide each voter with a sheet listing the name of each option and ask each of them to place their stickers there instead of on the posters or flip charts. You can then collect the sheets and transfer the votes to the displays to reveal how each of the options did.

Probe for maximum feedback and learning

When the voting is finished, what people think becomes immediately visible—almost like looking at a heat map. Now you want to gather even richer feedback through a focused discussion with the attendees. While there are many ways to go about this, we've found that asking people, strategy canvas by strategy canvas, why they did or did not vote for each blue ocean option serves this purpose well. "What specifically captured your imagination?" "What didn't?" "What's a drawback?" "What in the option's value or profit proposition should or could be sharpened?" If one strategy canvas received an overwhelming number of votes, ask what about it made people so passionate. Likewise, if one canvas received very few votes or no votes at all, ask people why they did not vote for it. "Were others just much better, or was there something about the option's value to buyers, or its economic benefits, that troubled you or turned you off?" As people recount their reasoning—the pluses, the minuses, and their doubts—take careful notes.

Taking the time to drill down into the attendees' responses is invaluable, not just in deciding which option to choose, but also because it can take a blue ocean offering up a level. Other times, you may learn that it was the tagline more than the actual strategic profile that captured people's imagination. That can tell you a great deal about what the team got right and what might need to be modified, so that the blue ocean option walks the talk.

When external guests are present, let them know that the organization's leadership will be calibrating all their feedback, as they decide which strategic move to pursue, and how it should be refined.

Decide which blue ocean option to pursue

Now it's time for the executive team to make the critical decision on which option (or options) to move forward with. Every executive team tends to have its own method of collective calibration and decision making. However, we've found that the decision-making process tends to work best when each member of the executive team starts by sharing their thoughts on each option, and then the whole team debates one another's assessments, noting areas where further clarification or refinement is necessary. Here are some key questions the executive team should explore:

> Given the feedback we've heard, should any of the factors on a to-be strategy canvas be modified or revised?
> Did the presentations or subsequent discussions reveal any missing essential component, which, if it were included, would multiply the offering's appeal to buyers?
> Does the offering fail to eliminate and reduce factors sufficiently to drive lower costs and break the value-cost trade-off?
> Is there a lower-cost way to deliver any of the factors proposed to be raised or created that could strengthen the offering's economic benefits?
> What capability gaps would need to be closed to execute this option? And what ideas are there for how the organization could close them effectively at low cost?

The executive team should make a short list of the strongest blue ocean options and select the one they think holds the highest market potential. As they do so, they should be sure they're carefully considering the voting and comments of all the fair's attendees. In the process, executives often see opportunities to merge two complementary and overlapping offerings into a single coherent whole.

Once they've reached their decision, the executive team communicates it to the blue ocean initiative team and the other organizational members attending the fair, along with their guidance on which aspects of the option need to be refined, based on their own deliberations and the comments made at the fair. We cannot overemphasize how important it is for them to provide sound and concrete reasoning to the team to support their decision.

Because the decision is usually very close to the voting, we have rarely witnessed people being puzzled by an executive team's selection. The team may initially be surprised if the executive team suggests that two offerings be merged into one. But once their reasoning has been explained, and they've been encouraged to ask questions, the team members soon come to understand the strategic logic the top executives are using. Once in a while, the most popular strategy at the fair does not make the cut. When this happens, it's usually because it appeals to what we call the "emotional" vote: An offering appears better than it really is only because it's so different. On deeper reflection, however, it becomes apparent that the difference is grounded less in a leap in value for buyers than in simply being original. Technology-driven companies often fall into this trap.

Inside a Global Consumer-Goods Giant's Blue Ocean Fair

What is a blue ocean fair really like? Let's observe what happened when Kimberly-Clark Brazil (KCB) set out to make a blue ocean shift in South America's largest market for bathroom tissue. When it comes to a highly commoditized, hyper-competitive industry, few industries are redder than the US$1.5 billion–plus Brazilian toilet tissue market, which numbers more than 50 competitors and 200 brands. But what can you possibly do with a product as simple and basic as toilet paper? KCB was about to find out.

The entire Brazil executive team, the Latin American continental leadership team for the bathroom tissue category, and the senior and mid-level leaders from every KCB product line were gathering in the large, modern, air-conditioned ballroom of a São Paulo hotel for the blue ocean fair. The objective was not only to select the strongest blue ocean move with the best profitable growth potential, but also to mobilize the willing cooperation and commitment of leaders at every level of the organization to ensure its effective implementation. Since bathroom tissue was the focus, there was no shortage of buyer experience in the room: Everyone was a customer. Counting the blue ocean initiative team, almost 100 people were present. Then two external board members also arrived, increasing the profile of the occasion and the nervousness of the blue ocean initiative team.

Curiosity and expectations were both high. The initiative team sat at the front of the ballroom. The CEO of KCB, João Damato, who was also the category leader for bathroom tissue for the whole of Latin America, welcomed everyone to the meeting. He briefly set the scene by describing how highly commoditized the market was, and how difficult it was to stand out and achieve an acceptable margin, especially given the power retail trade could exert over commoditized products—brands notwithstanding. He then reminded everyone about the purpose of the initiative: to propel a leap forward in KCB's profitable growth and margin.

The blue ocean initiative leader then outlined the industry's current red ocean reality in more detail, provided an overview of the blue ocean shift process, and recounted the chronology of the initiative, which had kicked off only three months earlier. Murmuring broke out when the industry's current strategy canvas appeared across a large screen and the pain points on the buyer utility map were revealed. A large percentage of first-tier noncustomers expressed their frustration, which was aptly summed up in one characteristic comment, "You need a math degree just to select your toilet paper, the choice is so overwhelming. Yet nothing stands out."

The initiative team then gave a spirited and sometimes highly amusing pitch for the blue ocean options they had developed. Each of the six strategic options, which ranged from *Just a Hug* to *Funny Paper*, elicited its share of "oohs," "aahs," and other sounds of appreciation. The applause increased after each presentation. Throughout, all the attendees made notes on preprepared sheets designed to gather their feedback on what they loved and hated about each offering as well as their ideas on how to improve each strategic alternative.

When all six options had been presented, the team leader pointed to the six stations set up around the perimeter of the ballroom, each displaying an offering's to-be strategy canvas, its ERRC grid, a summary of the benefits to buyers, and an overview of the option's economic benefits to KCB. The initiative team had taken it upon themselves to create rough prototypes of each offering, too. They handed stickers to each of the attendees, and told them they could give a maximum of two votes to their most highly rated strategic option. With that, people got up, walked around, looked, asked questions, made recommendations, wrote Post-its with their thoughts and stuck them onto the flip charts or simply gave their feedback to the team at the station, voted, had coffee, came back, and sometimes changed their votes or had another exchange with a team member. In the space of one to two hours, all 100 attendees gave feedback and had in-depth conversations with the team.

As the heat map of the most highly rated strategic options emerged from the myriad of small colored stickers, team members breathlessly compared notes:

"Hey, Claudio...Congrats, my friend! It looks like you got the most votes."

"Ha—thanks! Listen...I was just presenting the idea! It really belongs to all of us, especially Mario. I got so many questions about changes to the production line, I was delighted I could refer them to Sergio, who gave answers that seemed to ease their doubts."

"There's no technical problem we can't solve: What we've always struggled with isn't so much the engineering side as it is creating product offerings that unlock innovative value."

"I've never talked to so many leaders or received so

much good advice in the 12 years I've been here. It was just amazing—my best day at work, I can honestly say!"

When all the voting was done, the flip charts were moved to a separate room where the board members, and the executive and category teams could deliberate. They sat around a large conference table with the charts in front, while the initiative team sat behind them so they could listen attentively to the deliberations, clarify points if needed, and take notes on issues to be resolved. Everyone else went out to make calls, check their email, and have more coffee.

Addressing the blue ocean initiative team, the CEO opened the debate. "This is amazing. For such an apparently simple product, where all the potential means to stand apart appear to have already been tried, you came up with an ocean of ideas on how to make it stand apart." Then, addressing his fellow decision makers, he continued, "We can see that the top two ideas received considerably more votes than the other four. What I would like to hear, in your own words, are not only your major takeaways but, importantly, your concerns about these two ideas and, especially, what wisdom you can offer to ensure that we create a leap in value for buyers, increase the rate of profit and growth, and lower our business risk. Also, if you see aspects of the other blue ocean options that would increase the value and margins of these choices, please say what they are."

The discussions quickly zoomed in on *Just One Hug*, which had the largest share of votes. Just One Hug took a roll of toilet paper and significantly reduced its size—but not the amount of paper it contained—through compression. People had only to give it a hug, and—voilà—the compressed roll would pop back to a round toilet paper roll for easy use. Just One Hug's packaging also had a strong but simple plastic strap to make carrying it even easier.

"With many Brazilians going to supermarkets via public transport or on foot, and many traveling long distances to get to a hypermarket, carrying toilet paper is a nightmare, which has somehow escaped the entire industry's radar," observed one executive.

"What Brazilian hasn't struggled," another chimed in, "with a kid in one hand, a bag of groceries in the other, and a large pack of toilet paper tucked precariously under his or her arm? Come on. We've all been there. Many Brazilians struggle with this every week. It's a fact of life for the bulk of the market that's lower income, which we've never been able to tap into."

"It's more than that," added a category team leader. "I can tell you from my own experience, people struggle to store toilet paper once they get it home. We all buy these bigger packages so we don't have to run out to buy more every few days. But there just isn't room for it in our small apartments' limited cupboard space. Just One Hug's compressed size addresses that problem, too. Yet the whole industry is focused on embossing toilet paper, or adding scents, or providing low-quality, one-ply tissue. No player addresses these very real challenges. No wonder the vast majority of Brazilians buy toilet paper almost exclusively on price. The industry hasn't given people on tight budgets a compelling reason to do otherwise."

"What's more," another executive added enthusiastically, "Not only is Just One Hug's size markedly smaller but, with its distinctive packaging and carrying strap, everyone can immediately *see* just how different it is, allowing it to stand out easily in the sea of white paper, and saving people time and anxiety in making their selection."

"Last week, in one of the trade magazines, I saw that a secondhand vacuum-packing machine was available in Italy for a really low price," another manager added. "If we make a decision quickly, I'm sure we could still get it. That would bring our costs down even further, increasing our profit margins and lowering business risk."

"Great idea," said the legal counsel. "By the way, I'm going to check the patent situation immediately when I get back to the office. I know the team looked at this, but we want to make sure no one can easily imitate our idea. It's so simple—but it's pure genius.... I am very excited!"

The product development executive drew the discussion back to the other blue ocean options. "In terms of good ideas, why wouldn't we combine the environmentally friendly component of Ecko (the option with the third-largest number of votes) with Just One Hug? With Just One Hug's packaging reduction and leap in shipping transportation efficiency, it already has a strong inherent environmental component. The compelling value of Just One Hug plus eco fiber should give us much more leverage with large retailers, who are increasingly challenged on sustainability. Its smaller size will also drop our needed shelf space and costs."

"You just stole my point," laughed the supply chain director.

One by one, the decision makers voiced their concerns, insights, and pledges of support. The team members all made notes about what was said. After the fair, if their proposed offering was chosen, the team would take three weeks to both test the offering on the streets of Brazil, using the simple prototype they had created for the fair and further flesh out the business case they had already been developing for the new offering.

After a fruitful 90 minutes of deliberation, the decision makers stretched their legs, while the other attendees (who had used the opportunity to organize multiple business meetings in and around the hotel) reassembled in anticipation of the announcement. The CEO outlined the decision taken—to pursue Just One Hug with eco fiber; explained why it was taken; and summarized the guidance given to the initiative team. For the next 20 minutes, many of those present offered their personal support, expressed whatever concerns they had along with their ideas for addressing them, and offered additional suggestions for increasing the offering's profit and growth potential.

As the blue ocean team members rolled up their flip chart sheets and tucked their prototypes under their arms, the CEO huddled with them as if they were a soccer club. He repeated his congratulations and deepest gratitude for the outstanding job they'd done—all in a matter of less than three months— as well as for the insights into the existing market they'd so clearly revealed and the compelling and "never a boring second" way in which the new ideas had been presented.

Conducting Rapid Market Tests

Following the fair, the KCB blue ocean initiative team conducted 210 face-to-face interviews in which people were chosen at random on one of São Paulo's main streets, taken to a booth, shown the Just One Hug prototype, and asked for their feedback. While the team had already conducted ample market fieldwork in the process of developing their blue ocean options, this rapid market test with an actual prototype allowed them to confirm the strength of the offering, learn about any needed adjustments, and assess the offering's mass market potential, which was considerable: 80 percent of the interviewees said they would love to buy it. KCB followed this market test with a small-scale launch of the actual offering in Brazil's Northeast. This test launch was to not only cross-check and validate the market test's positive reaction in São Paulo but also further evaluate the offering's mass market potential. With these rapid market tests, the team refined the move and sharpened the heart of the pitch to buyers and to retailers as to why Just One Hug opened up a new value-cost frontier in the red ocean of toilet paper.

In 2009, several months after the new packaging machine

arrived from Italy, KCB used Neve, one of its key brands, to stage a full-scale launch of Neve Naturali Compacto, the trade name given to Just One Hug. The pack of compressed rolls contained the same amount of toilet paper per roll as standard ones, but its smaller size made it easier to carry and store. It was a breeze to identify at the point of sale. And it sold at a competitive price that drew demand across every segment of the market, including buyers who had previously bought only from the "value" range of the market. And since it was made with sustainable and recyclable fibers, it was environmentally friendly to boot.

As for KCB's costs, the compressed size led to a 15 percent drop in transportation costs—especially significant given Brazil's large size, a 19 percent reduction in the amount of packaging material used, and a drop in returns due to damage, all contributing to gross margins greater than 20 percent—unheard of in the industry.

Apart from creating unbelievable value for buyers and higher margins for KCB, the product proved to be a win for retailers (in this case Walmart), which saw a unique opportunity in being able to list Neve Naturali Compacto as an environmentally friendly product, due to its far lower carbon footprint as well as its reduced packaging and use of eco-friendly fibers. Several months after the new product was introduced, KCB was named the "Best Sustainability Supplier for Walmart," a deeply significant honor and achievement. (It later became the most sustainable product in the whole of Kimberly-Clark globally.) Last but not least, Neve Naturali Compacto's leap in both value to buyers and environmental sustainability increased KCB's negotiation power with retailers.

The new value-cost frontier the offering unlocked inspired KCB to roll out the "Compacto" format across every one of its major brands like Scott, providing a leap in value for its entire line of toilet paper. First launched in 2009, the blue ocean

Compacto format, born from the fair, remains the industry standard in Brazil and a star performer for KCB, despite the eventual entry of followers who imitated it.

Requiring your initiative team to *rapidly* market-test the prototype of the selected blue ocean offering with potential buyers you want to turn into customers—the way that KCB did—is crucial. This will not only allow you to understand the optimal way to position the offering to buyers and supply chain partners (or to the public or donors, where relevant), but also to learn about any additional adjustments you might need to make. *Rapid* is the operative word here. Which is to say, test your blue ocean offering in a short, specific amount of time as soon as possible after the fair is over. Why? The fair will have created momentum, which you don't want to kill by waiting too long to start testing or by taking too long to conduct the test. The more you delay, the more the team and your organization's technicians will also be tempted to build complicated, costly prototypes, which will add little to testing the offering's core idea and often overcomplicate it as well.

Completing the Move's Final Act for Launch

One of the most inspiring realizations that occurs at a blue ocean fair and, in our opinion, one of the most valuable is the profound shift in people's perceptions of their own and others' creativity and worth. Almost invariably, senior executives are taken aback by how creative the ideas put forward by their people are. It's common to hear them saying, under their breath to themselves, if not out loud to others, "I never knew our people were that good." And they mean it. Similarly, the people on the team are almost always surprised by their own creative competence—feelings that tend to get expressed in remarks such as "I didn't believe I could think beyond the industry's boundaries," or "I never knew I was that creative," or simply, "I can do it!" And with those feelings come increased confidence, and renewed mutual respect and appreciation. It is a watershed moment that has a profound effect on the organization's culture. When the team members and other attendees go back to their departments and share what they heard, saw, and learned, the authenticity and power of their words are palpable to others. This goes a long way toward building everyone's confidence in the integrity of the process and the blue ocean shift underway, further preparing the ground for effective execution.

Your blue ocean strategic move is almost ready to launch. The executive team has decided which option to pursue. The initiative team has conducted rapid market tests to confirm the market potential of the chosen offering and further tighten and refine it. Now the team is primed to formalize the big-picture business model of the move in a way that will maximize return and minimize risk for launch. Let's see how this final step unfolds to ensure that the business model for the new offering will not only offer a leap in value for buyers, but will also have compelling economic benefits for your organization.

CHAPTER 13

Finalizing and Launching Your Blue Ocean Move

WITH YOUR BLUE OCEAN move chosen, and its market potential confirmed, it's time to formalize your business model. The aim here is laying out the big picture: the economic logic that shows how the value and cost sides of your move interact and come together to deliver a leap in value for buyers in a way that generates strong, profitable growth for you. Such a business model allows you to appreciate and see how the individual operational tasks need to fit together to produce the bottom line. It will serve as an excellent road map while the move is actualized at the operational level. Once your big-picture business model is in hand, your blue ocean move is finalized and ready for launch.

To this end, the initiative team, with the mandate of senior management, now expands, pulling in and engaging people with the requisite operational expertise from across the organization, and shifting from part time to full time to ensure that team members have the capacity they need. The guide for their work is the to-be strategy canvas, which provides a clear picture of not only what to eliminate, reduce, raise, and create, but also the price the organization needs to hit to open the new value-cost frontier. It aligns people around what they will need to deliver on and be held accountable for, and empowers them to start thinking creatively about how that can be done with lower costs.

Fair process is just as applicable here as it has been thus far: By providing the wider organization with updates on the key takeaways gleaned from each step of the process, you've gone a long way toward keeping everyone up to speed, and priming the pump for cooperation and commitment. Now you need to continue to exercise fair process among all the people you'll have to engage, whether they are part of the expanded team or not.

Formalizing Your Big-Picture Business Model

By applying the four actions framework in creating your blue ocean move, the initiative team has already done a large part of the legwork needed to formalize your big-picture business model. On the one hand, they have identified the factors the industry currently competes on and invests in that can be eliminated or reduced, because they add little if any value to buyers and may even decrease it. While these decisions were based on buyer value, not on cost, in our experience most of what's identified for elimination or reduction typically lowers—often significantly—an organization's cost structure and has clear operational implications. At the same time, they've also identified the factors the industry currently under-delivers or fails to offer that should be raised or created, because they provide a decisive leap in value from the buyers' point of view. These factors, too, almost always have cost implications as well as direct operational implications. Only, here, the factors to be raised or created typically augment the organization's cost structure.

As an example, let's return to citizenM's affordable luxury hotels discussed in chapter 11. While its hotels enjoy

90 percent occupancy rates, and earn guest rankings on par with those of five-star hotels, citizenM's blue ocean offering strips out a host of costly factors—such as the front desk, a traditional lobby, bellhops, the doorman, the concierge, room service, and even full-service restaurants—which it didn't find to be decisive for the mass of frequent travelers. Every one of these factors citizenM eliminated directly cuts the number of hotel staff required (its hotels operate with less than half the staff of comparable, 200–400-room hotels) and, with it, overall staffing costs. By eliminating a traditional lobby and restaurant, and reducing room size by 50 percent, the costly factor of real estate is also significantly reduced. The impact goes well beyond the space that customers can see, because it means citizenM can also eliminate the space for a professional kitchen as well as all the associated costs that come with building out and maintaining a kitchen. Moreover, by reducing the guestroom variety to one standard format, citizenM is able to not only streamline building the rooms, which results in efficiency gains, but also, as we'll see below, make use of other, innovative, high-value and low-cost construction approaches.

At the same time, the citizenM team also identified three factors to raise: the sleeping environment of its rooms (with extra-large beds, fine linens, plush towels, quiet—or sound insulation—and strong showers); a prime city location; and connectivity for guests (with free high-speed WiFi and movies on demand as well as Skype phone rates, which are much desired by guests but actually cheap to deliver). And it identified three factors to create: simple self check-in kiosks; a unique and compelling communal living space, with a 24/7 bar and pantry; and multitasking ambassadors. Lastly, the team committed to deliver this experience at a price accessible to three-star customers. The result: an offering with the potential to attract the mass of "mobile citizens," regardless of whether they currently frequented three-star or luxury hotels.

The next step in formalizing your big-picture business model is to determine the target profit margin you want to earn to ensure a healthy win for your organization. What works best, we've found, is to start with a more aggressive profit margin than you think would be reasonable, given existing industry practices. Then your target costs—what your costs will ultimately need to be—can be derived by deducting this target margin from the strategic price the team has identified.

The more aggressive the target profit margin you set, the more aggressive your target costing will be. Challenging people to meet aggressive profit and cost targets stretches them to think beyond their usual practices and to search for innovations across their entire operation. Just as industries often compete on factors that buyers no longer value, standard industry operating practices often leave tremendous room for fresh thinking and innovations that can lower costs. So even though people may initially push back on aggressive profit and cost targets, we encourage you to hold firm. With some encouragement, they will strive to perform and deliver on their assignments in innovative, high-value, and low-cost ways, often with surprising results.

Unlike the more familiar practice of cost-plus pricing, in which prices are set by adding a desired profit margin to the organization's costs, target costing is based on price-minus costing. In our experience, organizations that fail to apply target costing to their blue ocean moves typically build out their business models only to find that their costs are too high to earn a profit at the strategic price set. So, they either raise the price of the offering or cut back on the value they intend to deliver—in both cases compromising the move and sending the organization drifting back into the red ocean. The lesson we've learned: Your to-be strategy canvas has to be nonnegotiable. What is negotiable is how your business model delivers it.

How to Hit a Challenging Cost Target

Beyond what organizations have eliminated and reduced in their blue ocean move to lower costs, there are several other ways organizations can pursue to hit their challenging target cost without compromising on their blue ocean offering to buyers. While there is no magic formula, there are several questions teams should explore, as they formalize their business model, to ensure the organization achieves the low costs required to actualize their blue ocean move: "Who can we partner with?" "How can we streamline and innovate operations?" And "How can we multiply people's positive energy and contributions?" Let's probe each of these in turn.

Who can we partner with? In bringing a new idea to market, many organizations mistakenly try to carry out every aspect of the operation themselves. Sometimes this is because they see the product or service as a platform for developing new capabilities. More often, however, it's simply because that's the way things have always been done, and no one thinks to question this approach. While doing everything yourself may give you more control, it usually takes more time and can be a lot more costly than partnering with an organization that's already more proficient and efficient in an area of your business model where you're a novice. By leveraging other companies' expertise and economies of scale, partnering (including making small acquisitions when doing so is faster and cheaper than other options) can pare costs and time, and close capability gaps quickly.

The citizenM team, for example, identified two important areas—food and housekeeping—where it could significantly lower its cost structure by outsourcing them in creative ways and enhance buyer value by benefiting from the proven expertise of others. While citizenM decided to eliminate restaurants and room service, it still aimed to provide healthy, fresh light bites in its communal living space. But food is a tough business: You need fresh ingredients, which requires volume; there is spoilage and waste; you need a kitchen, a good chef, and more. And yet, as Michael Levie observed, "Despite all that effort and cost, few hotels make food worthy of praise."

citizenM got around this dilemma by partnering with local boutique catering companies within blocks of each of its hotels. In this way, citizenM leverages the caterers' proven expertise and purchasing power to ensure that only the best fresh food will be delivered and restocked in its pantries throughout the day—think fresh sushi, salads, and tasty healthy sandwiches—resulting in lower costs and a higher-quality offering. citizenM also partners with an outside company for housekeeping and linens. But it doesn't stop there: Its partners also order all the guest amenities and cleaning supplies and store them on the partners' premises. Combined with the fact that citizenM's blue ocean move eliminates restaurants and room service, this affords citizenM the unique advantage of eliminating purchasing, receiving, and storerooms in its hotels, which simultaneously provides more space for additional guest rooms and significantly lowers operational costs.

The US-based retail chain Wawa, which serves over 600 million customers a year in more than 700 stores in six states, and has annual sales approaching US$10 billion, has been similarly savvy about partnering. Customers are so gaga about Wawa that some (like Jeremy Plauche) have even tattooed its logo on their arms. While Wawa's management team considered it a blue ocean company, in 2009 Howard Stoeckel, then its CEO, saw it drifting into the red ocean. The economy was tough after the global financial collapse, and competitors were catching up to Wawa. Determined to steer clear of the impending red ocean, Howard and his top team applied the blue ocean approach to open a new value-cost frontier. Up until then, Wawa's blue ocean had been created by the way it had perfected the intersection of its three businesses—convenience store, fuel retailer, and food service—under one roof, while delivering outstanding customer service. The perfection was apparent in the numbers: While not a convenience store per se, Wawa's in-store sales are more than three times those of the average 7-Eleven convenience store.

As Howard and the team worked with the blue ocean tools, and created what became known as their "blue ocean strategic plan," they identified food service as the weakest link in the company's overall offering and the one with the greatest profitable growth potential. As Howard reflected, "If you sell gas, people have traditionally assumed you can't be a high-quality food restaurant." As the team set out to make a blue ocean shift, it set its sights on completely changing this perception. It aimed to create a leap in value in the quality, freshness, and healthfulness of the food Wawa sold at the best possible price that would recast Wawa from a convenience store and gas station that also sells food, to a leading quick-service restaurant that also sells gas and convenience items.

The result was a total rethinking of what food to offer, how fresh and healthy it had to be, how to display it for it to be inviting and appetizing, and how to make the selection process easy and food fulfillment fast—all at the best possible price for buyers. Now Wawa offers freshly baked breads; fresh salads like kale and quinoa; healthy wraps and soups; made-to-order hoagies with fresher and more innovative ingredients; hot lunch, dinner, and breakfast sandwiches; and what is described by some as coffee nirvana. With this rethinking, food sales skyrocketed, as did the quality of the overall Wawa experience. The power of its blue ocean shift is reflected in the numbers: Today, Wawa's per-store food sales are ahead of McDonald's per-store sales. What's amazing, however, is the way the team built a business model for the new food and beverage offering, which simultaneously enabled Wawa to earn an aggressive profit margin and hit its aggressive cost target.

Wawa eliminates a number of things that other quick-service restaurants offer, such as in-store tables and drive-throughs. But what's key to its low costs and efficiency are the dramatic differences in its behind-the-scenes operations. It not only partners with grocery logistics leader McLane Company but also set up a daily fresh channel that allows Wawa to outsource its entire supply chain in food. It partners with bakeries for all its freshly baked offerings and with Taylor Farms and the Safeway Group for all the preprepared fresh food. To get fresh food delivered to every store, every day, Wawa partners with Penske Corporation, which manages a cross-dock distribution facility, where the perishable food made by Wawa's food partners is delivered daily. And Wawa operates none of these activities: Its involvement is limited to a small group of employees who work with its partners on communications and quality control to ensure reliable, high-quality deliveries.

As Howard observed, "By applying the blue ocean approach, we were able to identify what it would take to create a leap in the quality, value, convenience, and presentation of food for customers that would simultaneously raise the convenience and quality experience for Wawa overall. But we had no food preparation facilities and expertise in the league we were aiming to deliver on—which was world-class—to be able to make that happen. Rather than compromise our blue ocean offering, or make a costly attempt at developing this expertise in-house, we have partnered with the best to realize our vision fast and at low cost." According to Chris Gheysens, Wawa's current CEO, "Fresh food and beverage now account for more than 40 percent of Wawa's merchandise sales. We've grown from what had been a traditional convenience store to a restaurant to go with fuel. It's hard even to categorize us."

How can we streamline and innovate operations? Contained within this question are multiple possibilities for lowering costs without sacrificing buyer value. Subsequent questions teams can ask to uncover these possibilities include: "Can we replace raw materials with unconventional, less expensive ones?" "Can we eliminate high-cost, low-value-added activities and facilities or replace them with low-cost, effective ones?" "Can we shift the location of our offering to lower-cost real estate?" "Can we truncate the number of parts or steps in the production process?" "Can we factory-manufacture things that industry competitors construct manually?" "Are there off-the-shelf technologies we can use or activities we can digitize to reduce our costs?" The National Youth Orchestra of Iraq asked this question, for example, and answered it brilliantly by holding auditions via YouTube and using Skype for project management. These creative innovations not only eliminated the cost and logistical nightmare of attempting to do either task in person in Iraq, but also allowed NYOI to build a social media presence in the process.

Likewise, by delving into questions such as those listed above, the citizenM team discovered an innovative way to lower its building costs dramatically while simultaneously raising the quality of its rooms. In the hotel industry, construction is one of the largest cost factors. Because citizenM's blue ocean move envisioned only one type of guest room, the team was prompted to reflect on how other industries made standardized products. After all, that's what its guest rooms would be—standardized. Framed this way, the obvious answer jumped out at them: Standardized products are rarely made by hand; they're factory-manufactured. This led the team to question whether they could also manufacture citizenM's rooms, instead of using traditional construction methods. The answer was a resounding yes. Modular manufacturing would allow the rooms to be built at far lower cost and with greater speed, higher quality assurance and consistency, and, very importantly, optimized sound insulation and wiring using value engineering. So, although citizenM builds the lower floors of its hotels using traditional construction methods, its guestrooms are factory-manufactured. And because its blue ocean move reduces the size of the guestrooms significantly, they can arrive preassembled, so they can be easily stacked and snapped together. This innovation helped citizenM cut its room-construction costs by as much as 35 percent, compared to the average four-star hotel, and its overall construction time by around 35–50 percent, compared to other three-star and luxury hotels.

citizenM also realized it could further lower costs by eliminating call centers and phone reservations and replacing them with a simple, fast, online reservation system. For one thing, the growing mass of mobile citizens is tech-savvy and accustomed to doing things online. For another, most hotels' call centers and phone reservations are pretty annoying—a long message detailing which button to press for what, then pushing the right reservation button, then waiting for the next available receptionist while ads or uninspiring music play endlessly. Who likes that?

How can we multiply people's positive energy and contributions? The people who are the face of your brand, and ultimately determine a large part of your blue ocean offering's integrity, are the people who interact directly with your customers if you're a business, your donors if you're a nonprofit, or your citizens if you are a government entity. These customer-facing people need to walk the talk every day to create that tingly experience that gives their customers pause, makes them smile, and motivates them to come back again and again. Yet these very people are often viewed and treated as if they were the lowest level on the hierarchical totem pole. If you're serious about creating an offering with integrity and lowering your business model's costs, however, they shouldn't be. When the energies of the people on your front lines are engaged and multiplied, their productivity goes up, turnover rates drop, and their commitment to go the extra distance rises. This can be achieved by following a process that embraces humanness in the way you treat them. As discussed in chapter 4, such a humanistic process makes your front-line people feel recognized and appreciated for who they are as people, not because they are brilliant and perfect, but because they have something to contribute and want to make a difference. This humanistic approach is a powerful lever to explore as you finalize your blue ocean move. Let's see how it is put into action with customer-facing employees.

citizenM, Wawa, and NYOI, for example, all practiced this approach in formalizing their business models. One common denominator, which costs nothing, is the titles they give their people, which convey a sense of dignity. At citizenM you're not a front-desk clerk, or a bellhop, or a doorman, you're an "ambassador." At Wawa, you're not a convenience store cashier, or a deli worker, or a stock boy or stock girl. Every single one of its nearly 22,000 storefront employees is an "associate." As for the National Youth Orchestra of Iraq, its players were not only musicians but also "cultural diplomats" and "peace makers." All of these titles convey a larger sense of responsibility, grace, and purpose than merely getting a job done. Think of the impact any one of them could have on a person's sense of mission and pride.

The respectful message these titles send is reinforced by the ways the leadership sets the business model up to elevate customer-facing people in the corporate hierarchy. At citizenM, for example, the "reverse pyramid" is a central part of the culture, with hotel staff at the top of the organizational pyramid and top management at the bottom. At Wawa, every executive is expected to spend a minimum of one full day every month typically visiting 12 to 15 stores to talk with associates and store managers. At Christmas, it's a long-standing tradition for executives to spend the day visiting stores (with the majority dressed in Santa hats!), thanking associates for outstandingly serving customers 365 days a year. On every visit, management is there to listen, thank, learn about associates' concerns, and ask associates and store managers to share ideas for improving operations and stories of customers' delight. At NYOI, Paul MacAlindin assembled all the orchestra members and, using a facilitator from the Iraqi Peace Foundation who spoke both Kurdish and Arabic, invited them to define what they wanted their orchestra to stand for. The values, chosen by the players, were love, commitment, and respect. We can imagine no greater way for Paul to have demonstrated that this orchestra was about them, and that they had a mission to be a light of hope for their country as well as musicians.

Empowering customer-facing service staff and trusting them to use their best judgment when speaking with customers, instead of giving them scripts as though they were robots, is another powerful way to activate commitment and energy. Consider the way citizenM and Wawa hire, train, and reward their staff to make this possible. Both companies, for example, hire for attitude and values and train for competence. Among the sentiments echoed at both are "Skills we can teach. Attitude and values are tough to alter." And indeed, skills are taught intensively. But far more important is imbuing staff with a deep sense of what the brand stands for, and what its blue ocean move's promise to the customer is, and what their role is in making that promise a reality.

As Howard Stoeckel notes, "I tell all our associates, 'You may brew coffee, work the register, or make a sandwich. But your real job at Wawa is to help people have a better day.' There's no higher calling than that." Once hired, customer-facing staff get to interpret for themselves how to deliver on that brand promise, which is how and why they make authentic, inspired human connections with customers. Whether that means saying, "Hi, honey," or helping someone with the door, or asking a person who looks sad, "What's wrong?" they are on the case. This personal accountability for delivering on the brand's promise is reinforced and comes full circle with the bonus policies these companies follow. At citizenM, for example, ambassadors—not executives—can earn (or lose) a 30 percent bonus each month, based 100 percent on customer satisfaction. citizenM budgets for the full 30 percent. Why? Just look to its consistently high five-star guest satisfaction ratings, delivered by its multitasking ambassadors.

As for Wawa, it has one of the 10 largest employee stock ownership programs in the United States, based on the number of participants. Close to 40 percent of its private stock is owned by employees, with the greatest share of that held not by senior management, but by associates and store managers. With stories of dozens of associates who retired as millionaires to motivate them, associates take their stock ownership seriously. Meaningful performance incentives; hiring based on attitude; training customer-facing staff both for skills and, crucially, to internalize the brand's promise; and then empowering them to bring that brand to life through exceptional service—taken together, these practices multiply people's energy, engender a culture of strong accountability, create genuine and memorable experiences for customers, and lower the cost of staff turnover. It's a win all around. These organizations don't have customers; they have fans they delight, day in and day out.

Drawing the Big Picture

A big-picture business model shows how the value and cost sides of an organization's blue ocean move come together to generate strong profitable growth at the set strategic price.

Figure 13-1 depicts a big-picture business model, in this case for citizenM, and shows how its components interact. While the left side of the figure presents how the cost dynamics of the organization work to achieve its target cost, the right side shows what buyers receive to ensure they will have a compelling reason to purchase the new offering and an ability to pay for it. Directional arrows show how the elements on both sides of the model interact to create a profitable business model for the company and a win for its customers.

In the case of citizenM, through the big-picture business model presented in the figure, one can easily understand and see how it achieves strong profitable growth. In fact, citizenM's profitability outperforms all the traditional players with its

Figure 13-1

How citizenM's Business Model Works

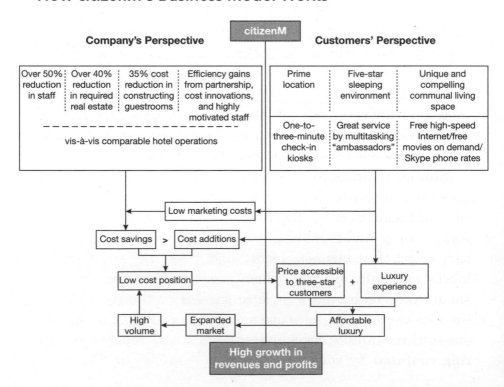

profitability per square meter being about twice that of comparable upscale hotels. This big-picture business model allows people to grasp the economic logic of the blue ocean move in one graphic and to appreciate how their individual operational tasks will fit together to produce the bottom line. It provides a road map for the organization to lay out the operational details and actions, including key milestones of what is to happen when and the objectives and deliverables for each function.

Together with the to-be strategy canvas, the big-picture business model focuses everyone on the same endpoint and prevents people from getting distracted or sidetracked as they translate the blue ocean move into a tangible offering. In essence, they act as an important "decision sieve," aligning the efforts of people across the organization, as they work out operational details.

Launching and Rolling Out Your Blue Ocean Move

The wisest rollout strategy is to start small, then go fast and wide. We can't emphasize this strongly enough. Apple, for example, didn't build 300 stores at once. They first built 2 and concentrated their efforts on ironing out the snags that inevitably get fully revealed only when a new offering goes live, in color. Soon thereafter, they built 25, and the rest is history. Today Apple has more than 490 stores around the world.

Similarly, citizenM built its first hotel in 2008 in its own backyard, at Amsterdam's Schiphol Airport. This allowed the citizenM team to carefully observe and analyze how the hotel was running, and to make any adjustments they found necessary to get their business model right. Were the self check-in kiosks optimally situated when guests entered the hotel, or should they be moved a little to the left or the right? Were the kiosk screens as intuitive as they needed to be to ensure one-to-three-minute check-ins, or were guests repeatedly getting confused by something? Was having one multitasking ambassador on hand when guests checked in sufficient to provide the warm welcome and genuine connection their blue ocean move demanded, or were more required? How about the factory-manufactured rooms: Did the wiring "snap together," as the value engineering in the factory prototypes showed, or did adjustments need to be made? Did the sound insulation specs actually achieve the desired level of quiet? And so on.

In this way, citizenM could quickly work out any kinks, from the way value was delivered to guests to its behind-the-scenes operations and business model, all the while conserving capital because the changes needed to be done in only one hotel. With the adjustments made, and its success clear, citizenM then launched a second hotel in the center of Amsterdam, building on the lessons learned, and providing another opportunity to validate its business model. With the Amsterdam citizenM hotel a tremendous success virtually from the get-go, citizenM management had confidence in the leap in value its hotels delivered and proof of the strong profit engine underlying it. With that, citizenM started to turn up the dial and roll out hotels in major cities around the world.

Wawa uses the same smart rollout strategy when it launches a new offering. It starts with a limited set of stores, works out the bugs, puts the offering into a few more stores to validate its strength and the effectiveness of its business model, and then hits the gas and rolls out fast across all its stores. This rollout strategy has distinct advantages on several grounds. For one, it acknowledges that there will almost always be points of refinement and correction needed in your blue ocean offering and business model. This helps keep people emotionally on track in the face of issues that arise when launching. It says, "Yes, we are aiming for the gold; but we shouldn't get discouraged or thrown when there are initial glitches. Rather, we should expect this, keep an open mind, refuse to get discouraged or look for someone to blame, see this as a valuable learning opportunity, and set about working through the bugs as fast as possible." This approach also minimizes financial risk, credibility risk in the market, and what we think of as demotivation risk with your people.

We've also seen what happens when organizations take the opposite approach, rolling out their moves far and fast, and then discovering the bugs. Only then, it's far more costly to fix the bugs and make adjustments, which leads to frustration and, typically, finger-pointing. And because the rollout is far and wide, the press is often fast to pick up on it. So when something goes other than planned, they are also fast to publish an overly negative review, which discourages people in the organization even further. Sadly, after that, many organizations throw up their hands, call the initiative a failure, and retreat, leaving egos bruised, money wasted, people demotivated, and an organization fearful of trying anything new again, when the glitches they encountered were no bigger or worse than those that accompany any new offering. It's just that they were magnified exponentially by the scale of the launch.

We suggest that you think about the launch and the rollout of your blue ocean move as though you were producing the next smash hit on Broadway. You've gone through the blue ocean shift process and come out with a compelling, original story line that everyone loves. People tell you they can't wait to see the play. And the people who've worked with you to create it can't wait to perform it at last. Moreover, by working through the big-picture business model, you've also worked out everything that needs to happen behind the curtain, from the stage sets, to the lights, costumes, and sound. But does that mean you don't need to practice and iron out the details, so the play will sing and the story line come alive? Of course not. To put on a smashing play, you need to first expect glitches, and then make minor modifications to get it right. When people say, after the first preview performance, "It still needs work," you need to listen carefully, take notes, eschew blame, and strive to unlock the magic of the script. You and your people need to fully understand that adjustments are the natural course of action for building excellence.

Now, you are ready to make your blue ocean shift. You have the tools and the process and the mindset to make this happen from start to finish. The world needs more blue oceans. We invite you to create yours.

A National Blue Ocean Shift in Action

WITH NATIONS AROUND THE world facing tight budgets and growing demands from their citizens, blue ocean shifts are as applicable for governments as they are for corporations, nonprofits, or start-ups. In this epilogue, we'll draw on the experience of Malaysia to illustrate a national blue ocean shift in action, discuss the issues it is addressing, how the process works, and the far-reaching results it has produced.

In the beginning of the new millennium, Malaysia was at a crossroads, stuck in the so-called middle-income trap. During the 1970s, Malaysia, Singapore, South Korea, and Taiwan had all been at a similar level of development, but that was no longer the case. In the intervening years, the other three countries had all become high-income nations, but Malaysia had not managed to make the jump. The country was facing differentiation challenges from developed nations and regions like the United States, Europe, and Japan, which offered higher quality, and low-cost challenges from emerging countries like China, India, Vietnam, and Indonesia.

Malaysia's leaders wanted to move the country out of this red ocean trap and thought that blue ocean strategy might provide the platform for achieving greater public well-being and higher national income. To test and validate their reasoning, the prime minister and the deputy prime minister invited us to engage in several rounds of discussions with different interest groups, ranging from informal small group sessions, to a three-day retreat with national leaders from the public and private sectors, to an official cabinet meeting chaired by the prime minister. After two years of exploration and probing, the government decided to apply the theory and tools of blue ocean strategy to create blue ocean shifts in the nation's economic and social sectors.

To this end, the government set up a nonprofit research organization, called the Malaysia Blue Ocean Strategy Institute (MBOSI), in 2008. The following year, it launched the National Blue Ocean Strategy Summit, an ongoing monthly gathering of Malaysia's top national leaders, its highest-ranking civil servants, including those from the nation's security forces, and selected leaders from the private sector. When the agenda doesn't require the direct attention of the prime minister or the deputy prime minister, the chief secretary to the government chairs the Summit gatherings. To ensure that the principles and process of blue ocean shift are properly applied, MBOSI has supported the Summit from the start.

By January of 2013, the National Blue Ocean Strategy Summit (hereafter referred to as the NBOS Summit) had launched more than 50 economic and social blue ocean shift initiatives. For these initiatives, *differentiation* was conceptualized in terms of delivering a leap in value, or high impact, to the country's economy and society, while *low cost* was defined in terms of the savings generated by reductions in the cost of providing government services. Since the public sector is notoriously slow, the *speed of execution* was added as the third measure of a successful shift, making the guiding principles of every NBOS initiative high impact, low cost, and rapid execution.

Following the successful outcomes of these initiatives and the rapid expansion of their scale and scope, the government established the National Strategy Unit under the Ministry of Finance to further support, accelerate, and monitor the initiatives in close cooperation with MBOSI. By 2017, the number of blue ocean initiatives launched at the national level totaled over 100.

How National Blue Ocean Initiatives Are Formulated and Executed

National transformation programs often fail because government organizations are unable to overcome deeply entrenched silos. With government ministries, departments, and agencies typically working in isolation, resources and information are seldom shared, and turf wars and lack of ownership are all too common. The NBOS Summit recognized that blue oceans could not be created unless these silos were broken down and the boundaries separating federal, state, and local government officials were dissolved. By encouraging people in these different silos and levels to work together and share their knowledge and resources, based on the tools and process driving a blue ocean shift, the Summit aims to expand national leaders' horizons on how to create and capture new economic and social opportunities for the public.

To this end, the NBOS Summit created two platforms to support the transformation—the Pre-Summit and the Offsite. The process begins with the NBOS Summit, which sets the strategic priorities for pressing national issues that need to be resolved, and specifies in what sequence they will be addressed. The matters the members discuss range from safety and security issues, like rising crime and global terrorism; to economic issues, like urban and rural development, and the need for more innovation and entrepreneurship, stronger infrastructure, and youth employment; to social problems and issues of public well-being, such as women's empowerment, inefficient government services, health care, low-cost housing, and environmental degradation, including wild animal poaching. Each Summit lasts three hours and ends with the announcement of new initiatives to pursue in addition to those already underway. The two supporting platforms then develop these initiatives in progressively greater detail.

With macro guidance from the NBOS Summit, the Pre-Summit, chaired by the chief secretary to the government, sets the scope, team members, and strategic direction for the new initiatives before handing them over to Offsite teams whom they've fully briefed. The Pre-Summit is composed of leaders chosen from government ministries, departments, and agencies who also prepare the Summit agendas and monitor the progress of ongoing initiatives to ensure their execution and resolve any cross-ministerial or cross-agency conflicts that occur during implementation.

Offsite platforms are made up of working-level teams tasked with executing the blue ocean initiatives. The leaders of these teams are also members of the Pre-Summit, thereby ensuring that their actions will be aligned. The teams develop detailed execution road maps, which lay out actionable tasks with clear time lines that each member can easily carry out and be held responsible for. Team members share their first-hand discoveries about on-the-ground realities in meetings, and they are empowered to adjust their execution road map accordingly, if necessary.

The chief secretary to the government and his team play a critical role across all three NBOS platforms by coordinating and orchestrating their efforts toward the country's goals. From the beginning, this work of national transformation has consistently benefited from the leadership of competent, determined, and devoted chief secretaries whose contributions to shifting the nation from red to blue oceans cannot be overstated.

So that everyone could follow the strategy discussions and develop a shared understanding of the road ahead and what would need to be done, a common language across the three NBOS platforms was essential. Visual tools like the strategy canvas, the four actions framework, and the eliminate-reduce-raise-create (ERRC) grid served this purpose well. For example, by looking at a strategy canvas with a compelling tagline and the four actions drawn on a single page, as shown in figure E-1, people at every level of government and in all the relevant ministries and agencies could easily see and tell if a proposed move was indeed a shift and likely to open up a new value-cost frontier. Figure E-1 depicts the strategy canvas of the

Figure E-1

Strategy Canvas of Malaysia's Community Rehabilitation Program

"Give a Second Chance Through Rehabilitation, Not Incarceration"

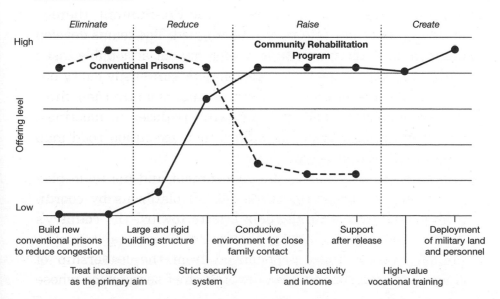

Community Rehabilitation Program (CRP), discussed in chapter 1, along with its tagline and four actions as presented at the Summit. As a quick reminder, the CRP was designed to rehabilitate petty criminals, who constitute the largest proportion of the country's prisoners. Since the shift, the recidivism rate has plummeted, families are thrilled, and society is safer. As for cost, a CRP center is 85 percent cheaper to build than a conventional prison and 58 percent cheaper to run. Based on current numbers, CRP is projected to deliver over US$1 billion in reduced costs and social benefits in its first decade. Perhaps its greatest gift, however, is the way CRP enables former inmates to transform their lives by giving them hope, dignity, and the skills to become productive members of society.

In formulating and executing initiatives, all NBOS platforms follow three overarching rules. One, to be considered, any idea or proposal must involve two or more ministries and be designed to meet the three blue ocean criteria of high impact, low cost, and rapid execution. Two, the principles of fair process—engagement, explanation, and clear expectations—need to be observed in all discussions and decision making. Three, market-creating tools like the strategy canvas, the four actions framework, and the ERRC grid are used, as applicable, and reflected in all discussions and reports. The Malaysia Blue Ocean Strategy Institute and the National Strategy Unit play important supporting roles throughout this process. The Summit takes the lead in driving the adoption of both the humanistic approach that earns people's voluntary cooperation and the blue ocean tools that build their creative competence.

How the Journey Began

Malaysia's blue ocean journey began humbly, in 2009, with a single initiative. Street crime was soaring. Snatch-theft was rampant, with thieves on motorcycles using rob-and-run tactics on pedestrians, mostly women. People wanted more police presence in the streets. While the police were doing their best to meet this demand, they lacked enough trained officers to staff more patrols. The police proposed building more training facilities to accelerate the number of recruits they could bring on. But with the world economy struggling to crawl out of the 2008 global financial crisis, and a rising government budget deficit, that option was off the table. The police were trapped in a red ocean of rising crime. Citizens were frustrated. And the competition—the criminal element—was winning out. The government recognized that conventional practices would not turn the situation around. A blue ocean shift was imperative.

As the Summit discussed the issue, it became clear that the Royal Malaysia Police couldn't solve the problem alone. The Ministry of Home Affairs and the Department of Public Administration had to join in. The Summit empowered a cross-ministry team and asked them to present their strategic action plans at the next Summit. To this end, the team ran an initial round of Pre-Summit and Offsite meetings to deepen their understanding of the realities on the ground and create viable blue ocean alternative solutions.

The team found that a great many trained police officers across the nation were doing administrative tasks, such as writing up reports, managing inventory, and filing documents. Officers traditionally performed these tasks, so no one had ever questioned the practice. But why, the team wondered, couldn't these activities be equally well performed by nonpolice personnel, freeing up the trained police officers for the patrols the citizens were crying out for? At the same time, by having members of the Ministry of Home Affairs and the Department of Public Administration on the team, the NBOS team found that the civil service had excess administrative staff on the payroll who had light workloads. A blue ocean opportunity existed to quickly move underleveraged, competent administrators locked in the "cold spots" of civil service departments to the "hot spots" at police stations. The team reckoned that such a move would allow the government to make an initial blue ocean shift, achieving high impact at low cost with rapid execution.

By then, the team was ready to chart specific strategies to execute the shift. But while the fair process practiced in all the platform meetings had aligned all the top-level people at the relevant governmental bodies, moving people across ministries and departments wasn't simple. It would stir up deep turf wars, involve issues related to relocation and incentives, and require widespread changes in people's mindsets and behaviors. Moreover, the Attorney General's Chamber would need to check whether moving personnel across the legal boundary between the police and the civil service would violate any existing rules and regulations. And if it did, the chamber needed to figure out how to address the problem within the bounds of national law.

Having listened to all these findings and execution challenges, the Summit added the Attorney General's Chamber to the team, approved the proposed approach, and asked the newly expanded team to map out and present an action plan with concrete milestones. At this point, the Pre-Summit and the NBOS Offsite platforms needed to be further mobilized to complete the task. The expanded team was also expected to show results within six months. A challenging time line like this would be used in all the subsequent NBOS projects, unless otherwise agreed to, as a way of creaing a sense of urgency and inspiring innovative approaches to speed execution. Clear expectations and a sound explanation were provided up front to all NBOS members.

The team reported their progress to the Summit monthly for feedback. In a period of six months, over 7,400 trained police officers who had been doing desk work were released to do street patrols, while 4,000 civil servants were placed at the police stations to take over the officers' administrative duties. Effiency gains identified in the course of the shift process accounted for the reduction in personnel and further lowered costs. Compared with a convential red ocean approach, where new police officer candidates were recruited, trained, and sent out on patrols, this cross-agency and cross-departmental move saved the government hundreds of millions of US dollars and had a rapid impact on street security. From 2009 to the end of 2010, reported street crimes dropped by 35 percent, and they have continued to go down since then.

Even more rewarding were the changes in people's attitudes and behaviors. New conversations, such as the following, began to take place: "I became a police officer the day I turned 22," one officer said, turning to the civil servant who'd taken over his administrative work. "I spent 15 years on a beat and had finally gotten a nice job sitting in a comfortable air-conditioned office [remember, the weather in Malaysia is hot throughout the year]. But when you came, I had to go back out on street patrols in the hot sun, and I wasn't happy about it." The civil servant looked at the officer and replied, "Oh, that's why you were so cold and confrontational when I started. But you're different now. You've become cooperative and supportive. Why?" The officer smiled and answered, "I saw you excel at administrative tasks, which isn't surprising, since it's your thing. And I felt good about your work. More importantly, though, once I got back in a police car, I realized I'd missed the patrols and the fun of reconnecting with the people I protect and serve, and monitoring the comings and goings in neighborhoods. NBOS brought us together and made us work on things we like and are good at." This exchange is not unique. While room for improvement still exists, and breaking down deeply divided silos will always take time and patience, it is not difficult to find positive exchanges like this across the country, as police officers and civil servants work together for the good of their country.

Similarly, some generals had initial reservations about the military's involvement in the CRP initiative. They were concerned that it could distract them from their core duty of protecting the country from external threats or invasion. After several rounds of discussions, however, they all agreed to give the CRP initiative a try. As we've seen, it has been a great success. At a recent Summit, the chief of defense forces, the highest-ranking general in the military, reflected on their journey, "We have come a long way, and we now wholeheartedly embrace the change that NBOS represents. Our duty is to serve our country, and we have found new ways of doing so while maintaining our core focus on keeping the country safe." Today, under NBOS, six CRP centers have been established and some 10,000 inmates rehabilitated.

Before NBOS the military and police almost never crossed the boundaries that separated their two institutions. That has changed. Multiple signs provide evidence that they now see protecting people and nation building as a common mission. For example, they have initiated joint patrols in crime hot spots, and the military has begun sharing their extra training facilities with the police. This has not only allowed the police to put trained officers on the streets more rapidly, but also resulted in significant cost savings by negating the need to build new police training facilities. "The police and military march at a different pace and salute in different ways," the inspector general of police observed at one of the Summits. But, he suggested, together with the chief of defense forces, "to signify the change in the way we work together for the nation, why don't we organize a joint graduation ceremony, so that the first batch of police recruits trained at military facilities will graduate side-by-side with military graduates? Such a ceremony would be a first in our history." Over 20,000 people came to witness this historic event, and the spirit of change was high and palpable.

The Evolution of the Journey

Since 2009, the Malaysian government has initiated more than 100 blue ocean moves, involving over 90 ministries and agencies from finance, to education, to rural and regional development, to agriculture, to urban well-being, to defence, to housing and local government, to women, family, and community development. The issues they've addressed range from safety and security, to economic and social development, to the environment and public well-being. You can learn about these blue ocean moves at www.nbos.gov.my and www.blueocean shift.com/malaysia-nbos. To date, the NBOS initiatives that have generated the widest demand among the citizenry are those focused on urban and rural well-being, entrepreneurship, and youth volunteerism. Let's look briefly at an example of each.

In June 2012, NBOS established the first Urban Transformation Center (UTC) in Melaka City, one of the country's state capitals. Since then, more than 20 others of varying size have been opened in main cities across the country. The UTCs are one-stop shops, where *all* government services are available under a single roof. Open seven days a week, from 8:30 a.m. to 10:00 p.m., they offer everything from passport renewals, licenses, legal permits, and registration forms to skill training programs, health clinics, social welfare programs, and official certificates of various kinds. The UTCs are soaringly popular—in a country with a population of slightly over 30 million, UTCs have counted nearly 50 million visits for government services in the first few years alone. In addition, people can also buy groceries, enjoy recreational facilities like fitness centers, and conduct their banking activities at the centers. Because UTCs are located in previously idling or underutilized government buildings, execution followed rapidly as soon as the Summit approved the idea. The first UTC building in Melaka was ready in just six weeks, and two weeks after that, the counters were open for business. Because ministries and agencies no longer need their own city offices, the UTCs will save the government billons of dollars in the years to come, while the gains in efficiency and convenience for the public, who no longer have to visit multiple offices, fighting city traffic all the while, are substantial. A similar model is at work in rural areas, where the NBOS Summit has established over 200 large and small Rural Transformation Centers (RTCs) to provide new economic, social, and educational opportunities that result in higher incomes for rural citizens.

The Malaysian Global Innovation and Creativity Center (MaGIC) is also a brainchild of the NBOS Summit. It brings together businesspeople, finance providers, domain experts, universities, and government officials to provide end-to-end support to both domestic and international entrepreneurs. Since its launch in April 2014, by then–US President Barack Obama and Malaysia's Prime Minister Najib Razak, over 15,000 start-ups have been established with its support. MaGIC not only orchestrates the entrepreneurial ecosystem of the country but also builds its creative competence by teaching blue ocean tools and methods to people from all segments of the society. The MaGIC Accelerator program, which is building a community of ASEAN (Association of Southeast Asian Nations)-focused start-ups, has become the largest in Southeast Asia.

The Summit's decision to create 1Malaysia for Youth (iM4U) has had a similarly transformative effect on youth volunteerism. Launched in 2012, the initative was designed to open up a new frontier of volunteerism by building young people's confidence and unlocking their energy and talent for the good of the nation. With about 3 million members, iM4U has become the largest youth volunteering organization in Southeast Asia and one of the biggest in the world. Its volunteers have carried out over 4,500 national and international projects to aid natural disaster relief efforts, provide supplementary schoolteachers, engage in charity work on behalf of the needy and elderly, perform local and regional community work, and more. This new and unprecedented level of youth volunteerism has impressed both the country's citizens and the regional public. As for the youth, they have seen first-hand the positive impact they can have on the well-being of others, which increases their confidence, their pride in their accomplishments, and their skills—all at low cost to the government.

These initiatives are game changers, not only in the way people work together to create new value-cost frontiers but also in how they think about and carry out their roles and responsibilities. During one of the Summit meetings, the secretary general of treasury said with a big smile on his face, "I am a finance guy. Having been assigned to lead and execute initiatives like UTC and MaGIC, I learned a lot about how to think and act in a blue ocean way. My fellow NBOS team members and I have realized that we need to both 'blue-ocean' these initiatives, and shift our mindsets. For me, this means being more than a numbers-driven finance guy. To deliver our national budget with high impact at low cost with rapid execution, I need to be a blue ocean strategist."

Since 2009, when the prime minister kicked off the National Transformation Journey where NBOS has played a pivotal role, the country's gross national income has grown by nearly 50 percent, and over 2 million jobs have been created. The global community, especially the governments of emerging and developing nations, has taken notice, and asked the Malaysian government to share its experiences with them. Malaysia and its leadership responded positively, and the result was an international conference on NBOS, held on August 16–18, 2016.

The three-day conference took place in Putrajaya, the country's federal administrative center outside downtown

Kuala Lumpur, and attracted 5,500 attendees representing 45 countries. Among the participants were heads of state, ministers, civil service leaders, and representatives from the United Nations, the Organization of Islamic Cooperation, the Association of Southeast Asian Nations, and member countries of the Commonwealth Association of Public Administration and Management.

The chief secretary to the government kicked off the conference by providing an overview of the NBOS initiatives. The prime minister then gave an inspiring keynote, explaining that "If we had continued with the old policies, we would have found the government and country swimming in an ocean of red. We knew that we had, instead, to make a paradigm shift, and create a new economic model; one driven by knowledge, creativity, and innovation—a 'blue ocean' of new opportunities." In the panel of heads of state that followed, the prime minister of Thailand built on this idea, noting that "Especially in times of economic uncertainty, countries tend to return to competition-based red ocean strategy," and urging the delegates to focus instead on "striving to innovate to create blue oceans."

After these opening events, the conference broke into sessions where participants discussed not only how the initiatives had transformed the formulation and execution of national policies but also how such changes affected the mindsets and behaviors of the people involved, their ways of working together, and the economic and social landscape of the nation. The Malaysian defence minister, who when he was home affairs minister, led the very first NBOS initiative, shared his view that "NBOS continuously reminds us that things have got to be shaken up from time to time, and that we should always keep an open mind and cooperate with each other." Given that the beginning of any change initiative is the most challenging period, his remarks, like his contributions, were especially resonant.

The conference also featured NBOS exhibitions, where participants could visit booths showcasing various initiatives and discuss what they'd heard. During the final day, they were also given the opportunity to visit one of the sites to experience firsthand how the initiative worked and how it affected people's lives. The CRP Center at Gemas was one of the options; visitors were able to see the new, income-producing skills the inmates were learning, and to listen as they described their work and achievements with genuine pride.

"Transformation requires people to work together in new ways, to think differently, and to take on new roles and responsibilities. These are not easy things to do, but they are rewarding. Throughout our NBOS journey, we have been creating new ways to serve people better and deliver on the things that really matter to them. NBOS has been transforming the entire nation. Blue oceans ahead!" said Malaysia's deputy prime minister in his concluding keynote address.

Today, at the Summit meetings, one can regularly hear participants talk about "blue-oceaning" initiatives and "NBOSing" their work. Presenting his vision for the nation at a recent Summit, the prime minister underscored the importance of this work, saying, "We aspire to be a top-20 nation in the world by 2050. For that, we need to persist on our blue ocean journey." With recharged energy, the chief secretary to the government is vigorously orchestrating all NBOS activities, motivating the participants and monitoring and communicating the results. In a recent address to the civil service, he reflected, "No doubt, change is not easy. But miracles can happen, given a positive mindset, as we have seen through NBOS. NBOS is a pivotal pillar in our nation's transformation journey." So, with renewed confidence, the blue ocean shift continues.

Notes

Chapter 1: Reach Beyond the Best

1. See NYOI 2009—Kickoff Year video, at 10:34, www.youtube.com/watch?v=5DCaqw0dasU (accessed March 30, 2017).
2. After six extraordinary years, in 2014 ISIS invaded Iraq. The rise of ISIS with its penetration in Iraq has endangered the country and forced the orchestra into hiatus. Yet, its message of hope, as documented here, can still be heard today, as even some of the greatest musicians around the world continue to celebrate the blue ocean it created.
3. Oprah Winfrey's tweet on ActiFry was posted at 1:46 p.m. on February 15, 2013. The full tweet reads: "This machine T-Fal actifry has changed my life. And they are not paying me to say it." https://twitter.com/oprah/status/302534477878554624?lang=en (accessed May 16, 2017). T-Fal refers to Groupe SEB's brand under which ActiFry is sold in the United States. Depending on the country, Groupe SEB markets ActiFry under different brands including T-Fal, Tefal, and SEB. For this reason, we simply refer to ActiFry as Groupe SEB's ActiFry in this book.
4. This is called environmental determinism, or the structuralist view. Its theoretical root stems from industrial organization economics, whose core argument can be summarized by its structure-conduct-performance paradigm. The paradigm says that industry structure determines organizations' conduct or strategy, which in turn impacts performance. See, for example, Bain (1959) and Scherer (1970).
5. This view of strategy is well articulated in the seminal work of Michael Porter, *Competitive Strategy* (1980).
6. That organizations can consciously shape industry boundaries and create new market space by breaking the value-cost trade-off are central arguments of our research on market-creating strategies. Among our other publications, see, for example, Kim and Mauborgne (1997a, 1999a, 2005, 2009, 2015a).

7. In his influential work, "What Is Strategy?", Porter (1996) formulated and used the concept of the productivity frontier to distinguish between operational effectiveness and strategy.

8. See Porter (1980).

9. The dashed curve will eventually form a new productivity frontier when its imitation and competition are in full swing.

10. See, for example, Kim and Mauborgne (1993, 1995, 1996, 1997a, 1998, 1999a, 2002b, 2004, 2005, 2009, 2015a), among others.

11. Since the launch of Groupe SEB's ActiFry and its great success, Christian Grob, who headed the initiative, unfortunately passed away.

12. See Global Footprint Network, "World Footprint: Do We Fit on the Planet?" (accessed April 3, 2017).

Chapter 2: The Fundamentals of Market-Creating Strategy

1. See Schumpeter (1942) for his seminal discussion on creative destruction.

2. Ibid.

3. While the intellectual origin of the concept of disruption is unclear, Richard Foster (1986) discussed what he called "technological discontinuities" in his book *Innovation: The Attacker's Advantage* and predicted that the phenomenon would only accelerate with coming tides of innovation. In his book, while the term disruption per se was not used, the phenomenon of "technological discontinuities" he described was about the disruption where upstart competitors abruptly overtook their well-run market leaders with new and discontinuous technologies. His research findings echo Schumpeter's insight about creative destruction.

4. Clayton M. Christensen (1997) has spurred the recent popularity of the term *disruption* through his influential work on disruptive technology and innovation. See his seminal work, *The Innovator's Dilemma: When New Technologies Cause Great Firms to Fail.*

5. Ibid.

6. In the context of new market creation, the term *disruptive creation* well captures the notion of displacement, whether it starts abruptly and destructively, with a superior technology, or slowly and gradually over time, with an inferior technology. Accordingly, we use the term *disruptive creation* to embrace both forms of displacement so that the process of new market creation through displacement can be fully, not partially, explained.

7. Our book *Blue Ocean Strategy* (2005, Expanded Edition 2015a) showed blue oceans of new market space were created both within and beyond the bounds of existing industries. We found that, compared with the blue

oceans of new market space created *within* existing industry boundaries, those created *beyond* the bounds often generated entirely new demand and growth without disrupting existing players and markets.

8. In a similar vein, Bhidé (2004, 2008) and Hubbard (2007) pointed out that Schumpeter's conception of creative destruction in economic growth missed a critical form of innovation and argued for the importance of what they called "nondestructive creation." They explained that nondestructive creation and entrepreneurship matter to economic growth. While their conception of nondestructive creation was in direct contrast with that of creative destruction without explicit consideration of disruptive innovation and their focus was more on the role of entrepreneurs and technology in the process of innovation and growth, their conception of nondestructive creation as a key form of innovation is insightful and is consistent with our research findings on market-creating strategies.

9. Unlike the entrepreneurship school of thinking on innovation and growth, the act of nondisruptive creation as defined here does not rely on entrepreneurs as it can be performed by any person, regardless of their entrepreneurial talent, with a systematic process. Such difference aside, Bhidé (2008) offers penetrating insights on the importance of nondestructive creation in explaining growth and innovation in the US economy.

10. C. K. Prahalad (2006) formulated the notion of "the bottom of the pyramid." There you can find more on why the "bottom of the pyramid" offers organizations ample brand-new opportunities as well as brand-new problems to solve.

11. For more on how technology innovation differs from value innovation, which is fundamental to an organization's ability to unlock commercially compelling new markets, as well as why value innovation is a distinctive concept from value creation, see Kim and Mauborgne (1999b, 2005, 2015a).

12. See, for example, Tellis and Golder (2002).

13. See Kim and Mauborgne (1999b, 2005, 2015a, 2015b).

14. See Heilemann (2001).

15. To get a free downloadable copy of our quiz, "Are you true blue or bloody red?" go to www.blueoceanshift.com/truebluequiz.

16. See, for example, Kim and Mauborgne (2005) and the work of Ries (2011).

Chapter 3: The Mind of a Blue Ocean Strategist

1. The theory of industrial organization economics proposes a structure-conduct-performance paradigm, which suggests a causal flow from market

structure to conduct (strategy) and performance. See, for example, Bain (1959) and Scherer (1970). Under this structuralist view of strategy, executives typically begin with industry and competitive analyses and then set out to carve a distinctive strategic position in the existing industry space, whereby their organization can outperform rivals by building a competitive advantage. The underlying logic here is that a company's strategic options are circumscribed by the market environment. In other words, structure shapes strategy. The seminal work on this is Porter (1980).

2. That industry boundaries are not fixed and that individual firms can create and re-create industries based on their conscious efforts is our central and long-standing argument. See, for example, Kim and Mauborgne (1997a, 1999a, 2005, 2009, 2015a).

3. Steve Jobs at NeXT Computer, Redwood City, California, 1995, https://www.youtube.com/watch?v=kYfNvmF0Bqw (accessed April 3, 2017).

4. Our 1997a *Harvard Business Review* article, "Value Innovation: The Strategic Logic of High Growth," first introduced the concept of the trap of competing. Our long line of research has since consistently argued that a focus on beating the competition and aiming to build competitive advantages frequently leads to imitative, not innovative, approaches to the market. For a quick summary of this argument see Kim and Mauborgne (1997b, 2003b).

5. See, for example, Kim and Mauborgne (1997a, 1997b, 2005, 2015a).

6. The central importance of noncustomers as a way to not only gain keen insight on how to create and re-create markets but also generate new growth has been a consistent finding of our research. See, for example, Kim and Mauborgne (1997a, 2005, 2015a, 2015b).

7. See Kim and Mauborgne (2015b).

8. See Kim and Mauborgne (1997a, 2004, 2005, 2015a, 2015b). See also Hill (1988).

Chapter 4: Humanness, Confidence, and Creative Competence

1. The concept we call *atomization* was first introduced in our article "Tipping Point Leadership" (2003a). Our follow-up research on it since then showed that atomization has a significant positive effect on people's motivation to take action, as it makes big challenges—like making a blue ocean shift—attainable to people. See, for example, Kim and Mauborgne (2005, 2015a).

2. Our research has consistently argued for the importance of firsthand discovery—not "outsourcing your eyes"—and conducting live market

research via "visual exploration." See, for example, Kim and Mauborgne (2002a, 2002b, 2005, 2015a).

3. Our research on fair process has demonstrated the critical role exercising fair process plays in strategy and management. We developed a model of fair process showing how it builds people's trust, commitment, and voluntary cooperation. See, for example, Kim and Mauborgne (1991, 1993, 1995, 1996, 1997c, 1998).

4. For a managerial summary of our fair process research see Kim and Mauborgne (1997c).

5. In Kim and Mauborgne (1998), we developed intellectual and emotional recognition theory. Our research found that the respect for people's intellectual and emotional worth that fair process engenders via engagement, explanation, and clear expectations triggers something at the core of the human spirit that builds our trust, commitment, and voluntary cooperation. It makes us want to "go the extra mile." The theory posits that, through fair process, people feel intellectually and emotionally recognized and valued and, in response, they mirror that recognition back to the organization and their colleagues.

Acknowledgments

We have had significant help in actualizing this book. INSEAD, our academic home, has continued to provide a unique and inspiring environment in which to conduct our research. We have benefited greatly from the truly global composition of our faculty, student body, and executive education participants, as well as the crossover between theory and practice that exists at INSEAD. Dean Ilian Mihov and Deputy Dean Peter Zemsky of INSEAD have provided enduring encouragement and institutional support. We would also like to acknowledge our former Dean Frank Brown for his vision to establish the INSEAD Blue Ocean Strategy Institute.

With our deans' support—including that of former INSEAD Executive Education Dean Sumitra Dutta who is now dean of Cornell SC Johnson College of Business, we have been able to create many blue ocean programs for INSEAD executives and MBAs that are carried out across the globe. Special thanks to all the INSEAD MBAs who have taken part in the Blue Ocean Study Group, the Blue Ocean Simulation Course, and the Blue Ocean Theory Course, and to all the executives from around the world who participated in the Blue Ocean Strategy Open Enrolment Program or Blue Ocean Strategy corporate-specific programs. Their challenging questions and thoughtful feedback clarified and strengthened our ideas. Special thanks also to the Boston Consulting Group (BCG), which has extended financial support for our research and has proven to be a great long-term partner dating back now for more than 20 years.

We are grateful for INSEAD's faculty who have taught blue ocean courses in the MBA, EMBA, and executive education programs at the school. Among the faculty are Professors Andrew Shipilov, Fares Boulos, Peter Zemsky, Guoli Chen, Jens Meyer, Javier Gimeno, Neil Jones, Mi Ji, James Costantini, Ben Bensaou, Michael Shiel, Narayan Pant, Loïc Sadoulet, Matthew Lee, Lauren Mathys, and George Eapen. Not only have they provided valuable feedback and rich discussions that have stimulated our thinking, many have importantly also become our dear friends. Thank you to all.

Along the trajectory of our research journey, many people have supported us at different points and we are thankful for all. However, there are two individuals who deserve special mention: Gavin Fraser and Marc Beauvois-Coladon. Over long years, both Gavin and Marc have provided feedback and put our ideas in practice often before they were even published. We are delighted and proud that two of the blue ocean shifts discussed in this book are the direct result of their powerful application of the ideas in practice. Gavin and Marc, thank you for your support and insight, the intellectual integrity you bring to your work, and importantly your friendship. Special thanks are also due to Jae Won Park, CEO of the Malaysia Blue Ocean Strategy Institute (MBOSI); John Riker, who skillfully led the Blue Ocean Strategy Initiative Center; and blue ocean senior experts Jason Hunter and Ralph Trombetta, whose experiences in applying our ideas in practice have directly contributed to our book. The dedicated work of all the directors and fellows of MBOSI including Jang Rae Cho, Gowrishankar Sundararajan, Lisa Carse, Tim Polkowski, Pamela Leong, Craig Wilkie, Julie Lee, Pallav Jha, and the rest of the MBOSI team serves as the backbone for the national blue ocean shift we lay out in the book's epilogue.

Thanks especially to our Blue Ocean Officer Kasia Duda and her team at MBOSI for their enthusiastic support and dedication. Kasia, thank you for being an unsinkable ship and great captain of the team. We appreciate all that you do.

Special thanks are also due to CEO of the Blue Ocean Global Network, Robert Bong, who also serves as chief advisor to MBOSI, and his team: Chin Chin Lim, Serena George, and Gan Kah Liang. Thanks also to the members of the Blue Ocean Global Network, a global community of practice on the blue ocean family of concepts—especially to those we were unable to mention here.

Warm thanks are also due to our outstanding team of executive fellows and researchers, current and recent past, at the INSEAD Blue Ocean Strategy Institute (IBOSI). In particular, Mi Ji, Oh Young Koo, Michael Olenick, Mélanie Pipino, Katrina Ling, and Jee-Eun Lee. Through the thought-provoking cases and firsthand original theory-based videos, today blue ocean concepts are used in over 100 countries around the world. Thanks also to our IBOSI coordinator Kim Wilkinson. Researchers beyond those already cited who deserve special mention are Zunaira Munir, Allison Light, and Amara Buyse.

Over the decade since our first book *Blue Ocean Strategy* was published, corporate executives, public officers, entrepreneurs, small- and medium-size business owners, and even high school students and religious organizations have set out to put our ideas and market-creating tools and frameworks into practice to make a blue ocean shift. To all these individuals—some of whom are contained in this book—we offer our sincere thanks. You have inspired us, sharpened our thinking, and greatly shaped the ideas in this book.

The Malaysian government has been applying the concept and tools of blue ocean shift to national development through its National Blue Ocean Strategy (NBOS) initiative. We are enormously grateful to Prime Minister Najib Razak and former Prime Minister Abdullah Badawi for their vision and inspiring leadership to create blue oceans for the nation.

Also, special thanks are due to Deputy Prime Minister Zahid Hamidi, Defence and Special Function Minister Hishammuddin Hussein, and all cabinet ministers who have spearheaded the cross-ministerial collaboration under NBOS.

The chief secretary to the government of Malaysia, Ali Hamsa, and the chairman of Petronas and former chief secretary to the government, Sidek Hassan, deserve our special appreciation for their excellent work in institutionalizing and nurturing the growth of National Blue Ocean Strategy within the Malaysian government. Other important contributors to NBOS include the secretary general of Treasury, Irwan Serigar; chairman of Permodalan Nasional Berhad (PNB) and former minister in the prime minister's department, Wahid Omar; governor of the Central Bank of Malaysia, Muhammad Ibrahim; director general of the Public Service Department, Zainal Rahim; chairman of Agrobank and former director general of the Public Service Department, Zabidi Zainal; inspector general of the police, Khalid Abu Bakar; chief of the Defense Forces, Raja Mohamed Affandi; former chief of the Defense Forces, Zulkifeli Zin; CEO of Petronas, Zulkiflee Ariffin; commissioner general of prisons, Zulkifli Omar; and director of the National Strategy Unit, Aminuddin Hassim, along with all the secretaries general and directors general of the Malaysian Civil Service and the leaders of the Malaysian security forces.

It would be remiss of us not to acknowledge the millions and millions of Malaysians who have contributed, either directly or indirectly, to creating blue oceans in Malaysia through various NBOS initiatives. We are very grateful to the numerous civil servants, teachers, students, generals and soldiers, police officers, professionals, businesspeople, entrepreneurs, youth, retirees, housewives, even inmates and many more besides, who have given their time, energy, and hearts as participants and volunteers. While there are far too many to mention their names here, it has been truly inspiring to witness the efforts made by citizens from all walks of life who have supported and played a crucial role in Malaysia's national development through NBOS.

We'd also like to thank President Obama's Board of Advisors on the White House Initiative on Historically Black Colleges and Universities. This work provided new impetus for us to apply and expand our blue ocean theory into the nonprofit sector.

In writing this book we have benefited from the comments of many people. In particular, we are grateful for the thoughtful comments and suggestions made by Nan Stone. Not only is Nan a dear friend we have known for over 20 years, she also served as the editor-in-chief of *Harvard Business Review* overseeing our initial HBR articles that are the seeds of our research. Thanks are also due to the valuable comments and feedback made by Andrea Ovans.

Finally, we would like to thank our publisher, Hachette Books. From the very start the entire team, in particular Mauro DiPreta, Michelle Aielli, and Betsy Hulsebosch, have believed in the ideas and been strong enthusiastic supporters, providing encouragement and inspiring ideas, and importantly, also being graciously patient as we struggled to get the manuscript done. We appreciate the dedicated efforts of Joanna Pinsker and David Lamb as well. Thanks also to Michael Pietsch, Hachette's CEO, for his full support and commitment to our book. We are grateful to all.

Bibliography

Bain, Joe S., ed. 1959. *Industrial Organization*. New York: Wiley.

Bhidé, Amar. 2004. "Entrepreneurs in the 21st Century—Non-destructive Creation: How Entrepreneurship Sustains Development." Lecture at the Royal Society of Arts, London, November 17.

———. 2008. *The Venturesome Economy: How Innovation Sustains Prosperity in a More Connected World*. Princeton, NJ: Princeton University Press.

Christensen, Clayton M. 1997. *The Innovator's Dilemma: When New Technologies Cause Great Firms to Fail*. Boston: Harvard Business School Press.

Foster, Richard, 1986. *Innovation: The Attacker's Advantage*. New York: Summit Books.

Global Footprint Network. "World Footprint: Do We Fit on the Planet?" http://old.footprintnetwork.org/en/index.php/GFN/page/world_footprint/ (Accessed April 3, 2017).

Heilemann, John. 2001. "Reinventing the Wheel." *Time*, December 2, 76.

Hill, Charles W. L. 1988. "Differentiation versus Low Cost or Differentiation and Low Cost." *Academy of Management Review* 13, July, 401–412.

Hubbard, Glenn. 2007. "Nondestructive Creation." *Strategy + Business* 27, Summer, 30–35.

Kim, W. Chan, and Renée Mauborgne. 1991. "Implementing Global Strategies: The Role of Procedural Justice." *Strategic Management Journal* 12, 125–143.

———. 1993. "Procedural Justice, Attitudes, and Subsidiary Top Management Compliance with Multinationals' Corporate Strategic Decisions." *Academy of Management Journal* 36, no. 3, 502–526.

———. 1995. "A Procedural Justice Model of Strategic Decision Making." *Organization Science* 6, February, 44–61.

———. 1996. "Procedural Justice and Managers' In-role and Extra-role Behavior." *Management Science* 42, April, 499–515.

——. 1997a. "Value Innovation: The Strategic Logic of High Growth." *Harvard Business Review* 75, January–February, 102–112.

——. 1997b. "When 'Competitive Advantage' Is Neither." *Wall Street Journal,* April 21.

——. 1997c. "Fair Process: Managing in the Knowledge Economy." *Harvard Business Review* 75, July–August, 65–76.

——. 1998. "Procedural Justice, Strategic Decision Making, and the Knowledge Economy." *Strategic Management Journal*, Editor's Choice, 323–338.

——. 1999a. "Creating New Market Space." *Harvard Business Review* 77, January–February, 83–93.

——. 1999b. "Strategy, Value Innovation, and the Knowledge Economy." *Sloan Management Review* 40, no. 3, Spring, 41–54.

——. 2002a "Why Seeing Is Succeeding," Inside Track, Viewpoint, *Financial Times*, April 15.

——. 2002b. "Charting Your Company's Future." *Harvard Business Review* 80, June 2002, 76–85.

——. 2003a. "Tipping Point Leadership." *Harvard Business Review* 81, April, 60–69.

——. 2003b. "Think for Yourself—Stop Copying a Rival." FT Summer School, *Financial Times*, August 11.

——. 2004. "Blue Ocean Strategy." *Harvard Business Review* 82, October, 75–84.

——. 2005. *Blue Ocean Strategy: How to Create Uncontested Market Space and Make the Competition Irrelevant*. Boston: Harvard Business School Publishing.

——. 2009. "How Strategy Shapes Structure." *Harvard Business Review* 87, September, 72–80.

——. 2015a. *Blue Ocean Strategy, Expanded Edition: How to Create Uncontested Market Space and Make the Competition Irrelevant*. Boston: Harvard Business Review Press.

——. 2015b. "Red Ocean Traps: Mental Models That Undermine Market-Creating Strategies." *Harvard Business Review* 93, March, 68–73.

North American Industry Classification System: United States 1997. 2002, 2017. Lanham, VA: Bernan Press.

NYOI 2009—Kickoff Year video, at 10:34. www.youtube.com/watch?v=5DCaqw0dasU (Accessed March 30, 2017).

Porter, Michael. E. 1980. *Competitive Strategy*. New York: Free Press.

——. 1996. "What Is Strategy?" *Harvard Business Review* 74, November–December, 61–78.

Prahalad, C. K. 2006. *The Fortune at the Bottom of the Pyramid*. Upper Saddle River, NJ: Wharton School Publishing.

Ries, Eric. 2011. *The Lean Startup*. New York: Crown Business.

Scherer, F. M. 1970. *Industrial Market Structure and Economic Performance*. Chicago: Rand McNally.

Schumpeter, Joseph A. 1942. *Capitalism, Socialism and Democracy*. New York: Harper & Brothers.

Tellis, G., and P. Golder. 2002. *Will and Vision*. New York: McGraw-Hill.

Index

About the Authors

W. CHAN KIM and **RENÉE MAUBORGNE** are professors of strategy at INSEAD, which is consistently ranked in the world's top business schools, and co-directors of the INSEAD Blue Ocean Strategy Institute in Fontainebleau, France. They are fellows of the World Economic Forum and were named among the world's top five best business school professors by *MBA Rankings*. Kim is an advisory member for the European Union and serves as an advisor to several countries. Mauborgne served on President Barack Obama's Board of Advisors on Historically Black Colleges and Universities (HBCUs) for the president's two terms. They advise, consult, and speak to governments and companies worldwide, and have published numerous bestselling articles in *Harvard Business Review* and *Academy of Management Journal, Management Science, Organization Science, Strategic Management Journal, Administrative Science Quarterly, Journal of International Business Studies, MIT Sloan Management Review,* the *Wall Street Journal,* the *New York Times,* and the *Financial Times,* among others.

They are the authors of *Blue Ocean Strategy: How to Create Uncontested Market Space and Make the Competition Irrelevant* (Harvard Business Review Press). *Blue Ocean Strategy* has sold over 3.6 million copies and is recognized as one of the most iconic and impactful strategy books ever written. It is being published in a record-breaking 44 languages and is a bestseller across five continents. *Blue Ocean Strategy* has won numerous awards including "The Best Business Book of 2005" Prize at the Frankfurt Book Fair, was selected as a "Top Ten Business Book of 2005" by Amazon.com, and was chosen as one of the 40 most influential books in the History of the People's Republic of China (1949–2009) along with Adam Smith's *The Wealth of Nations* and Milton and Rose Friedman's *Free to Choose.*

Kim and Mauborgne are ranked in the top three management gurus in the world in the Thinkers50 global list of thought leaders and Mauborgne is the highest placed woman ever on the list. They have received numerous academic and management awards around the globe, including the Carl S. Sloane Award for Excellence from the Association of Management Consulting Firms, the Leadership Hall of Fame by *Fast Company* magazine, the Nobels Colloquia Prize for Leadership on Business and Economic Thinking, and the Eldridge Haynes Prize by the Academy of International Business for the best original paper in the field of international business. They are the winners of the Prix DCF 2009 (Prix des Dirigeants Commerciaux de France 2009) in the category of "Stratégie d'entreprise." *L'Expansion* also named Kim and Mauborgne as "the number one gurus of the future." *The Sunday Times* (London) called them "two of Europe's brightest business thinkers." *The Observer* called Kim and Mauborgne "the next big gurus to hit the business world." Kim and Mauborgne won several Case Centre awards including "The Global Top 10 Bestselling Case Writers (2015/2016)," "All-Time Top 40 Bestselling Cases" in 2014, "Best Overall Case" in 2009 across all disciplines, and "Best Case in Strategy" in 2008.

They are the founders of the Blue Ocean Global Network (BOGN), a global community of practice on the Blue Ocean family of concepts that they created. BOGN embraces academics, consultants, executives, and government officers. For more about the authors and BOGN see www.blueoceanshift.com.